THE VIEW
FROM
HERE

SOUTH SHORE
ESSAYS

VERNON OICKLE

The View From Here
© 2025 Vernon Oickle

Cover design: Rebekah Wetmore
Editor: Andrew Wetmore

ISBN: 978-1-998149-87-2
First edition September 2025

Moose House Publications,
2475 Perotte Road
Annapolis County, NS B0S 1A0
moosehousepress.com
info@moosehousepress.com

Moose House Publications recognizes the support of the Province of Nova Scotia. We are pleased to work in partnership with the Department of Communities, Culture and Heritage to develop and promote our cultural resources for all Nova Scotians.

We live and work in Mi'kma'ki, the ancestral and unceded territory of the Mi'kmaw people. This territory is covered by the "Treaties of Peace and Friendship" which Mi'kmaw and Wolastoqiyik (Maliseet) people first signed with the British Crown in 1725. The treaties did not deal with surrender of lands and resources but in fact recognized Mi'kmaq and Wolastoqiyik (Maliseet) title and established the rules for what was to be an ongoing relationship between nations. We are all Treaty people.

Also by Vernon Oickle

One Crow Sorrow
Two Crows Joy
Three Crows a Letter
Four Crows a Boy
Five Crows Silver*
Six Crows Gold*
Seven Crows a Secret Yet To Be
    Told*
Eight Crows for a Wish*
Nine Crows for a Kiss*

Life and Death after Billy
Friends & Neighbours: a collection
    of stories from the Liverpool
    Advance
Busted: Nova Scotia's War on Drugs
Queens County
Ghost Stories of the Maritimes
    (volumes 1 and 2)
Dancing with the Dead
Great Canadian Ghost Stories
    Volume II (co-author)
Disasters of Atlantic Canada: stories
    of courage and chaos
Canada's Haunted Coast: true ghost
    stories of the Maritimes
The Editor's Diary: the first 13
    years
Angels Here Among Us
Red Sky at Night
South Shore Facts and Folklore
I'm Movin' On: the life and legacy of
    Hank Snow

Beaches of Lunenburg-Queens
Nova Scotia Outstanding Outhouse
    Reader
Red Coat Brigade
Ghost Stories of Nova Scotia
Kiss the Cod!
Strange Nova Scotia
Newfoundland and Labrador
    Outrageous Outhouse Reader
Where Evil Dwells
How to talk Nova Scotian: the
    Bluenoser's book of slang
The Nova Scotia Book of Lists
My Nova Scotia Home
We Love Nova Scotia: a people's
    portrait
More Ghost Stories of Nova
    Scotia
Queens County: a history in
    pictures
The Second Movement: Nova
    Scotia's outrageous outhouse
    reader No. 2
So you think you KNOW Nova
    Scotia?
Forerunners: Harbingers of
    Death in Nova Scotia
Through Rain, Sleet or Snow:
    rural mailboxes of Nova
    Scotia
Grandma's Home Remedies
Even More Ghost Stories of
    Nova Scotia

* available from Moose House Publications
moosehousepress.com

Foreword

Kim Kierans

These days, as the media landscape shifts, the long-standing idea of journalism as a public service is under attack. This timely collection of columns by Vernon Oickle—an international award-winning journalist and author—highlights the vital role of local newspapers as hubs around which communities unite.

Twenty years ago, almost every town in Nova Scotia had a weekly newspaper, and reporters like Vernon were out and about in their community. Their stories and editorial columns celebrated progress and success and pointed out what needed to be fixed.

Local weeklies had it all—council decisions and debates, development issues, platforms for electoral candidates, fishing and farming news, sports scores, where to shop and what's going on this weekend. The editorial columns raised issues, reflected on and made sense of events and offered advice. Residents could rely on their local paper for factual and timely information to help them make informed decisions. The local paper was an important community anchor, a secular church bulletin with an edge.

Consolidation and closures over the last 25 years have left news deserts in most smaller communities across North America. In Nova Scotia, weeklies like The Digby *Courier*, Middleton *Mirror Examiner*, Bridgetown *Monitor*, Shelburne *Coast Guard*, Scotia *Sun*, Liverpool *Advance* and Amherst *Citizen* have disappeared or been absorbed into regional or provincial newspapers.

Most towns no longer have a newspaper office on Main Street with a dedicated reporter and editor. Reporters now work out of their home and cover large geographic regions, often by telephone. It's impossible for one journalist to report on the municipal politics and health events, uncover wrongdoings, and document high-school sporting events and community successes in every town. The disappearance of weeklies has created an information vacuum and opened the door to online mis- and disinformation that erode community life.

Through all this flux, Vernon has been a steadfast champion for community journalism. He has spent more than 40 years as a reporter, editor and columnist at weekly newspapers on the South Shore of Nova Scotia. He is rooted in the historic town of Liverpool, where he was born and raised, where he and his wife Nancy raised their two boys, and where he researches and writes award-winning books and columns.

As you will discover, this collection of columns is rich with observation, personal perspective and opinion. Each story reflects Vernon's deep connection to community and his readers and eloquently brings past issues and events to life and taps into our shared humanity and experiences—love, loss, laughter, struggles, outrage and optimism.

For example, the column **The walls came tumbling down** is a meditation on progress, mixed with nostalgia for his old high school. "I watched the heavy demolition equipment slowly and methodically dismantle the place where I spent four years of my young life." As Vernon walks us down the school halls and recalls his struggles with his studies and mean kids, we are transported back to our own high school days. When he reflects on what he learned, he invites us to take stock of how our high school years shaped us.

In 2015 Vernon wrote a column from Alberta, where he received his college's Alumni Community Leader Award. **From Liverpool to Lethbridge** recounts his journey out west 33 years earlier to study journalism and the culture shock of leaving home for the first time. "I had no idea where I was going or what I was doing. I knew no one and, as I wandered the halls of the college trying to figure out if I had done the right thing, I wondered what the heck had I gone and gotten myself into." Sound familiar? This column opens a door for us to remember our life journey and assess where it has led us. For Vernon it was a reporting job at his hometown newspaper, *The Liverpool Advance*. Given his successful career, one could say the rest is history.

This book is full of memories—some painful, others playful, always engaging. Vernon Oickle is a master storyteller, Nova Scotia's town crier of text. These columns will have you smiling, laughing, nodding, thinking and talking.

For me, this collection is evidence of the important role that local voices play in nurturing community. It's also a rallying call to support local independent media so that community voices like Vernon's can find a home in our homes.

And, as Vernon says at the end of his columns, "That's the view from here."

Kim Kierans is a journalist, educator and author of
Journalism for the Public Good: The Michener Awards at 50

A career, a lifestyle, a passion

When I was a youngster growing up in the town of Liverpool on Nova Scotia's South Shore, I remember the excitement every Wednesday morning when the local newspaper would arrive in our household, usually brought home by one of my parents following a trip to the corner store.

Wednesday was Advance Day in Queens County and, while I didn't realize it at the time, I would come to appreciate how important this newspaper was to so many people and the role it played in their lives. For some people, *The Advance* was their only source for news and their link to other people and the outside world.

I don't know that, as a child, I ever really thought that someday I would end up working for my hometown newspaper, let alone eventually becoming the editor, but in time I grew to appreciate the importance of our community's newspaper. Indeed, it was the common thread that held our community together, sharing the news—both good and bad—and creating memories that people often cut out and pasted in family photo albums and scrapbooks to be passed on to future generations.

At one time, one could find everything you needed to know in the local newspaper—what was on sale and where the deals could be found that particular week; who was getting married or celebrating an important life milestone; who had died and who had a baby; what community events were coming up; and what decisions were being made by local councils and school boards that would impact our lives.

The Advance also carried news of tragic events in our neighbourhoods, such as major motor vehicle accidents and fires, natural disasters (seemingly not as common years ago as they are today) and serious crimes that had occurred in our community.

These sad and distressing events were often news that some people didn't want to know, but by reporting on all the happenings, the newspaper was meeting its mandate, which was to be a mirror of the community and to record all the news for historic purposes so that future generations would have a record of our successes and failures, and of our foibles and triumphs.

If a newspaper was achieving its mandate, then it usually meant that people in the community always felt fully informed and up to date. Such was the case for *The Advance,* and the level of excitement that one would experience every Wednesday was palpable.

Life happens and, as the years went by, I eventually determined that I wanted to work in newspapers. After I spent several years in Lethbridge, Alberta studying journalism, my career path led me back to Liverpool, where I began a reporting job at *The Advance.*

It may be the romanticized version of the story, but there was something very provocative and alluring about going to work for one's hometown newspaper. When I was given the opportunity to do just that, I threw myself into it, giving myself over to the job 110 per cent.

I'm a firm believer that, while we may be able to teach someone to be a writer, you can't teach someone to be a reporter. I believe that is a skill and talent that you're born with.

That belief has gotten me into trouble on more than one occasion over the years, but I still argue its validity. I am thankful that, as Jock Inglis— my first editor at *The Advance*—often told me, he believed I was born to be a reporter. While I have had several mentors throughout my more than 40-year career in the newspaper industry, I believe that had it not been for Jock's faith in me, I most likely would have ended up in some other field, doing God only knows what.

Throughout my career, I've reported on a variety of news events— some great and some not so great—and I've had the pleasure of meeting some extraordinary people along the way, and through it all, I always endeavoured to do the best job I could. I've been rewarded for that commitment many times over and I consider myself to have been truly blessed for having enjoyed such a remarkable career in a job that I truly loved.

In thinking back over my years in newspapers, I would be hard-pressed to identify one type of story I prefer over others, because they've all had their highlights and lowlights.

There have been times when the job had been gruelling and depressing, but, in pushing through the challenges, I was able to deliver the story to the readers and I'm proud of that. I am also proud that, as my journalism career progressed, I eventually became editor of *The Advance,* a post I seriously relished. I can honestly say that it was a proud moment for me when I donned the editor's hat of my hometown newspaper.

In the latter half of my career, as I worked for other publications, I was given the opportunity to write editorials and columns, which I enjoyed beyond words. I especially embraced the idea of writing a weekly general-interest column because it gave me the freedom to explore any topic that piqued my curiosity or ignited a spark. Nothing was off-limits, and I liked that.

The purpose of an opinion piece is to help shape the public discourse on any given topic. I always told readers that while I did not expect them to agree with everything I had written, I did hope they would keep an open mind and appreciate the fact that a column was just my opinion and it was my objective to offer a different perspective to the issues of the day.

Unlike news stories where reporters must stick to facts, opinion pieces were just as the name underscores—one person's opinion. However, to be taken seriously, that opinion must still have its merits and be anchored in facts and truth.

I've written hundreds of columns throughout the course of my career and for different publications. Between 2014 and 2024, I wrote a weekly column called "The View from Here" that appeared in *The South Shore Breaker* and various other publications throughout Nova Scotia. I enjoyed the experience very much as it allowed me to write about my favourite topic—the place I call home.

On the following pages you will find a collection of my favourite columns from that period in my newspaper career. They represent my views on a variety of issues and in a lot of ways, this collection serves as the exclamation mark on my life's journey working in the newspaper business. Thank you for welcoming me into your homes every week for the past four decades.

On that note, then, for what could be the very last time I write these words for publication—that's the view from here.

Vernon Oickle
June, 2025

Dedicated to

the memory of a special lady, Georgia Fooks. You gave me the skills and encouragement to chase my goals, even when I was a fledgling journalism student.

And to

Aya Roller. Even though we are miles apart and haven't seen each other for decades, thank you for getting me through those collage years and for the life-long friendship.

We are grateful to the *The Chronicle Herald* and Saltwire, owners of *The South Shore Breaker*, for giving Vernon the opportunity to write these columns, and for permission to use them in this book.

The View From Here

Vernon Oickle

The view from here on

My Nova Scotia home

Vernon Oickle

Seven Wonders of the South Shore

July 9, 2014

I've always considered myself fortunate to have been born and raised on Nova Scotia's South Shore, a place second to none anywhere else on the planet, as far as I'm concerned.

Sure, there are places where the temperatures are warm and balmy year-round, where it never snows and where the grass always seems greener, but that doesn't make them any more attractive than the South Shore. This is my home, and it's where I hope to remain.

I appreciate that, in recent decades, the region has fallen onto economic hard times and, as a result, faces many challenges, but the one thing that has always impressed me about the South Shore is the ample supply of resilience that exists here. Through all the difficult times, there remains an undercurrent of persistence and optimism, and a survival instinct that bodes well for the region.

We've weathered a tough economic storm that essentially started back in the 1980s with the collapse of the traditional ground fish industry. Ultimately, that led to the closure of many processing plants throughout the southwest region and beyond.

The hard times culminated two years ago with the mothballing of the former Bowater paper mill in Brooklyn, Queens County. The impacts from the loss of one of the region's largest employers were far-reaching and are still being felt. In fact, those losses will reverberate well into the future, affecting not only those who were directly employed at the mill, but also those who worked in the forestry industry supplying fibre to the paper maker and other residual industries.

In the midst of this upheaval, the region's economy was thrown another curve ball almost five years ago, when the former NDP government killed the subsidy that was helping to keep the Yarmouth to Maine ferry service afloat, a decision that had serious and sweeping negative implications for the entire southwestern region of the province, leading to the near collapse of the tourism industry, a sharp rise in unemployment

19

numbers and the closure of many businesses.

'Devastating' is the one word that best describes this scenario and, in the end, the former government paid the price when voters rejected the NDP in record numbers last October. Now, with the ferry sailing once again, the future looks much brighter, indeed.

However, despite this turmoil, all the ups and downs, and all the uncertainty, the people of this region soldiered on with a determination that is to be celebrated and revered. Giving up has never been an option for the people of the South Shore. We've seen tough times before and, with pure grit and utter determination, we've pushed through them.

And we'll do it again.

This region has a great deal going for it, but the key is to stop dwelling on what went wrong. Instead, we must turn our attention to the future and embrace the opportunities, because no one else will do it for us. The days of government handouts have long since passed, meaning it's up to us to clap on and take hold.

In looking to that positive future, I've done an inventory of those things that I like to call the Seven Wonders of the South Shore:

1. Topping any list of assets must be the people who live and work here. I certainly can't call myself a world traveller, so maybe my view is limited, but I consider the people of the South Shore among the finest anywhere. I've known them to be hardworking and resilient and never easily back down from a challenge. They may get knocked down a few times, but I've seen them pull themselves up, regroup and face their challenges head-on. That's a powerful resource on which to build a future.

2. It almost borders on cliché, but there is no denying that the region's unspoiled natural beauty is also one of its strongest resources. As the world continues to shrink, people elsewhere will seek out places such as ours, places that can offer a brief solitude and reprieve from the spoils of modern technology and industry. Our challenge is not only to protect and preserve these natural assets, but to also find a way in which to capitalize on them. This must be done with care, but surely there is a way.

3. Another strong asset is the region's rich and diverse heritage, starting with Yarmouth's proud history in shipbuilding and sailing, Shelburne's proud Loyalist and African-Canadian heritage, Liverpool's unique privateering legacy and Lunenburg County's

distinct connection to the sea, including the world-famous *Bluenose* and the Town of Lunenburg's designation as a UNESCO World Heritage Site. Add all of this together with the varied history in all other nooks and crannies of the South Shore and we've got a unique heritage experience. Let's package it all as one adventure and sell it to the world.

4. As the region's traditional resource-based industries fall on hard times, it is essential that we find new opportunities to take their place. Fortunately, the South Shore is known to be a unique ecosystem with a climate ripe for new and exciting agricultural opportunities, such as growing grapes to bolster the wine and cranberry industries, and the Hascapa berry operation based near Blockhouse in Lunenburg County that is quickly making a name for itself. These are the types of industries on which we must build our future.

5. I've often felt that those of us who live on the South Shore take way too much for granted, like our relatively safe communities. Think about it. Compared to some places, the towns and villages in this region offer a safe, enriching and nurturing environment ideal for raising a family or for those looking for a comfortable location in which to retire. Do not underestimate the value of this resource.

6. We've seen this region go through and survive some very tough times, so our track record is another important asset. We should not dwell in the past, but we must learn from it. Draw upon the strengths and chart a course that includes the positives. There are many. The challenge is to find them and to hang onto them, but that's the best approach, as clinging to the negatives will get us nowhere.

7. And, finally, I would count our collective resolve to fight through the obstacles and overcome the hardships as another of our assets. It can be a slugfest for one person or even a small group of people to rise above the difficult times, but together, as a community, we can achieve a great deal. The desire to work as a cohesive group and draw upon each other's strengths, knowledge and experience is a huge benefit if we harness it.

It's true that this region faces many challenges, but we can decide either to give into the pressures and roll onto a slow demise, or to accept the reality and move forward. I'm not sure about the rest of you, but I believe that, with a positive and supportive attitude, we can overcome. When you put these assets into their proper perspective, you can see that we have a lot going for us.

Or, at least, that's the view from here.

The changing face of rural Nova Scotia

July 16, 2014

When I heard that a small corner store in Milton, a tiny community just outside of Liverpool, had closed, the news hit me hard. As it sunk in that the store was gone, memories of my childhood flooded back. It was like a dam had broken and I was quickly washed back in time.

The Corner Store, as it was known, was strategically located on the main route inland to North Queens, which meant no matter where one was heading, be it to Greenfield, Caledonia or across the province to Digby and the Annapolis Valley, it was necessary to drive past the store, and so the first leg of the excursion often began with a stop to pick up a few things one needed to make the trip all the more pleasurable.

This pit stop was especially a must if you had children in your car, be-cause everyone knows that you can't go for a pleasurable Sunday drive without keeping the little ones content. What better way to do that than to ply them with treats? That may be frowned upon today, but I grew up in an era when it was okay to reward your children with treats, so please don't lecture me.

I can remember, as a youngster, enjoying many ice cream cones that came out of that little green store. Chocolate was my favourite, but of course my parents were never excited about that on a hot day with the car windows down, as they knew I'd end up with more ice cream on the front of my shirt than in my belly.

Fortunately, my mother always packed spare shirts for my sister and me whenever we left home, as I usually had to do a quick change once the ice cream was gone and then we'd be on our way to whatever adven-ture awaited us that day.

I also have fond memories from my childhood of travelling with my grandparents. They liked to ride the back roads and explore out-of-the-way places far removed from the beaten path. They'd often stop and check out old treasures that appealed to them and while, at a young age, I may not have appreciated how they spent their idle time, today I relish those memories I made with them. And, like many other excursions, my adventures with my grandparents always started with a stop at that little green corner store in Milton.

Now, I will admit that when it came to snacks, my grandparents had quirky and eclectic tastes. Their regular purchase included a half-dozen bottles of Pepsi, maybe a bag of plain potato chips for me, and always a pound or two of small bologna because my grandfather loved that stuff. At some point on our trip, we'd find a quiet spot, maybe beside a river or lake and pull over, and everyone would have a hunk of bologna and chase it with Pepsi.

So they were the good ole days. They were special memories for sure. But the point is that, for many in my community, the Corner Store in Milton was a part of their infrastructure, just as so many other small stores were important to other rural neighbourhoods throughout the province.

These stores had everything a body could want, from essentials such as bread and milk to canned goods and produce, to confectionery items and freshly-butchered meat, to food staples such as sugar and flour. And, yes, even treats and snacks for the youngsters.

If you needed something in the evening or on a Sunday and the larger grocery stores were closed, as they were years ago, then you could always find it at your friendly neighbourhood corner store. And, as the name suggested, convenience stores were practically located almost on every corner of town. But those days have long since passed.

I did a quick count of the independently-owned corner stores I can remember being in the Liverpool area when I was a child and came up with 14. Do you know how many small corner stores are located in that same geographic area today? Three. I did not count corporate-owned stores such as those operated out of the Irving garages, as they really aren't the same thing.

It's sad when you think of these corner stores disappearing, but there are many reasons for their demise, including competition from the larger supermarkets that are open practically 24-7. A shrinking population, which ultimately means fewer customers, and the rising costs of running a small business, are also contributing factors.

I'm not a retail expert, nor would I ever suggest that anyone could make a fortune from running such a business, but maybe, with the right mix of products and the right strategic location, someone could make it work. I hope so and I wish them well.

Corner stores truly reflect the essence of rural living, but it appears these independent, family-operated businesses are a dying breed and could actually be on the verge of extinction. Sad, indeed. However, their fate is a reality of the era in which we live.

Another sign of the challenges facing rural communities is the growing number of abandoned and repurposed churches throughout the region. Shrinking congregations has emerged as a serious trend in recent years, a reality that in some cases actually threatens the collapse of many local parishes and certainly poses a challenge in maintaining any physical structure. With fewer people to fundraise for and maintain these buildings, numerous congregations are faced with the tough choice of letting go of their physical structures, despite their historical significance to their communities.

To me, communities of worship, no matter the religion or faith, are the lifeblood of any community, and while it is disheartening to see so many historic church buildings being put on the real estate market to eventually be sold and perhaps remodelled, we must remember that the church building is just a structure. People can practice their faith without a building. In fact, the ability to worship doesn't require a building, although a church structure does provide a focus around which a congregation can gather to celebrate in the good times and to provide comfort and strength in the hard times.

Church buildings then, just like the small corner stores, are facing an uncertain future as rural communities restructure and look to the future.

Other casualties of this restructuring of rural communities are the small, rural schools.

We could debate the pros and cons of closing small schools, but I'm not going to do that today. I will, however, say that, like many institutions in rural communities throughout Nova Scotia, small schools face an uncertain future amid rising costs and shrinking populations.

These are simply the facts. The challenge for our communities is to figure out how to do more with fewer resources; maintaining the status quo with less money and fewer resources is no easy task. Is closing an option? That possibility always exists, but it does not have to be the only option. Coming to grips with the realities of a changing society that demands more from our students, combined with fewer dollars to deliver upon those demands, is the ultimate challenge.

It's time to move away from the adversarial approach that has divided communities for decades. This change will require strong government leadership and support from the school communities. For anything to work effectively, it must be a team effort.

We also must keep in mind that what may have worked for one generation, may not necessarily work for our current needs. For instance, most small corner stores have outlived their need, or they wouldn't be disappearing into the dust of history. This is true because society has adjusted its shopping patterns around the larger supermarkets that have seen what the market demands and have provided it.

That may not sit well with some of us, but it is evolution, and that's the view from here.

If there's one thing I hate...

July 16, 2014

People who know me, know that if there's one thing I detest it's the phrase "come from away" or "CFA" to describe people who were not born and raised in our wonderful community.

I appreciate that, in some cases, the phrase is used accurately to describe people who have relocated to our piece of paradise for whatever reason, be it family, retirement, health, business, or employment opportunity, but I feel that it's sometimes used in a derogatory manner to assign blame or even to ridicule others.

Most of the time I find its usage to be offensive and even confrontational. This is especially true in a group setting, when ideas and information are being exchanged. I've seen this happen in public forums and functions when it's thrown out to the gathering as a verbal form of finger pointing when someone doesn't agree with an idea or suggestion.

How often have you heard, "What do you know? You're a CFA"?

What exactly does CFA mean, anyway? If you have relocated here, what exactly is the cut-off date after which you are no longer considered a CFA? Is it five years? Is it 10? Maybe 25 or 50?

Aren't we all essentially CFAs? Yes, some of us may be second, or third, or fourth or even fifth generation Nova Scotians, but the only people who are essentially native Nova Scotians are First Nations people. Technically, everyone else is a CFA.

For me, it really doesn't matter how long you've lived here, because as soon as you move to the province you should consider yourself a Nova Scotian as should others around you.

I choose to label those individuals as "HBCs": "Here by Choice."

It shouldn't matter where anyone came from or even why he or she relocated here unless they're a master criminal. What matters most is that someone was so impressed with the beauty and the positive attributes of our area that they chose to move here, and we should be happy about that.

With these people come new ideas, new energy, new vision and a new insight that, in most cases, they are willing and anxious to share with their new neighbours. It's up to us to embrace these individuals and to welcome them into the fold.

We can learn a great deal from these individuals if we let them into our communities and make them feel as though we appreciate their contributions. In fact, in many cases, the ideas from these individuals have breathed new life into local events and into the community itself.

There are many positives about this arrangement, as people who have relocated to our neighbourhoods often see things from a new and different perspective. Many of us who have lived here our entire lives may lack the ability to see new angles, and our ideas may become stale and outdated. We also tend to look inward and with blinders, so sometimes an infusion of new ideas can breathe new life into our events and the community.

This isn't to say that all our local ideas are bad ones, nor to suggest that all the ideas from people who move here are good, because that is not the case. However, it does mean that we should meet in the middle and find ways to cooperate. After all, the result we want is success in whatever we do. The key is to end up with the best ideas, regardless of where they came from or who suggested them. In that way, we all benefit.

That said, the onus of this cooperation does not rest solely with those of us who grew up here. It's a two-way street, and I, too, get irritated when new people arrive with an attitude that suggests that they believe they know what's best for us and the communities we've called home for many years. That is not the way to make friends and encourage cooperation.

It's also off-putting when these individuals suggest that they may have moved here because they were attracted to the romanticized image of a small, rural community. They sometimes resent change because it goes against their Anne of Green Gables vision. By the same token, we don't appreciate anyone telling us that they know what's best for us.

Open and honest dialogue is the best approach as we work toward solutions that benefit everyone.

Most of us "locals" will agree that change is sometimes necessary for the survival of our communities, and we know that if we don't grow and evolve with new ideas and initiatives, we run the risk of growing stagnant and perhaps even regressing. We should encourage our new neighbours to express their views, and welcome the input with open minds; but in the end, regardless of where the idea originated, we must do what is best for our communities.

Those of us who have been fortunate to grow up in this wonderful part of the world take a great deal for granted, but the fact that we are attracting many new people to our region should be proof that we do have lots to offer. That being said, we must be willing to share and accept new ideas, regardless of where they originated, or at least that's the view from here.

Our community is only as strong as we make it

January 14, 2015

Those who know me know that I like nothing more than talking about the many great communities here on the South Shore, the place we call home.

I had the chance several times to do just that over the recent holiday season because, no matter where I found myself, the conversation managed to wind its way to that topic. Naturally, I piped up and offered my opinion, as I'm known to do.

My philosophy is a simple one—our community is only as a strong as we make it, and we do that by working together. I also believe that, despite some major challenges and setbacks over the past few years, the communities of the South Shore can have a bright future if we are supportive of each other and embrace new ideas and initiatives, no matter how far-fetched they seem or even if they differ from our normal way of thinking.

Over the years, I've heard of too many good ideas that couldn't get off the ground because the initial reaction from others was not positive or supportive. Some of the best ideas may have seemed far-fetched to the first people who heard them, but once they took shape and got off the ground, they seemed brilliant.

Just because you can't see the bigger picture doesn't mean the picture isn't worth painting, so, for the sake of our collective futures, when you hear a proposal you don't like, let's just hold back on the negative rhetoric until we have given the idea a fair hearing.

As we move forward, we must also be more respectful of the change that is afoot and stop dwelling on setbacks. We all know what's happened in the past, so let's do ourselves a collective favour—let's leave those issues in the background.

I'm not saying we can just shrug it off, but whatever has happened in the past has happened, and we can't rewrite history. However, we can write our future together and we can collectively chart a course for that future. We may have to navigate some rough waters along the way, but let's make a promise that we will stay the course and not jump ship when things get tough.

Okay, now that we've made that commitment, let's start by doing an assessment of what we have going for us. No matter where you live on the South Shore, there can be no arguing that the region's strongest asset is the people who live and work here. We've seen them bounce back from much adversity and I think we're well on our way to seeing that happen again. I believe our "can-do" attitude will carry us through again. However, it won't happen if we don't pull together.

By together, I include every community in our region. To enjoy success, we have to eradicate any remnants of past protectionism that may exist, because the truth is, what's good for one part of the South Shore is good for the entire region.

For example, if the Yarmouth ferry attracts tourists to that end of the region, the entire South Shore reaps the rewards. There was much proof of that fact this past summer when, for the first time in several years, most tourist operators throughout the region reported a major upswing in business.

While each town in the region could benefit from the establishment of a major employer, the fact remains that if, for example, a major industry is created in Shelburne, other communities such as Lockeport, Liverpool and Barrington will benefit from increased traffic and spending. The same can be said for Lunenburg and Bridgewater and other places in between.

It may be natural for each community to want to protect its territory, but we must embrace the idea that our community no longer consists of smaller geographical areas that are separated by invisible boundary lines. Shrinking populations and dwindling resources demand greater participation, void of any protectionism, which means increased co-operation is the first order of the day. We've seen that trend in recent years.

In an effort to move forward, we have to use our ingenuity and be creative. I believe that the tourism industry holds one of the greatest opportunities for growth and development for the South Shore, but, despite current successes, many opportunities remain untapped. The region's deep and rich heritage is truly one of the greatest assets at our fingertips, but we must take the initiative and figure out how to best utilize that resource.

I think of Liverpool's privateering heritage, Shelburne's Loyalist and Black heritage and Yarmouth's rich seafaring history as areas that hold great opportunities that, to a large degree, have remained largely untapped. While the annual festivals in those communities and some exhibits are good first steps to celebrating that history, think of what we could offer the world if we can break into the vault.

The new Black Heritage Centre currently under construction in Birchtown to highlight the arrival of Black Loyalists in that part of the region several hundred years ago is a good example of grabbing onto our roots and capitalizing on their full potential.

Imagine how exciting it would be to see a Privateer Interpretive Centre in Liverpool or a Loyalist Interpretive Centre in Shelburne or a shipping museum in Yarmouth. Think of the tourist potential those facilities would provide for three South Shore towns currently in rebuilding mode. The possibilities are as endless as our imaginations.

Would turning these ideas into reality be easy? Not likely. Would there be many obstacles? Without question. Would people support these ideas? They would if their true potential were recognized.

It all comes down to vision and commitment and it would take a united effort to build even one of these facilities but imagine the positive impacts such a facility would have on any one of these communities.

Living in Liverpool and being a student of local history, I have long imaged what a centre devoted to our privateering heritage would do for our town. After all, Liverpool was once known as the Privateer Capital of North America.

The same can be said for Shelburne and its Loyalist past, but I can envision the tourism potential of these centres and I think of the positive economic and cultural impacts they would have on our towns.

So here we are back to the main point—it would take a community to make any one of these ideas a reality, and by community, I mean all of us, you and me, and all three levels of governments, or at least that's the view from here.

25 reasons why I love Nova Scotia

January 28, 2015

I'm a proud Nova Scotian and I always welcome the opportunity to talk about my home province so when someone recently challenged my enthusiasm by betting me that I could not list 25 reasons why I love Nova Scotia I quickly accepted the bet.

How dare they, I thought. What audacity.

Without hesitation, I took up the challenge.

Let's see if you agree with my observations or if you can come up with other points that I've overlooked. Feel free to pass along your ideas.

1. Generally speaking, Nova Scotians are kind, caring, generous and supportive of others.
2. Neighbours are willing to help their neighbours, especially those who are less fortunate or those who may have fallen onto hard times.
3. In comparison to other locations, Nova Scotia is a safe place to live and raise a family.

4. Unspoiled beauty abounds in Nova Scotia.
5. The natural, pristine environments in Nova Scotia are second to none.
6. Our rich and diverse heritage creates an interesting setting to live and raise a family.
7. The eclectic mix of cultures creates a diverse and rich society.
8. The resiliency of the people to keep on fighting in the face of adversity and seemingly insurmountable odds has always been an inspiration to me.
9. The ingenuity of people to create their own solutions to their problems.
10. The can-do attitude that permeates the entire province is often contagious.
11. The determination that has pulled the province through some tough times and will do so again is palpable.
12. The unique and traditional food we enjoy such as Rappie pie, blueberry grunt, sauerkraut and Lunenburg pudding offers something for everyone.
13. The abundance of folklore and traditions add layers to our lives.
14. The ease with which rural and urban communities meld together makes living in Nova Scotia a unique experience.
15. The natural talent that abounds in Nova Scotia most notably in the arts is truly inspirational.
16. The fact that Nova Scotia is a natural habitat for so many birds and wild animals and further that as a society we place great emphasis on protecting their habitats.
17. For the most part and despite the occasional occurrence that draws negative attention, the majority of Nova Scotians are tolerant and accepting of people who are "different."
18. Nova Scotia is the cradle of democracy and freedom of speech in North America, something for which we should all be proud.
19. Nova Scotia has produced a long line up of outstanding and distinguished political, business and civic leaders throughout its history that should inspire us all.
20. Even though the weather can be harsh at times, by and large it is one of the most moderate regions in the country.
21. We live in a place of relative safety free of exploding bombs, errant bullets and dissidents wanting to do us harm.

22. Nova Scotia is well positioned to provide any type of outdoor experience one desires, from experiencing the ocean or a freshwater lake, to enjoying the ski slopes and the inland, wooded regions.
23. Nova Scotia has a diversified economy that has been built on natural resources, agriculture, construction, industrial and the arts that provided many opportunities to both attract and build success.
24. I like the fact that Nova Scotia is one of the oldest regions of Canada and as such that gives us bragging rights that the roots of our great nation begin right here.
25. And finally, I am proud and happy to call Nova Scotia my home because my family roots and those of my wife's family are firmly planted in the province. It's also the place where we raised our two wonderful children, so as our home the province is an important link to our past and future.

And so, there you have it folks. A list of 25 reasons why I'm a proud Nova Scotian and you know most of these reasons can be adapted to anyone's list.

The real message here, as far as I'm concerned, is that those of us who are fortunate to live, work and play in Nova Scotia are, indeed, lucky. The real tragedy, however, is that many of us take these qualities for granted, or at least that's the view from here.

What is community?

March 25, 2015

Anyone who reads this column regularly will know that I am proud to live in the wonderful town of Liverpool and I'm equally proud to call the much larger South Shore Region my home. This part of the world has so much to offer so there is no need to go anywhere else.

I grew up here, raised my family here and have chosen to stay here even when other opportunities came along in the past that would have taken me elsewhere. Although faced with some challenges (what part of the world isn't?), the South Shore is a great community to live, to work and to raise a family.

To coin an old phrase, the pasture always seems greener until you're there grazing so I stayed, and I have no regrets about putting down my roots here.

While Liverpool, just like every other community on the South Shore, has had its fair share of ups and downs in recent years, largely based on the collapse of traditional resource-based industries and outside economic influences over which we had no control, I see a strong and vibrant future.

While admittedly it continues to be a struggle, I see the town rebounding, but it won't get there overnight, and it won't get there without a great deal of hard work and cooperation from everyone and without innovate thinking and strong leadership from our leaders and governments at all levels.

However, I firmly believe that with the right approach and the right attitude, our towns and villages will bounce back and will become hubs of activity once again, but we must have faith, work hard, remain united in our efforts and be supportive of each other. We must reject the tendency to dwell on the negative and pull together as one cohesive force of change.

During a recent conversation about Liverpool and the South Shore with a group of people whom I respect, someone asked what I think defines a community. Although, when considering such a question, our first instinct might be to think about the number of businesses that exist within our geographical boundaries, the number of storefronts that line our main streets or the number of houses that make up our neighbourhoods, the reality is that "community" has nothing to do with any of that.

Don't get me wrong. I understand that a community needs businesses to survive, and to grow and prosper. And it needs people to reside within its boundaries, but a community isn't about bricks, boards and mortar, a healthy community is about the people who occupy those buildings and who operate those businesses.

It's about the people who reside in those homes and who do the volunteer work that needs to be done. It's about businesspeople having enough faith in the area that they will invest in us.

A community is a group of people with common interests living in a particular area (such as a town or a region). It's a group of people linked by a common history, common principles, a common set of challenges and common objectives. A community is a group of individuals who have a shared vision and who are united and unified in achieving a group of shared goals.

Right now, in Liverpool and all along the South Shore, our shared vision is to see the region grow and prosper, to attract and nurture business, and to become a place where our young people can find employment and our seniors can retire in comfort. That is our goal and that is the thing that makes us a community.

So then, with all of that being said, let's take a look at what makes a "true" community.

Being part of a community not only means recognizing when your neighbour needs a helping hand, but also means extending that hand to help without waiting to be asked.

Being part of a community also means knowing that when the chips are down, your neighbours will be there to help lighten the load. Sometimes you may have to ask for help, but being part of a community means you aren't afraid to do so.

Being part of a community means taking pride in where you live and doing everything you can to protect, guard and enhance that environment.

Being part of a community means supporting another person's idea even when you think, in your humble (sometimes not-so-humble) opinion, it's not such a good idea.

Being part of a community means embracing initiatives when they're launched and promoting the efforts as good news.

Being part of a community means celebrating the success of your friends and neighbours and spreading the word. It also means crying with them when they experience failure, as we all do at some point in our lives.

Being part of a community means demonstrating your pride through your actions and by what you say.

Being part of a community means doing your share of the heavy lifting instead of criticizing those who are brave enough to step up to the plate.

Being part of a community means nurturing young citizens and helping them realize their full potential. It also means showing respect and appreciation for the wisdom of those who came before us.

Being part of a community means learning from past mistakes and using those lessons to move forward, together.

Being part of a community means listening to and accepting constructive criticism when it's offered.

Being part of a community means helping to build up instead of tear-ing down.

Being part of a community means being part of the solutions instead of contributing to the problems, or at least that's the view from here.

Who says you can't go home again?

May 13, 2015

There's an old saying that suggests you can't go home again, and while I've never been sure what that really means, I've always thought it was suggesting that we can't go back to a familiar place and expect things to be the same as they were when we left.

To me, it suggests that change is inevitable and that we should never return home (or any familiar place) following an extended absence and expect things to be as they were the last time we were there.

It makes sense. Things change. Places change and people change. It's part of the aging and maturing process. It's a natural evolution of life and societal development.

This point was recently driven home to me when I returned to my old stomping grounds in Lethbridge, Alberta, where I studied journalism from 1980 to 1982. I was honoured to return to my former college to re-ceive the Lethbridge College Distinguished Alumni Community Leader Award, given to graduates in recognition of their careers and their con-tributions to their communities.

It's a prestigious award and I am deeply grateful to all of those who supported and endorsed my nomination. I won't name you publicly, but you know who you are.

Being singled out by your peers is a humbling experience, especially when such an award is in recognition of your life's work, as it provides an opportunity to reflect upon your past accomplishments and to assess what you've done. It also causes you to look ahead and ask what you have to offer and accomplish in the future.

Have you achieved everything you wanted to achieve in your life?

Have you done the things you wanted to do? Have you met the goals you set for yourself when you began this journey? What more can you and will you do?

I am grateful that I have been able to answer in the affirmative to most of these questions, but obviously there's still more that I want to do. I certainly don't feel as though I'm done yet.

Among the highlights of the experience for me was the chance to visit Lethbridge and the college where I studied, and to reconnect with some old friends I hadn't seen in a very long time. I hadn't been back there for over 30 years, and the changes I encountered were remarkable.

Clearly, life in southern Alberta is good. The growth and development in the city have been tremendous, with commercial, residential and industrial projects exploding throughout the region, but that's what happens in a place where the economy is robust, attracting people from across the country and beyond.

As well, the college has undergone a complete metamorphosis and looks nothing like the place where I studied in the early 1980s.

Having the opportunity to return to Lethbridge College was much akin to a rebirth for me. After a challenging year of unexpected changes (most of which I now believe were for the best, as they provided me with real insight into myself and a better understanding of how some people function), it gave me the opportunity to refocus, regroup and to put things into perspective.

As they say, when times get tough, it's often good therapy to get back to your roots, and that's sort of how I viewed this excursion. I hoped that by reconnecting with my past, I would find a way to focus on my present situation with an eye to the future.

When I first went to the college in 1980, I went as a young, naive kid who had no idea what he was getting into or what the future held for him. Going into this strange world, I only knew that I had a dream of having a career in newspaper journalism. I had no idea what achieving that goal would entail, but I was prepared to give it my best shot.

This time, I returned with almost 35 years' experience in my chosen profession. I returned as a successful journalist, author of 21 books (and more to come), a dedicated community volunteer, and as a husband and the father of two wonderful children.

I expected that the college had much to offer me upon my return visit, but this time, with a career and life experience in my back pocket, I also felt I had a lot to offer the college. So, it was a mutually beneficial experience.

I'd be lying if I said that winning the award wasn't anything special because, in fact, it was a big deal; and while I knew it was a privilege to be recognized, I also I felt important to be singled out from the thousands of students who have graduated from Lethbridge College over the past 50-plus years.

Everyone likes to win awards. I don't know of too many people who would not embrace such an honour, but it's equally prestigious in that this particular award recognizes two important aspects of who I am: my career and my dedication to my community.

On anyone's list of important things in life, family comes first. After that, my career and community share equal billing on the list, so to be recognized by my college for those attributes is, well, it's simply special.

Lethbridge was home to me for several years, and I will always have a special place in my heart for Lethbridge College and for the city. So, it was important to make this return visit as I felt a need to get back to where it all started; but in the end, Liverpool and Nova Scotia are where I truly belong. I knew that in 1982 after I graduated, and I knew that following my recent trip.

I will admit that it's great to travel and to experience other parts of Canada and other countries, as it gives us a different perspective on our own lives and communities, but it's also wonderful to return home, or at least that's the view from here.

What would you like your community to be?

April 13, 2016

It's no secret that I love my community, the place where I was born and raised.

My ancestors lived for many generations in Liverpool and Queens County (now the Region of Queens), so my roots run deep here. It's also the place where my wife and I raised our two children, so it is near and dear to us. It's our home and, while we've visited other places, it's always wonderful to return.

It is also the place where I was educated and where my journalism career took root, so I'm thankful for the professional opportunities my community has provided me.

And because my community is so important to me, I felt the need to give back, so over the years I've invested thousands of volunteer hours into a variety of causes, chief among them education, health and tourism.

However, despite the affinity I feel toward my community, I admit to pausing for several minutes recently when someone asked what I'd like my community to be like 10 or 20 years from now.

I truly believe that great potential awaits our communities here on the South Shore (and all of Nova Scotia, for that matter) and that we are on the cusp of something extraordinary. However, I also know we won't achieve that potential if we don't work together and harness our visions, strength, abilities and, yes, even our weaknesses so that we can deal with them. It's very important to keep it all in perspective.

The vision that I have for my community is that it will achieve the greatness that I know it is destined to achieve. I want it to be a place where new and innovative ideas can take root and grow, a place where everyone's vision will be embraced and given proper consideration.

The solution to our challenges may just be one crazy idea away, so that's why I think it is imperative for all of us to embrace and nurture new ideas when they come along. Instead of ridiculing someone's idea because it's never been tried before or because you don't think it will work. It is imperative that we be supportive and offer encouragement.

With all that being said, I still want my community to be a place where we can express our opposing or dissenting views and opinions without fear of reprisal from those with whom we disagree.

I want it to be a place where disagreements can be had without fear of backlash or ridicule, but that can only happen if those views are honest, sincere and based on legitimate arguments and not simply just because you don't like how something sounds.

Looking ahead, I want my community to be a warm and welcoming environment for people who come here from other places, be it from another area of Nova Scotia, another province or another country.

We must keep an open mind about those who choose our community as their home and as a place to do business. Let's invite them into the fold and help them put down roots. Let's help them understand our way of life, while at the same time making an effort to understand their beliefs and traditions.

I want my community to be a place where we treat our neighbours with respect and dignity, without being judgmental. We need our community to be a place that allows people of all races, nationalities, religions and sexual orientations to be who they are. This is imperative if we are going to see our communities grow and prosper.

I want my community to be a place that treats our senior citizens with the respect and dignity they deserve. We can learn a great deal from those who came before us, and we would do well to tap into that wisdom and experience. After all, there is no one better to teach us than those who have already experienced the trials and tribulations of life.

As we chart a course for the future, it is also imperative that we understand our past, because those roots keep us grounded. We can learn from our history, and there is no better way to connect with our past than through our senior citizens. They are an important resource that often goes underutilized, so we must change the focus and make them part of the conversation.

I want my community, then, to be a place where mutual respect and understanding between all age groups is an everyday occurrence.

Likewise, I want my community to be a place that fosters youthful vision and allows young people to be part of the solutions. Let's call it the great age divide, but far too often, I believe, we dismiss the younger age group simply because we don't understand them. We must break down these barriers and try to understand that, while our views may differ, we're still in the same boat, with similar goals.

Furthermore, we must accept that today's younger generation will someday be the decision-makers and we will depend upon them to maintain and build our community for future generations. It's the cycle of life perpetuated.

I want my community to be a warm and inviting place for those who are here by birth and those who are here by choice. I want my community to be a place where businesses flourish and prosper, and volunteers are recognized for the excellent work they do and the contributions they make. And I want it to be a safe, nurturing environment for every resident, no matter his or her demographic.

I believe many opportunities await us. I believe our communities can be as strong or as weak as we make them, but the simple fact remains that we can control the future if we work together and support one another, or at least that's the view from here.

Vernon Oickle

The view from here on

Important milestones

Vernon Oickle

The walls came tumbling down

June 18, 2014

For almost a week, I stood by the fence each day and watched as my old high school was levelled to a pile of broken bricks, twisted metal, shattered glass and splintered wood. The images brought mixed emotions.

On the one hand, it was sad to see a building that had played such an important role in the lives of so many people being reduced to rubble, but on the other hand it was exciting because the removal of the old school signalled progress for the community of Liverpool.

Furthermore, contrary to some disgruntled observers who lamented the building's demise, the facility had outlived its usefulness and it was, without question, time for it to go.

I appreciate that we tend to cling to old buildings, especially one like the former Liverpool Regional High School that had been a community centre since it opened around 1957. Throughout the decades, the school was an integral part of so many lives and bore witness to so much of the town's history that it's difficult to see such a facility bite the dust.

During its lifetime, the school graduated thousands of students who went on to achieve great success in their chosen fields, not only in the local community but farther afield. Many accomplished great things in the provincial, national and international arenas, including those who excelled in the arts, sports, business, politics, medicine and science. The honour roll is long and impressive.

Over the years, the school also boasted many successful teams in a variety of sports; for many generations, LRHS was especially known for its basketball squads, many of which were legendary in varsity circles. LRHS was also known for the talented students who excelled in music and for its high level of academic achievements.

Without question, the residents of this community have ample reasons to be proud of those who passed through those hallowed halls.

While all of this success speaks volumes about the dedication, talents and hard work of the students who received their education at the school, it also speaks to the level of guidance, support and instruction the teaching staff demonstrated throughout the decades.

To accomplish greatness, a school requires two key components: students who want to learn and a teaching staff that knows how to reach not only those eager to learn, but, almost more importantly, those who are reluctant learners. Throughout its lifetime, LRHS was fortunate to have many examples of both groups.

However, like many aging buildings, the old LRHS—which had become a junior high school about 20 years ago, when the new high school opened further up the road—had passed its expiration date. In fact, it was time for it go ten years ago, if not before. But, despite the pressing need for a new middle school, the effort to win government support for such a project was long and drawn out, requiring us to jump through hoops. Such is the political process.

We made a strong case, though, and the provincial government approved the project about four years ago. Today, a modern, state-of-the-art middle school stands next to the site of the old high school. Housing Grades 6, 7 and 8, and boasting a new approach to teaching, the South Queens Middle School is a shining example of what a community can accomplish when people work together for a common goal.

There are times when it makes sense to preserve old buildings, but this was not one of those times. Some had suggested that the government should have invested money to refurbish the building, but it would have taken millions to renovate the structure and bring it up to modern codes and expectations. It made more economic sense to construct the new facility and remove the existing building.

With the demolition complete and the debris finally hauled away, the site will eventually become a soccer and multi-purpose field that will benefit not only the students at the South Queens Middle School but the entire community. It's never easy to let go of the past, but we must consider this to be progress.

I attended the old LRHS from 1975 to 1979, and while I have many fond memories of my time there, I also have some not-so-great memories of my high school experience. That's probably one of the reasons I had so many mixed emotions as I watched the heavy de-molition equipment slowly and methodically dismantle the place.

Among the good memories are of the friends I met, many of whom I remain friends with today. Some of my not-so-great memories include the struggles I had with my studies and of the bullies who roamed the halls. Yes, forty years ago, long before social media and texting became the tools of harassment for this modern generation, bullies made life difficult for some, so while overall I would say my high school years were a good experience, it wasn't all roses.

But, despite the ups and downs, my experiences at LRHS con-tributed to the person I am today. The successes I enjoyed proved to me that good things can come with hard work and determination, while the struggles I faced taught me to persevere in the face of ad-versity.

Through the tough times, I learned to turn weaknesses into strengths, and I refused to give up even when it might have seemed easier to just turn and walk away. It was in high school that I learned the road of life is sometimes bumpy, just as it's sometimes smooth and level, but I understand now that we can control our own destiny with the right attitude, hard work and a boatload of determination.

When I think of my high school years, it seems like a lifetime ago, and, in truth, I guess it was. So much has changed since I graduated in 1979. The world today is filled with challenges that I could not even begin to imagine back then. Today's students must be prepared to meet those challenges, and it is for that reason that I'm glad to see the old building removed because, in the end, education isn't about bricks and boards. It's about the students and about them having access to the best facilities and programs available.

To give the students at the new middle school those opportunities, the former school had to be removed. That's not something to ridicule or lament; that's something to celebrate.

They may have torn down the old building, but they didn't wipe out our memories, or at least that's the view from here.

From Liverpool to Lethbridge

April 22, 2015

As you're reading this column this week, I am reliving a part of my past. I'm thousands of kilometres away, in Lethbridge, Alberta, where I attended college in the early 1980s. Earlier this year, I was honoured to learn that my *alma mater*, Lethbridge College, had chosen me to receive the Alumni Community Leader Award, and now I'm here for the ceremony.

It has been many years since I was in Alberta, and I was excited to be finally going back. I anticipated a great deal would have changed, as the world was a different place back then. The city of Lethbridge has expanded, the college has morphed into a wonderful institution of higher education, I've lost most of my hair and gained a few pounds, but beneath all this change are the memories of a terrified young man who, almost 35 years ago, had never been west of New Brunswick before I went to Alberta.

In August, 1980, when I boarded a train in Halifax and headed west to study journalism at what was then Lethbridge Community College (LCC), I had no idea what the future held for me. I had no idea where I was going or whom I would meet.

I will admit to being apprehensive at the time about heading out on my new adventure to a part of the country that was foreign to me. I would essentially be a stranger in a foreign land, but at the same time I was also very excited by the opportunity to explore new things. I will also quickly admit to having a few bouts of homesickness during my first few weeks there, but I do not recall ever having any regrets about my decision.

We did have journalism schools in Atlantic Canada back then and, over the years, I have been asked many times why I chose to attend a college so far from my home. The answer is simple. After carrying out some research (which wasn't as easy almost four decades ago as it would be today with computers and the internet), I determined that the journalism program at LCC offered everything I was looking for.

I remember the first day I walked into the college. I had no idea where I was going or what I was doing. I knew no one and, as I wandered the halls, trying to figure out if I had done the right thing, I wondered what the heck had I gone and gotten myself into.

It's one thing to attend a college or university two hours from your hometown, but it's a completely different experience to attend college in a town more than 2,000 kilometres way.

Talk about culture shock. There was no hopping in the car and going home on the weekend for me, but I think that was a good thing in that it taught me to grow up and mature in ways that many of my contemporaries could not even begin to understand. So, there I was in a strange world that was foreign to me, but I was determined that I was going to make the most of it and make the most of it I did.

It had been several decades since I attended LCC, but I am thankful for the success that I found there, for it gave me the foundation on which to build my career and the tools with which to be successful.

I started working full-time in community newspapers upon my graduation in 1982, when newspapers were still printed solely on paper. A great deal has changed in the time since.

When I started in journalism, there was no Internet, World Wide Web or social media and our computers were as large as a table. We had not heard of texting, skyping, face time, Facebook, or tweeting. Sounds almost obscene, doesn't it?

Heck, when I started in the business, our newspaper office didn't even have a fax machine. In fact, I can remember that when fax machines first arrived, we thought we had finally gone high-tech.

Our office was one of two locations in town where you could go to fax something or to receive a fax. We charged 10 cents to send a fax and 25 cents to receive a message, since we were using our paper.

My, how times have changed. Today, fax machines are practically antiques.

I've seen many changes in the newspaper industry, from using hot wax, Exacto knives and a light table for paste up to full page pagination on a computer screen; from photographers using a darkroom to develop their pictures from rolls of exposed film, to digital photos that can be sent around the world in the blink of an eye; from reporters rushing back to their offices to write and file their stories before deadline to reporters standing on the street corner and instantly publishing their stories on the internet.

Times certainly have changed, and dinosaurs like me are quickly becoming extinct, or at the very least redundant. We're being put out to pasture in favour of computer-savvy youngsters who can easily navigate the Internet and social media, but I guess that's called progress. Some even call it evolution but think of the knowledge and experience us old guys have. Technology can never replace that.

I've had a wonderful career, one that has given me many interesting experiences. I've had the pleasure of meeting and interviewing celebrities, world leaders and headline-grabbing newsmakers. I've had the challenge of reporting on national and international stories, including murders, the drug trade, political corruption, abductions and even a major plane crash in 1998 that left 229 people dead. Above all, I've had a rewarding and exciting career and never had to leave my hometown again.

It has been a whirlwind, that's for sure, but it was important for Nancy and me to remain in our home community, where we could raise our two sons. I am thankful that my journalism exploits in the weekly newspaper world have allowed us to do that.

Since graduating in 1982 and establishing my journalism career, I have come to appreciate the important role our communities play in our lives. It is with that understanding that I have made it a priority to help make my community, Liverpool and the South Shore, continue to be a great place to live, work and raise my family.

I believe we all have a responsibility to contribute to our society and we can do that by helping to build strong and vibrant communities, or at least that's the view from here (in southern Alberta this week).

Memories from a two-room schoolhouse

September 27, 2017

I'm sure we all have fond memories of our early years in school. We also probably have some not-so-happy memories, but let's not dwell on those today. Instead, let's think happy thoughts and save those nasty ones for another day.

Two recent events caused me to start thinking about my early childhood experiences in a two-room schoolhouse. The first was actually the coming together of two different things—my 56th birthday and the beginning of another school year earlier this month.

Perhaps it has something to do with my age, but even though my children are both fully grown and out of school, I always get reminiscent each September as other children head back to the classroom. It's especially heartening to observe the really young ones, full of vim and vinegar, as they line up early in the morning to get on the big, yellow school bus for the very first time.

The mix of excitement and nervous apprehension plastered across their young, innocent faces is priceless. Their expressions of angst and exhilaration are almost palpable. On that first day of school, both the children and their parents experience a wide range of emotions as the little ones embark on what we hope is the beginning of a life experience filled with learning, happiness and, most of all, fun.

Most are awestruck, others are sad to be leaving the routine they've known for the first four or five years of their lives. From that first step onto that school bus, their whole world changes and the future is theirs to behold and experience.

How exciting is that?

When I started school for the first time in September, 1966, I didn't go on the school bus. The children from my neighbourhood at the end of Wolfe Street in Liverpool walked to school each and every day, no matter the weather conditions, and that brings me to the second event that prompted this little stroll down memory lane.

I started my formal education in a two-room building called Riverview School because, as the name implies, the building overlooked the beautiful Mersey River. From the tops of the high concrete steps that were located at the front of the school, there was a tremendous panoramic view of the river.

It was stunning; let's get that right.

I was reminded of that building just recently when my wife and I drove by the land on which the school was located. The property, owned by the Region of Queens Municipality, has remained empty, except for the alders and underbrush growing there, since the building was demolished in December, 1995. Now they've put it up for sale.

The Riverview School, which opened in October, 1951, was a manifestation of its era. It was built at a time when the area's population was so great that many smaller communities each boasted their own school. It was a trend throughout Nova Scotia at the time, as buildings were erected to meet the needs of these bursting populations of Baby Boomers.

Today, however, most, perhaps all, of these smaller, nondescript, square white buildings have been phased out as educational institutions. Many of them, long ago determined to have outlived their original purposes, have either been torn down or converted into multi-use facilities that have served their communities well over the years. They dot the countryside, their glory days as places of learning long ago faded into the dust of history.

Riverview's fate was sealed when it closed at the end of the 1966-67 school year. That was my primary term, my first and last year at the school, but I remember it well.

There were two classrooms in the upper level of the building. One room housed Grades Primary, 1, 2 and 3. The older students, Grades 4, 5, 6, 7 and 8, were housed in the second classroom. The washrooms were in the basement of the building and there was a tiny, tiny staffroom for the two women—Mrs. Tarr and Mrs. Farquhar—who taught there at the time. They were both wonderful teachers; I still remember them well and with much fondness.

The class sizes weren't large. In fact, there were only five of us in the Primary grade the year I started school, but the mixed and combined class setup allowed us to interact with the older kids, maybe even learn something from them on a good day. I believe there are mixed opinions on the effectiveness, or not, of that approach to education, but that debate is best left for another day.

Life at Riverview was interesting, as one might expect in a small, rural, two-room school, with its high points and its low levels, but I can guarantee that education was the top priority. The philosophy of the era was simple—the teachers were there to teach, and the students were there to learn.

But we also had many fun times at Riverview. In those days, we were expected to go outside and play no matter the weather conditions. While there was a large lot at the front where the students could play during recess and lunch breaks, there was also a small area behind the school where we could play and unwind, where kids could simply be kids.

It may have been a few years ago, but I recall there was a brook that flowed next to Riverview, one that dumped into the nearby Mersey River. I remember the warnings from the teachers: "Stay out of that brook," they would command.

And of course, what do children do when an adult tells them not to do something? They do it because, well, children must be curious and explore. If I had a nickel for every child who had to be sent inside that building because they disobeyed the teachers and slipped into the frigid brook water, I might not have ever had to work a day in my life.

I also remember a few good ole fashioned playground fights that took place behind the Riverview School. I remember one particularly bloody affair when one young upstart left the play area with a pretty good bloody nose, but he survived. In fact, we all survived and left the school with not only a good educational foundation but also with lots of fond memories.

Riverview School closed the year I completed Primary and all its students were then bussed further into Milton, to a new school that had been built there. I stayed at that school until I completed Grade 8, and then it was off to high school in Liverpool, but through all those experiences, I still remember my time at that little building nestled on the bank of the picturesque Mersey River.

Eventually, the building found a new life and, throughout much of the next two decades, Riverview was used as an upgrading school for adults wanting to improve their education. But in time, that program was phased out and the building was shuttered one last time. It then remained empty—except for a period when it was used for the local food bank—for many years until the Region of Queens had it unceremoniously torn down.

What a waste.

Yes, as they say, them were the good ole days. But in fact, they were just that. In this era when we all go full tilt, it's often therapeutic to sometimes dip a toe into the river of time and let the memories carry you away, or at least that's the view from here.

The Halifax Explosion, 100 years later

December 6, 2017

It was Thursday, December 6, 1917. The day dawned bright and clear. It was a sunny, but cold winter day, the kind that would make a person hasten their step as the snow crunched underfoot.

The port city of Halifax was a busy place with ships coming and going as they transported their cargoes of troops, relief supplies and munitions in support of the war effort overseas.

At approximately 8 a.m. the *Imo*, a Belgian relief ship, headed up Bedford Basin toward the Atlantic Ocean. At about that same time the *Mont Blanc*, a French supply ship, steamed up Halifax Harbour to meet a convoy that would accompany her across the treacherous Atlantic Ocean.

The *Mont Blanc* was laden with explosives—35 tons of benzol, 300 rounds of ammunition, 10 tons of gun cotton, 2,300 tons of picric acid (which is used in explosives), and 400,000 pounds of TNT.

The *Imo* was a much faster ship than the *Mont Blanc*, and was travelling too fast and in the wrong channel as she headed quickly into the Narrows. It was then that the *Mont Blanc* first spotted the *Imo*, moving quickly in its direction and in its channel.

The *Mont Blanc* signalled that she was in the correct channel, but the *Imo* replied that she was not changing course. The *Mont Blanc*, expecting the *Imo* to swing towards the Halifax side of the harbour, signalled that she was intending to pass on the starboard side.

By this time the *Mont Blanc* was precariously close to Dartmouth and had slowed to a snail's pace. However, instead of turning towards Halifax, the *Imo* maintained its course. This left the *Mont Blanc* with only one course of action, to swing to port, in the direction of Halifax herself, a move that would take her directly across the bow of the *Imo*, thus allowing her to pass on the starboard side.

This might have worked had the *Imo* not, simultaneously, signalled full speed astern. The *Imo*'s bow swung right, striking the *Mont Blanc*.

The colliding ship missed the TNT cargo but struck the picric acid stored directly beneath the drums of benzol. The impact of the two ships cut a gaping hole in the *Mont Blanc*, creating sparks in the process.

Amid the resulting blaze, the crew of the *Mont Blanc*, aware of their deadly cargo, abandoned ship, and leaving the burning vessel heading in the direction of the city of Halifax.

It was now approximately 9:05. The ship burned for twenty minutes, drifting until it rested against Pier 6, in the Richmond district, the busy, industrial north end of Halifax. The spectacle was thrilling, and drew crowds of spectators who were unaware of the danger.

The *Mont Blanc* finally exploded very close to the shore of Halifax, resulting in the largest man-made explosion prior to the nuclear age and sending a powerful shock wave for miles in all directions.

The human and monetary cost was tremendous, staggering in fact, even by today's rich standards. More that 1,900 people were killed instantly, and within a year the death toll climbed to more than 2,000 victims. It was estimated that a further 9,000 people were injured from the explosion and approximately 325 acres—almost the entire north end of Halifax—were devastated. The structures left standing following the explosion were eventually consumed by the resulting fire.

As for the *Mont Blanc*, the 3,000-ton ship was totally destroyed, her shattered remains being flung several kilometres in all directions. The barrel of one of her cannons landed three-and-a-half miles away, while part of her anchor shank, weighing over half a ton, flew two miles in the opposite direction.

The shock wave had tremendous force, shattering windows some fifty miles away. Reports from as far away as Sydney, Cape Breton revealed the blast was even felt that far away.

Within hours, relief efforts began, but not surprisingly hospitals could not cope with the wounded. And to make matters worse, a terrible winter blizzard struck Halifax the following day, depositing more than sixteen inches of snow on the ruins of the once-bustling city and, more importantly, on the human sufferers.

In time, however, the city was rebuilt, and today there are few survivors of the now-famous Halifax Explosion who can tell their tragic stories. Catherine Gertrude (Gert) Roy was born in 1896 in Halifax. She moved to Liverpool in 1917 following the explosion. She was one of those who witnessed the catastrophe and lived to talk about it.

Gert is deceased now, but I had the opportunity to interview her many years ago and, as we observe the 100th anniversary of this tragic event in our province's history, I would like to share some of her memories from that tragic day.

"I can say without hesitation that it was the most horrible day of my life," Gert recalled. "It was like the entire world stood still for us. Everyone thought the Germans were bombing us. After all, we were still in the middle of the First World War."

She recalled, "I remember hearing once how someone suggested that a German warship had been anchored just off the coast and fired a bomb at us, but that story turned out to be false. But it was terrible just the same. I remember when the explosion happened, all I heard was a terrible crash, or boom, sort of like thunder but three times louder than thunder....A lot louder. Then that was immediately followed by the sounds of breaking windows and doors slamming and wood twisting and buildings crashing down around us, and people screaming and crying out for help. It was the worst thing anyone could ever image. Anyone who survived those first few minutes was lucky to be alive."

Or maybe not, Gert quickly added.

Married for only a few months at the time of the explosion, Gert and her husband, Ralph, had been living in Black Court in the north end of Halifax, about a mile and a half from the explosion site. Stating that she can remember the event just as if it had happened yesterday, Gert said, "The explosion was so strong that it shook the whole city, and they say they felt it way down here in Liverpool, so you can imagine how it felt in the city."

She continued, "It was just terrible. So many people died or were injured that day. I had a sister who lost an eye, but my family were pretty lucky that more didn't happen to them. Some families were not as lucky. Entire families were wiped out. That's a sad thing to think about. In just a matter of minutes, entire families were destroyed....Mothers, fathers, sons and daughters were all gone. How does anyone recover from that?"

As with Gert's sister, eye injuries were among the most common injury reported from the explosion, as many Halifax residents rushed to their windows to see the burning ship just prior to the blast. When the explosion occurred, hundreds of people were sprayed with shards of glass from the shattering windows. Gert said she could remember hearing stories of people removing glass from under their skin even years later.

It was the memories of death and human suffering that remained with Gert her entire life, in vivid detail, through the years. "The injured children are what I remember the most, and they all seemed so lost. There were hundreds of them wandering aimlessly around the ruins, crying and looking for their mommies and daddies, but for many of them, their parents were never found."

Gert described how on the days following the explosion she saw "little white caskets lined up row upon row on the city streets, holding the bodies of hundreds of children that had been killed in the explosions or later succumbed to their injuries or to the cold." Schools and other buildings became makeshift morgues.

Corpses, body parts, dead horses and dogs were everywhere, and Gert said that along with that came the terrible smells that stayed with her for a long time, especially the odour of burning flesh.

"It's just a terrible thing. It gets in and burns your nose. I remember smelling this sickly, sweet smell in the air and I had no idea what it was," she recalled. "Later, I found out that it was the smell of human flesh being consumed by the fires that burned uncontrollably for days."

Trying to describe the scene after the explosion, Gert said it was even worse than anyone can imagine. "Total, absolute destruction. The entire north end of the city was wiped out. Streets were gone. Buildings were levelled. People were killed and injured and bleeding and in need of medical help which couldn't keep up. It was total hell."

For the survivors of the explosion, Gert said trying to pull their lives back together was extremely difficult because they could not forget about the people who had been killed or injured, and all those who lost family members. But, she added, time passes, and the scars do eventually heal. "It's impossible to forget something that killed and injured so many people. You just can't do it, but you find a way to go on. You might try to forget, but pictures like those get in your head and they're buried there forever."

That's the view from a hundred years ago, when disaster struck this province.

The night the world fell from the sky

September 12, 2018

I could not allow the 20th anniversary of the crash of Swissair Flight 111 to pass without observing an event that shook the entire province and, in many respects, still reverberates in the region more than two decades later.

I worked full-time for community newspapers back then and I recall the events well.

It was as if the world fell from the sky on September 2, 1998, when the plane plunged into the cold, unforgiving waters of the Atlantic Ocean near Peggy's Cove, killing all 229 people on board. The disaster forever changed the lives of all those who responded to the emergency, many of whom continue to live in this region.

I have vivid memories of that night, memories that I am sure I will never forget.

I recall that it was dreary and foggy, the kind of night ripe for tragedy when, just before 11 p.m., I received a call telling me that emergency crews were rushing to the scene of a reported plane crash somewhere near Blandford. At that point, no one had any idea how serious it was or what type of plane had crashed. Two decades later, we know the full scope of this disaster as its legacy is still felt today. While those who died in the crash were the obvious victims, the tragedy also had an overwhelming impact on many other lives, including emergency personnel and those who reported on the story.

Media from around the world converged on the South Shore in the wake of the tragedy. I can say without hesitation that covering the aftermath of the Swissair crash was one of the most emotionally draining stories I've worked on in my entire career.

I had covered other tragedies and disasters including murders and deadly car crashes, but I had never reported on anything of this magnitude. Reporters covering the catastrophe experienced sights, sounds and emotional sensations that left us numb. I still shudder at the thought all these years later.

To be sure, the crash devastated the lives of the families and friends of those who perished, but it also caused a long-term emotional impact that the residents of these communities will never forget. And I am sure that for some of those touched by the tragedy, the memories are as fresh today as they were twenty years ago.

An army of volunteers immediately sprang into action. Brave fishermen took to the water in a valiant attempt to rescue any survivors. They stayed on to help in the recovery effort once it was determined there were no survivors.

Volunteer firefighters, search crews, police and all the recovery personnel suffered from the stress associated with such devastation. Still others, such as the Red Cross, church groups, local residents and even schoolchildren, reached out to embrace all those who needed a helping hand. The local response was nothing short of inspiring, but that is our way.

At the height of the rescue/recovery efforts, our emotions were often stretched to the breaking point. Reporters are supposed to be objective, but in covering this tragedy, we were constantly tested as we faced sights and sounds unlike anything we could have imagined. This was a heart-wrenching story, well beyond our comprehension. We hear of such tragedies occurring in other places, but we never believe it will happen here.

There were times in the days following September 2, 1998, that reporters, just like members of the general public and everyone connected to the tragedy, felt overwhelmed by the facts, but we pushed forward. However, some things get in your head, and they stay there. This tragedy left a legacy of painful memories that are impossible to forget.

I recall, during one of my visits to Peggy's Cove in the days following the crash, witnessing one young woman, a grieving family member, pass her infant to a man standing next to her and then try to throw herself into the cold Atlantic. But for the quick actions of those nearby, she too might have become a victim.

And I will never forget an elderly family member screaming, "My God! My God!" as he was carried away by stretcher. Obviously overcome by his grief, the man had collapsed on the rocks while visiting the site not far from where his loved ones had died.

Above all, the sights and sounds of the memorial service held a week after the crash are forever fixed in my mind and heart. I cannot erase the images of mothers, fathers, wives, husbands, sisters, brothers, sons and daughters crying over their terrible loss as the list of names of those who died in the crash was read.

If these sights have left such an indelible mark on me, I cannot begin to imagine what those more closely associated with the recovery of the crash victims are feeling even twenty years later. Their lives will never be the same again.

Whatever the tragedy, the world does keep on spinning and somehow, we manage to move on. In time, while we don't ever forget, we do find a way to cope, and we come to terms. Somehow, we accept that such tragedy is part of our lives. The challenge in the face of such horror is to hang on, even when it feels like you are falling off, and that's the view from here.

A dark day that changed the world

September 11, 2019

There are days that stick in our minds with memories that are so vivid and so stark it's as though the events happened only yesterday.

59

These events usually revolve around marriage, births, deaths, graduations, retirements and other family-oriented milestones involving loved ones.

On a much grander scale, there are events that are so profound that we never forget what we were doing when they occurred. Whenever we hear of those momentous events, we immediately recall what we were doing on the day we first heard the news.

People recall the day President John F. Kennedy was assassinated, the day Martin Luther King died, the day the first man walked on the moon, the day Elvis Presley died, the day the Space Shuttle Challenger exploded on takeoff, or the day Princess Diana was killed. They remember where they were, what they were doing and whom they were with. They remember these events in such vivid detail that it's like a moment frozen in time.

For each era, these milestones are different. Earlier generations have vivid memories of the day Pearl Harbor was attacked, or when Canadian troops were first deployed in combat in each world war, or when the atomic bombs were dropped on Japan, the day the war ended or when the Titanic sank.

Depending upon one's age, such events will hold different meaning, but even with the passing of time they continue to shape our collective psyches and impact society years after they occurred.

In recent history, nothing has had a more profound impact on daily lives in the United States and Canada than the terrorist attacks on the on September 11, 2001, when four planes were hijacked and turned into missiles of mass destruction and death. Surely, no one who was alive that day and able to form memories will ever forget the horrific sights and sounds of those jetliners ramming into the two towers of the World Trade Center, the impacts of which reverberated around the globe and which, are still being felt today.

A total of 2,977 civilians in the World Trade Center died, as did 87 passengers and crew members aboard American Airlines Flight 11 that hit the North Tower. Another 60 passengers and crew aboard United Flight 175, which hit the South Tower, also died that day.

Of the brave men and women who rushed to the scene of mayhem, 343 New York City firefighters and rescue workers, 23 New York

City law enforcement officers, 47 Port Authority workers and 37 Port Authority police officers lost their lives while attempting to save the victims in the World Trade Center.

The attacks didn't stop in New York. In fact, the terrorist plot extended to Washington, where 59 passengers and crew aboard American Airlines Flight 77 were killed when the plane crashed into the Pentagon and another 125 people died in the building. A fourth plane, also aimed at a Washington target, never reached its destination, but a total of 40 passengers and crew aboard United Flight 93 gave their lives stopping four hijackers over Pennsylvania.

In total, more than 6,000 others were injured in the attacks. Even eighteen years later it takes our breath away to recall the death and destruction of September 11, 2001. In truth, it's still difficult to calculate the total impacts of these attacks.

In the days, weeks, months and years that followed the events now known collectively as 9-11, North American society underwent a major transformation and we saw a seismic shift in how North Americans view the world. While we were once secure in our belief that North America was immune to the horrors of such senseless violence, in one day the terrorists brought it to our backyard and now we live in a different world. It's a place where increased security measures, mass paranoia (and sometimes hysteria), invasion of privacy and government intrusion have become the order of the day. We are constantly reminded never to drop our guard and that the world will never be a safe place again.

Following the horrendous attacks, we witnessed much of the world go to war in Afghanistan as the U.S. and its allies launched an offensive designed to wipe out the terrorist threat that led to the attack on U.S. soil. Canadians were touched by the events, many of them close to home and many of whom continue to suffer the impacts of the war.

While the physical dust has cleared and the actual rubble has long been removed from the attack sites, the fallout from 9-11 is still being felt and the images of that day are forever ingrained in our collective memories. To witness such an event and to try to put it into perspective is not an easy thing to do, but somehow, we must find a way to move beyond these events and to end the hatred that these attacks represent.

Society still has a lot of work to do in that regard.

Today, as we mark the 18th anniversary of 9-11, we wonder if the world will ever recover, and we like to think that yes...yes we will. However, the stark reality is that there has been such a shift in public policy and thinking over the past eighteen years that it's impossible to imagine a world free of fear that the next major attack may be just around the corner.

Above everything else that has transpired in the nearly two decades since 2001, that is the true legacy of 9-11 and, in that sense, the terrorists keep on winning long after the smoke has cleared, and that's the view from here.

The wheels on the bus go round and round

November 18, 2020

When I was a youngster, oh so many years ago, I took the bus to school, and I remember those experiences very well. In fact, I remember them so well that it almost seems just like yesterday.

My school experience didn't start with the bus. In fact, when I began in grade primary, I walked to school every morning along with a few other kids from the neighbourhood and my older sister, Heather. At noon, following morning classes, we would walk back home for lunch, as we were not permitted to stay in the building.

At home, we'd scarf down a quick bite to eat, turn tail and make the trek back to school. Once again after classes were finished, our feet would carry us back home in the afternoon. The next day, we'd do it all over again.

This routine happened in all kinds of weather because there was no bus service in our part of the county, not to our school, at least.

After my first year of school, the old building was shuttered, and we kids were bussed further away to a bigger school with larger classes and more opportunities.

I don't know, though. Overall, I would say it was a positive move, but in many ways, I missed the little two-room school with the smaller, more intimate and closely-knit classes. However, the opportunity to ride the bus was very exciting for a little kid starting Grade 1.

I remember the first day of taking the bus was filled with excitement and some apprehension. I had never ridden on a school bus before that first day of my Grade 1 year in September 1967 and I had no idea what to expect. All the other kids from the neighbourhood and my sister were making the trip with me, so there was some comfort in that fact.

However, once the door slammed shut and the wheels on the bus started to turn, any early angst was quickly eradicated. This was exciting for a six-year-old kid and within the first few minutes of the bus pulling away from the stop, any fear and apprehension that I had felt were quickly eroded and replaced with excitement and yes, even awe.

It wasn't long before I came to appreciate the bus ride to school every morning and back home every afternoon, especially during inclement weather. I rode the bus from my Grade 1 year through to the end of Grade 8, after which I was required to walk because the distance from our home to the high school I attended was considered within walking range by those who make such determinations.

It really wasn't, though, and today, the children from the same neighbourhood where I grew up are bussed to all their schools, as they should be. I remember walking to high school in some pretty nasty weather. And it's not that I was lazy, but during those days, I recall thinking how great it would be to be able to take the bus.

When we were kids, we took the school bus for granted. As an adult who watched his own children take the bus every day, I came to appreciate how important the school bus truly is.

I bring this up as an objective observer because today, while I watch from my dining room window as the youngsters line up every morning to wait for the bus and then to see them excitedly scamper on board—some of them so tiny their legs can barely reach up to the next step—I realize that we don't give the bus drivers enough credit.

Think of the onerous responsibility they have. We entrust them with the safety of our children, and it is their job to transport that precious cargo to school in the morning and then to return them safely home in the afternoon. It's not a job to be taken lightly and I do believe bus drivers are among the unsung heroes who get very little recognition for the important work they do.

I recently came to that realization while watching the bus pick up the neighbourhood children and noticed how attentive the driver was as the youngsters climbed on board and took their seats. Watching those kids, all of them wearing face masks in accordance with current pandemic safety regulations, I saw that they all knew exactly what they were doing, and it was clear to me that the kids respected the driver and, in turn, the driver respected their young passengers.

How wonderful is that, I thought.

When I see children behaving in such a respectful manner, it speaks volumes to me about how well the driver does the job. We should tip our hats to bus drivers and say thank you for a job well done.

Almost by coincidence, later that same day, someone made a post on Facebook about a driver who failed to stop for a school bus that morning even though the red lights were flashing and the stop arm was extended. This could have been a tragedy and, fortunately, the driver caught the idiot on video. The post further said that charges were forthcoming.

I say, good for the bus driver. I also say, throw the book at the other motor vehicle operator and impose the highest fines possible. The fool could have killed a kid or badly injured someone. What in the heck could have been so important that the driver would speed past a stopped school bus that was picking up children?

There is no excuse for such behaviour, and the incident further confirmed to me that bus drivers have an important job, and some days I'm sure most of them think they deserve a medal for what they do.

By my way of thinking, they really do, and that's the view from here.

Vernon Oickle

The view from here on

This, that, and every other thing

Vernon Oickle

Why?

October 1, 2014

Okay, so I'm having one of those weeks where my mind is all over the place, which means it's difficult to focus on one thing.

I find that the mind is often like an impetuous child in that, no matter how hard you try to control it, sometimes it's best just to let the old chestnut have its own way. So, as I sat down to write this column, I decided to let my mind do its own thing and this is what it came up with.

Why is it that people who say they're so busy have all the time in the world to sit in front of their computers and write on Facebook about how busy they are?

Why do people buy tickets to major sporting events and then sit in the stands watching the game on their tiny phone screens?

Why can't people sort their garbage properly in public places when the signs giving them precise directions are displayed right in front of them?

In the same vein, why do people continue to litter when trash bins and waste cans are strategically placed throughout most communities?

Why is it we try to go out the in-door and in the out-door?

Why do people have to ruin what's left of summer and even the fall by continuing to harp on how many days to go until Christmas? Believe me, it will get here quick enough.

Why is it we complain about the roads being in such poor shape and then when the work crews move in to fix them up, we complain about the delays and the mess? We can't have it both ways, people!

Why do people continue to use cell phones while driving, even though it's been against the law for several years now?

Why is it just as soon as you make a doctor's appointment you start feeling better or when you make an appointment with the dentist, your tooth stops aching?

Why do people say, "Oh, you're home," when you answer the phone? Of course I'm home, or I wouldn't be answering the phone?

Why do grocery stores post signs that say, "2 for $4 or 1 for $2?" All I can say is, "Huh?"

Why would anyone fall for that buy-one-get-one-free sale in which the price of the first item is jacked up to cover the cost of the second "free" item?

Why do stores make shelves so high? It's particularly challenging for vertically-challenged people like yours truly.

Why do drivers think it's safe to operate a motor vehicle with a dog draped across their laps or hanging out their side window?

Why is it that when I'm standing ready to enter a crosswalk, many motorists keep right on trucking through the intersection? It's like they are oblivious to the pedestrian waiting to cross the street.

Why is it that in a country as rich and powerful as Canada, there is so much crippling poverty and rampant homelessness?

Why, with all the smarts and ingenuity we have in this country, do we still have such staggering rates of unemployment?

Why is it people don't talk anymore? Oh yeah, they text instead. Silly me.

Why is it that some people always seem to find the negative in everything?

Not only that, but why is it that these negative people are the ones who speak the loudest and are always heard?

Why, in this supposed era of inclusion, do we still marginalize and ostracize people with the use of labels to describe their race, culture, intelligence, colour, age or sexuality? Are we all not just human beings?

Why would anyone purchase any of those new-fangled drugs they try to push on television after hearing about all the possible side effects, which, to me, often sound worse than the original illness itself?

Why do politicians, officials and so-called experts refer to everyday people like you and me as "ordinary Canadians?" What exactly makes an extraordinary Canadian? No matter how rich and famous you are or what job you may hold, aren't we all just Canadians?

Why do we drink our water from plastic bottles when Canada has one of the largest supplies of fresh, clean water in the world?

Why do people who complain they don't have enough money to pay their bills and cover all their living expenses, continue to smoke?

Why do we, as a society, continue to rely on government for everything that needs to be done? Isn't it time that we all step up to the plate and take a swing for the fences?

In this modern, affluent society, why can't we find a way to spread the wealth around so that the haves continue to have what they've always had, while the have-nots end up having what some of the haves have? Did you get all of that?

Why do Canadians have to wait until October 2015 for the next federal election? Can't we just have the election this month and get it over with before the Harper Conservatives do more damage to our national institutions and destroy our international reputation?

Why can't we find a way to appreciate what we have right here in our own backyards instead of dwelling on the things that we don't have?

Why do other parts of Canada refer to Atlantic Canadian provinces as have-not provinces? Indeed, we have a great deal. They would do well to remember that richness isn't always measured in money. They'd also do well to remember that old adage—what goes around comes around—as someday the tables could be turned. After all, there was a time when Atlantic Canada was considered a "have" region.

Here's one that boggles the mind. It's that age old question that every person asks at one point in his or her life—why can't people learn that the proper way to put the toilet paper on the holder is to put it on so that it rolls over the top?

So, you see, it is true what they say. The mind does move in mysterious ways and sometimes, as I've discovered this week, it's best just to let it do its own thing, or at least that's the view from here.

Who says they have it easier?

November 12, 2014

How often have you heard someone say kids today have it so much easier than we did when we were younger?

What nonsense. In truth, such a statement is so inaccurate it hardly justifies a response. However, I feel compelled to address this serious issue because if left unchallenged, such thinking becomes accepted wisdom, doing a great disservice to our youth.

I will concede that, in this hi-tech, modern world in which our youth are connected to a vast array of information and seemingly endless opportunities, it may appear as though they have it easier; but in fact those opportunities come with many challenges and obstacles. Cyber bullying, for instance, is just one negative side of this new era of instant communication and connectability.

But the challenges our youth face aren't solely connected with the internet or technology.

Since modern technology can link us to the rest of the world in just a matter of seconds, one might think that an unlimited wealth of opportunities awaits today's youth when, in fact, just the opposite is true. While information and knowledge can be the keys to success, oftentimes they aren't enough, and I bristle every time I hear someone say that kids nowadays have it a lot easier than earlier generations, because that's just not true.

Different challenges and, perhaps, enhanced opportunities, yes. But easier? No way. In fact, not only do they not have it easier, but I would also suggest that on some levels they actually have it a lot harder than previous generations.

It may seem to some that young people these days have it easier because of all the material things they possess and the seemingly-endless list of opportunities that lie before them, but the fact remains that along with those things come new stress levels and certainly higher levels of expectation and subsequent pressures.

These are different times from when you and I were children, just as the years of our youth were different from those experienced by our own parents and grandparents and those who came before them.

While we tend to compare the lives of our children with our own childhood experiences, our observations are usually way off the mark. The truth is, every older generation draws these conclusions about the youth of the day, because it is often easier than taking the time to understand the challenges and obstacles of today's youth.

As the father of two, I speak from personal experience when I say young people don't have it easier. I have witnessed firsthand the angst that young people are often put through not only because of peer pressure, but because of parental expectations and a system that expects them to grow up and mature much more quickly than when I was a teenager.

Trust me, those pressures do not make their lives any easier.

It's true that we do give our children more material things than we may have enjoyed in our youth, but that is primarily because the means and technology exist for us to do so. However, it is also true that with those things, we expect our young people to mature and succeed at a quicker rate. In many cases, our children are not allowed to have a childhood.

In fact, by the time our young people hit junior high school they are practically supposed to know what they want to do with the remainder of their lives so that they can make the right curriculum choices. How can they possibly know such things at age 14? Hell, I know some adults who still don't know what they want to do when they grow up, and they're over 40.

But pressures from within the school system are only one source of angst experienced by the younger generation. In truth, today's youth growing up in this high-tech, computerized era of instant communications and technology are constantly bombarded with challenges and opportunities that many of us couldn't even imagine when we were their ages.

And if that isn't enough, along come dear ole mom and dear ole dad who, while meaning well, heap their own doses of pressure onto the shoulders of their offspring. I'm sure we all want the best for our children, but expecting our sons and daughters to become rocket scientists or superstar NHL players before they can walk and talk hardly seems like gentle prodding.

Now, add to all of this the normal pressures of growing up such as our sons and daughters' personal insecurities and feelings of inadequacy and the social stresses of trying to fit in with their peers and you have a potent cocktail for inner turmoil that seems more profound today because of the modern technology such as cell phones and computers, that serve up, non-stop, stories of anguish other people are suffering.

I cringed a few days ago, while standing in the lineup at a local supermarket, when I overheard several individuals of a senior persuasion waxing poetic about the evils of this generation's young people and lamenting about the lost youth that we are raising.

Now while I agree that there are many bad apples running amok in our communities (every generation has them), I also argue that there are far more members of the younger generation who are blossoming into fine, upstanding and contributing members of society. It's just that we tend to dwell on the negatives.

I know many young people who, through their long and varied list of activities in their schools and community involvement, could put many of their elders to shame. It's true.

Some young people defy explanation. They are exemplary students, outstanding athletes, dedicated volunteers and all-round wonderful kids, yet some of the senior generation seem determined to label the lot of them as lost youth. Such stereotypes are wrong, and they are, simply, unfair. While some young people may be responsible for some of the problems in today's society, adults are equally culpable, so it is inaccurate and misleading to paint all young people with the same brush.

If the pressures of technology and society are not enough, think of the other obstacles getting in the way as our young people look to the future. Growing unemployment rates and escalating student debts are just two more of the alarming realities they face. Anyone who thinks the youth have it easier today is sorely misinformed and mistaken.

The truth is that life is scary and we—I mean all of us—have a role to play in helping the younger generations to overcome these obstacles. The youth must be part of the solution, but clearly, they cannot overcome these issues without our leadership and guidance. The next time you start to suggest that today's youth have it easier, I urge you to think about you're saying.

It behooves us to become better informed about those youngsters before we write them off. And, above all, never, ever assume that the young people of today have it easier because that is simply not the case, or at least that's the view from here.

If I could save time in a bottle

November 19, 2014

Earlier this year, while I was giving a talk at the Colchester Historeum in Truro about my book on country music legend Hank Snow, my attention was drawn to an interesting exhibit that displayed the contents of a 137-year-old time capsule that had recently been removed from the northeast corner of the old Normal College building.

Located in downtown Truro, the municipal and provincial heritage building is currently undergoing extensive renovations to become the new home for the town's library.

Although much of the capsule's contents had been destroyed with the passage of time and because of water seepage, the display had been causing considerable discussion among the locals about some of the items that were sealed up in 1877, most notably some of the old newspaper clippings from that era that were still legible, and a few old coins that were a curiosity.

As I viewed the Truro items, I wondered what it would be like 100 years from now if future generations opened a time capsule from this time period and discovered how we lived. Wouldn't it be fun to be there to observe the reactions and to hear the comments from those who would be opening the capsule?

So now I'm planning my own time capsule, that I hope won't be opened for at least 100 years.

At first, I thought about including a CD or memory stick containing all kinds of information about our generation and what our world is like today. I also thought that I would include an iPod with hundreds of songs on it, but then I realized it's very likely that future generations will not have the equipment to access the information stored on such devices, as our current technology will be obsolete by then.

Besides, I'm sure that our descendants will be able to access all that material from large data banks that will likely be stored on super computers. Including anything along that line in my capsule, then, would be rather redundant and a waste of precious space.

No, my time capsule must contain more personal things. So, this is what I would include:

> An actual newspaper, preferably one that includes something I've written (maybe this column), but a real newspaper nonetheless because chances are pretty darned good that in 100 years newspapers on newsprint won't exist. Instead, the news will be dispensed through some sort of electronic gadget, one that will probably be no bigger than a fingernail.
>
> Additionally, I'd include a real book because those aren't likely to exist 100 years from now either, except maybe in museums or private collections. It will have to be an important book, however, and I haven't yet decided what it will be. I'll only have room for one, so I must choose carefully.
>
> I think I'd also throw in some currency and coins because there's a pretty good chance that, a century from now, all our financial transactions will be done electronically and there will be no need for real money. Heck, we've seen that happening even today.
>
> I think stamps are also likely to go the way of the dodo bird as we rely more and more on the internet to communicate, so I'll include a sample of those. Certainly, I'll put in several different ones from Canada, but maybe also a few from other countries just for

good measure.

I'm thinking it would be fun to include a toy, one each for a boy and a girl. I'm talking about real toys, though, not some electronic gadget. I'm thinking just simple toys such as a truck and doll because, if current trends are any indication, it's very likely that such hands-on toys that require a child to have an imagination may no longer exist in the future.

In that same vein, I'd also include a Monopoly board game, because that never grows old even with the popularity of video games.

I think I'll put in a rock, a seashell and some sand from the coast of Nova Scotia as it exists today because, if global warming continues, chances are good that the coastline will be someplace else further inland a century from now.

I'm also thinking that a picture of every lighthouse along the South Shore will be of interest to future generations because it's likely that, 100 years from now, these structures will have disappeared. It might also be a good idea to include a current map of Nova Scotia because, a century from now, there's a very good chance most of the province could be under water.

And as a good Nova Scotian, I'll also include a bottle of Alexander Keith's beer because of its historical relevance to the province, as well as a bottle of the Captain, the drink of choice of many Bluenosers.

Since I'm a movie buff and a huge fan of Tom Hanks, I'd also include a selection of his movies on Blu-ray and pray to God that a century from now they'll have the technology to watch them. Speaking of entertainment, I'd also include every season of "The Big Bang Theory" on disc just so that future generations can see what made millions of people laugh 100 years earlier.

I'd include a sample of my handwriting, but I've been told that it's so bad that no one will be able to read what I've scratched out, so that seems rather futile. Instead, I think I'll ask someone prominent to write a message from the past to the future.

I'm still deciding on whom I should ask to contribute, but I am sure it will be someone who can write something inspirational and convey our hopes for the future and express our regrets for the mistakes we've made.

I'm not sure if they'll still be around 100 years from now, but just in case they're not, I will also include some Post-It notes in my time capsule because anyone who knows me will also know that I think they're the greatest invention from the 20th century. No? You haven't seen my office.

I think I'd also include a cellphone so that future generations can have a hands-on experience with the device that literally destroyed the art of face-to-face communication.

On a personal note, I'd also stick in a bottle of my mother-in-law's homemade chow because she makes the best chow I've ever tasted. I'm not saying it will still be good enough to eat 100 years from now, but it's so good that it's worth taking the chance. I'll also include the recipe so they can make their own in the future.

And finally, because I'm sure whoever opens my time capsule will wonder just who the heck I was, I will include a personal journal with details about myself and some thoughts about our lives in this period of time.

But honestly, despite all the material things one could place in a time capsule, I think the most important thing we could pass on to future generations is the message that they must learn from the lessons of the past. They must study our mistakes and successes and understand where we went wrong so they don't go down the same road, or at least that's the view from here.

Things that make me go, 'Huh?'

January 21, 2015

Okay, it's a new year and everyone seems so serious these days. Call it the lack of sunlight from the dark days of winter, the string of negative news items that have dominated the press in recent weeks or after-the-holiday blues, but I've noticed that people just seem to be in a bad mood.

Taking all of that into consideration and responding to the requests of readers and fans (yes, I have one or two), I've decided to take a decidedly lighter approach to this week's column by writing about things that have made me go, "Huh?" in recent weeks.

Don't get me wrong. Lots of serious news also makes me go, "Huh?", so it's not all fun and games. However, while examining the world around us, we've also got to appreciate the lighter side of things.

For example, I went, "Huh?" several days before Christmas when I went to the mailbox and found a card telling us that we could go to our nearest Sears outlet and pick up our Spring and Summer catalogue. *Really?* I remember thinking. Not only had we not even celebrated Christmas yet, but the day that the card arrived was December 21, the winter solstice. Talk about getting ahead of ourselves.

I recently went, "Huh?" while shopping in one of the region's large supermarkets and discovered, all in the same isle, Christmas items, products to celebrate Valentines Day and items for Easter. Now, if that's not getting our wires crossed, then I don't know what is.

I go, "Huh?" each and every time I walk into a grocery store and see the rising price of food. Wow. Enough said.

I go, "Huh?" every time I hear of someone else getting in trouble because they've been caught posting inappropriate comments or pictures on Facebook or on some other social media platform. Seriously, folks, in this day and age of instant and mass media, when it's impossible to do anything without leaving an electronic footprint, you'd think people would know better. There is no excuse for poor judgment, and if anyone makes inappropriate posts or sends offensive texts, then they deserve whatever fallout they suffer. Sorry, boys, but we live in a new age.

The falling price of gasoline causes me to go, "Huh?" every time I put gas in my vehicle or call the oil delivery man for a fill up, but in a good way.

I also go, "Huh?" when I note the higher price of gasoline from one area of the South Shore to another and wonder why the prices can't be uniform so that everyone pays the same no matter where we live and work.

I go, "Huh?" every time I hear more accusations against comedian Bill Cosby, which have been making headlines in recent months over allegations of his sexual assault against at least 15 women. The 77-year-old former star of *The Cosby Show* who, at one time was revered as America's top father, has never been charged with a crime stemming from the accusations, which resurfaced last October, but the scandal has tainted his entire legacy and destroyed his career.

I went, "Huh?" the other day when I read that Hollywood was actually considering making *Triplets*, a sequel to *Twins*, the 1998 film that stared Arnold Schwarzenegger and Danny DeVito as twin brothers, and this one may also star Eddie Murphy as the third sibling. Who in their right mind would think that was a good idea? I mean, seriously, I wouldn't exactly consider *Twins* to be a classic deserving of a sequel.

Recent news that Tim Horton's and McDonald's were both eliminating items from their menus received some attention, but the idea of Tim Horton's without Timbits and McDonald's without the Big Mac caused me to go, "Huh?" I'm not a big eater of these items, but the idea of a world without either of those products somehow seemed wrong to me. It would be like Burger King without the Whopper or KFC without the chicken. As it turns out, only one flavour of Timbit will be eliminated, and the Big Mac news turned out to be a hoax. Whew, I mean, "Huh?" After all, we all need a guilty pleasure once and awhile.

News that three masked gunmen stormed the offices of the satirical newspaper *Charlie Hebdo* in Paris on January 7, killing 12 people in the attack and injuring several others, caused me to go, "Huh?" as we cringed at the thought that these agents of free speech could be slaughtered in such a cold and callous way. Is this the new normal we live in?

I went, "Huh?" a while back when the region experienced its first major snowfall—two centimetres—and people were demanding that school should be cancelled. I'm all for putting the safety of children first but come on. It's a no-win situation for whoever is responsible for making this call.

Speaking of snowfall and winter driving, I always go, "Huh?" when I see people driving without fully cleaning off their windshields or their vehicles. Don't they realize how dangerous that is? It really boggles the mind.

When I saw that one of the region's major broadcasters lead its newscast with the story of another university sex scandal instead of the story that Halifax police were investigating a double, and possibly triple, homicide I went, "Huh?" I consider myself to be a newsman, but when did inappropriate sexual behaviour between a professor and student become more important than homicide? Says a lot about the society in which we live.

I went, "Huh?" a few weeks ago when I read a news item that pointed out as many as 200,000 Canadians will experience homelessness each year and that, according to the Canadian Homelessness Research Network, on any given night, about 30,000 Canadians are homeless. I'm not naive and I know Canada faces many serious social issues, but how can it be that in such an affluent country, there are people forced to live and sleep in the streets? We must do better.

So, there you are. In a world where doom and gloom control the everyday agenda, we also managed to put a light spin on the table. There is a lot of negativity in the world today, but I think it's important to also maintain our sense of humour, or at least that's the view from here.

Time for short, fat, bald men to unite

May 27, 2015

I'm short, fat and bald. By some standards, that's three strikes against me.

If I were in a game of baseball, I'd be out. But does that mean in our society, which is so unnaturally obsessed with superficial beauty, that someone with such less-than-desirable physical attributes would automatically be out?

Based on the flurry of recent television ads I've noticed this spring for yard products, I'd not only be out but I'm also in need of some serious psychological and emotional, if not physical, help. But I try not to take these attacks personally, even if they are clearly aimed at the short, fat and bald members of the male population.

We hear it all the time that women are pressured to look a certain way and to maintain a certain weight. That attitude is confirmed every time we open a magazine, turn on the television or watch a movie, but men also suffer from stereotypes. We just don't hear about it as often because men don't complain about such things for fear of being labelled as wimps.

Well, guys, I'm speaking up this week, as I'm tired of the not-so-subtle innuendos from these commercials that men who don't fit a certain mould are losers.

There seems to be general consensus that Hollywood's image of the "perfect" woman is not only insulting to the average female, but is also unhealthy. There is also the real fear that society's obsession with wafer-thin bodies sends the wrong message to young, impressionable girls and may lead to a variety of eating disorders.

These are all valid points. So why then is it okay to tell men that, in order to be successful, they must be over six feet tall, have a full head of thick wavy black hair, have a six pack and sport two days of stubble? Surely there's something wrong with that and I'm calling on all short, fat and bald men to take a stand.

So, my pudgy, vertically-stunted and follically-challenged brethren, let's unite. I'm fed up and it's time to shoot down the stereotypes.

For starters, guys, don't you find it insulting that a commercial for a ride-on lawn mower suggests that only hunky men right off the cover of *GQ* can use these products? What's up with that?

It's all about perception. Playing on the insecurities of us guys who would never think about pursuing a career based on our looks is a tried-and-true marketing strategy. As this new commercial opens, it shows a dumpy, bald guy wearing an ugly polo shirt and plaid shorts trying to start his push mower. Even I'll admit this poor schmuck looks like a lost cause.

While this "loser" struggles with little success to start his mower, he glances casually across to his neighbour's well-kept yard and watches, almost lustfully, as the guy next door emerges from his garage sitting high and proud on the seat of his ride-on.

Like a brave king on his mighty steed, he is grinning from ear to ear. His eyes sparkle with that not subtle message which says, "If you want to look like me and not that loser next door, you need to rush out and buy one of these mowers."

Yeah, right. Like that's going to happen! Surely my old mower has a few more summers in it.

But it doesn't end there. If the manly stud with the well-chiselled features doesn't convince you to buy this particular brand of mower, then perhaps another of his well-toned cohorts will persuade you to buy a new brand of miracle seed that apparently will make grass grow anywhere.

That's right. Not only have the manufacturers engaged the hunks to push their mowers, but they've also employed these pretty boys to pitch grass seed.

Like the mower commercial, this one for the grass opens with the average Joe inspecting his front yard that's riddled with patches of brown grass and barren spots. To his rescue comes the tanned and good-looking neighbour, armed with this miracle grass seed. Will the injustice never end?

What's wrong with the dumpy guy being the one on the mower or the one flogging the grass seed?

Nothing really, but that commercial wouldn't sell so well largely because these weak male versus strongman stereotypes have been ingrained in our culture for generations.

You may remember those magazine ads depicting the scrawny weakling on the beach being the target of a muscle man who kicks sand in his

face. In the next few panels, the skinny guy undergoes a major metamorphosis and transforms his body into a well-cut muscular specimen,
confronts the bully and gets the girl in the end. Miraculously, even his facial appearance changes.

Thus begins the age-old lesson that's been preserved and perpetuated
for generations, that the only way for men to succeed in our society is to
be buff and brawny, but that's not the case. Just like the concern we express for women who may be so brainwashed by the unhealthy image that
Hollywood promotes about them, we could be equally concerned for
young men.

As short, fat and bald men around the world will attest, we can't all be
eye candy or sex symbols. Instead, we should be encouraging young men
to be the best people they can be, to be healthy, to eat well, to exercise
regularly and to maintain a healthy attitude about themselves and life in
general.

These commercials with their subliminal messages that looks are important don't do much to help this cause. Society's unhealthy fascination
with the beautiful body doesn't help either.

You might say that, as a middle-aged bald man, I'm being overly sensitive or maybe even envious. You might be right, but we can't change who
we are. You can change how you look, if you have lots of money and willpower, but no amount of plastic surgery, liposuction or hair implants can
change the person you are on the inside.

Move over George, Brad and Johnny. It's time for short, fat, bald men to
unite. We must take a stand and that's the view from here.

Is it just me, or...?

October 14, 2015

Have Canadian elections become more like United States elections, with
negative attack ads that target individuals and distract voters from the
real issues?

Regardless of which party one supports, it's important to pay attention
to the issues, get to know the candidates in your electoral district, and get

all the facts.

Am I hearing more and more people saying they aren't voting in this upcoming election? Why is that? Why do people feel so disenfranchised?

Remember, it's your democratic right to vote. True, it's also your right not to vote, if you so choose. However, elections are your opportunity to pass judgment on an existing government, either by giving it a new mandate or by giving it the old heave-ho, so make sure your voice is heard on October 19.

Does it seem to cost more to buy groceries these days than it used to?

Even the food items that were once considered cheap, such as hamburger, are no longer cheap, and don't even get me started on the price of beef, chicken and fruit. Whoa!

Are there more Blue Jays fans around this year than over the past 22 years?

It must be true that everyone loves a winner. No bandwagon for me. I've always been a fan. Go Jays!

Does it seem that this year is just flying by?

Maybe it is true that, as my parents were fond of saying, as we get older time goes faster. My theory to explain this phenomenon is that the older we get, the more we pay attention to what's coming, such as our monthly bills or the next important date on the calendar. That means, as adults, we're never in the moment or the day and, since we are always looking ahead, the time zooms by, or so it seems. Remember, it's sometime important to stop and smell the coffee.

Does it seem that when it storms these days it REALLY storms?

Torrential rainfalls that lead to flash flooding, and record totals like they experienced in parts of New Brunswick a few weeks ago, suggest there's more going on than the normal cycles of the climate. Is it possible that global warming isn't a made-up conspiracy or the figment of someone's imagination? Whatever the case, something in the air has changed.

Are there more careless drivers on the roads these days than ever before?

I'm talking about those reckless individuals who pass on solid lines, refuse to adjust their speed to the weather conditions, talk on cellphones while driving and continue to put the lives of people at great risk. Remember, you're not alone on the highways.

Does it seem like there's more litter around the roads this fall than in the past?

I hate it when I see trash thrown on the ground. It's such an eyesore and this blight on our countryside is so unnecessary, as there are plenty of trash receptacles around our communities. To me it signals two things: people have no respect for anyone else and/or they're just too lazy to find a trashcan. Either way, there is no good excuse for littering.

Does it seem that the line between what is considered reality and what's not real is becoming more and more blurred?

Is it this fast-paced world of mass communications in which we live, or is it some of the crap that passes as entertainment on television these days?

Does it seem that the fine art of personal, one-to-one communications is becoming a dying life skill? Seriously.

People don't talk anymore. Instead, they text.

Does it seem that many politicians expect us to put our faith in them even though their track records suggest we shouldn't trust them?

If any elected representative wants our trust, then they must earn it, but many just take the electorate for granted. This attitude is wrong on many levels.

Does it seem there have been more visitors around the South Shore this tourist season?

Is it possible that the increase in numbers might have something to do with the increased marketing efforts in the U.S., the availability of the Maine to Yarmouth ferry or the lower value of the Canadian dollar in comparison to the American dollar? Perhaps it's all of these factors combined, but whatever the case, it's good news for the region.

Does anyone else cringe when Donald Trump appears on television talking about how he will improve the United States once he's elected president?

I know that while we're in the midst of our own federal election, I shouldn't be paying so much attention to American politics, but the truth is, what happens in the U.S. has a major impact on our Canadian economy and, generally speaking, on our society. And furthermore, is it remotely even possible that our friends south of the border would elect Trump for president?[1]

Do you find that nowadays a large percentage of the population is apathetic about becoming involved in their communities?

It is true that it's easier to complain than to take action, but I've always thought that if people stepped up to the plate and made an actual contribution instead of sitting back and complaining about things or ridiculing what other people are doing, then our communities would be doing very well, thank you very much.

Do you find that more and more people are complaining about what they don't have instead of being grateful what do they have?

I appreciate that these are difficult times for a lot of people, but complaining about things instead of being thankful for the positive things in our lives serves no purpose and helps no one, especially not yourself or those close to you. My philosophy is simple: if you don't like something, then change it. And if you need help to make that change, then seek it out.

Does it seem like cellphone companies are trying to get us to buy new phones every year?

Come on. Do you really need an upgrade every 12 months? Besides, what do you do with your old phones? Throw them away? Stick them in a drawer? Give them to a friend? Put them in a museum? Send them to the moon? Seriously, who needs to change their phone that often?

Are you as excited as I am to see the new *Star Wars* movie that's coming this December?

I've been a huge fan ever since I saw the first *Star Wars* in 1977. Movies don't get much better than that classic.

Do you think our federal government has dropped the ball on the Syrian refugee crisis?

There was a time when Canada was recognized as one of the first countries in the world to respond to a humanitarian crisis, but not so

---

1 I guess so.

much anymore, as Prime Minister Harper would have us all but turn our backs to the problem. We must do better by these people.

Are you tired of waiting in the drive-through lineup to get your coffee or tea while the people in the car ahead of you have ordered a full course meal?

I'm all for parking the car and going inside to get my order, but when I'm in a hurry, I don't want to wait behind someone who has ordered everything but the kitchen sink. To me, a drive-through is for quick orders.

And does it seem that we've come to the end of the line for this week? It certainly does, or at least that's the view from here.

When did that happen?

November 21, 2015

As an observer of people and the world around me, I'm always on the lookout for things that irk me or kind of hit me the wrong way.
Things like these, for example:

When did a sports team losing two games in a row become a losing streak as I heard one radio announcer recently announce? Really? Two games is a streak? A bad patch, maybe, but not a streak.
When did it become okay for homes and businesses to decorate for Christmas before Remembrance Day? This trend seems to be increasing every year and it is not okay. Simply stated, this is not acceptable and should never happen. As a sign of respect, the least we can do is wait until November 12 before pulling out the colourful lights and ornaments.
When did we finally have gender parity in the federal cabinet? In 2015. Way to go, Prime Minister Justin Trudeau.
When did commercialism take over the world? Seriously? Who wants to see Christmas ads running on television before Halloween?
When did the government of Canada recognize global warming as a real

threat and not some conspiracy contrived by a group of dooms day prognosticators? Oh, wait. That was about a month ago, when the new federal government was sworn in and we welcomed the new Minister of Environment and Climate Change. Finally, we have a government that admits the truth.

When did it become acceptable to sit in a Remembrance Day ceremony and use your phone for texting? Oh, wait. It hasn't become acceptable, and all I can say is, shame on you. Is nothing sacred anymore?

When did it become acceptable to throw lit cigarette butts out the window of your vehicle so that they smack into my windshield? I'm not judging you for smoking, but please stop doing that. If your vehicle doesn't have an ashtray, then find one and use it.

When did it become acceptable for physically-abled people to use parking spots designated for physically-challenged people? Never! So, people, please stop using them. If you're parked in one of the clearly-designated spots and someone who really needs it can't get one, then they are forced to park further away from the building. Handicapped parking spots are reserved close to buildings for a reason, and being more convenient for people who can more easily get around isn't one of them.

When did it become okay to throw your litter out the car window? Well, we all know that never happened. Come on, people. There's no need to ruin our beautiful countryside with litter and garbage. It's your trash. Take it home with you for proper disposal, and don't litter.

When did it become acceptable to make a turn without using your single lights? It's one of the most basic rules of the road. Too bad so many people seem to forget it. Be safe. Drive defensively.

When did children stop going outside to play? Oh, wait. Didn't that happen with the arrival of home computers and video games?

When did children start asking for iPhones and iPads for Christmas? Does that mean trucks and dolls are no longer in fashion? It's a different world, indeed.

When did our world become such a dark place that we can no longer go an entire calendar year without some horrible terrorist attack, bombing or shooting? We live in a sad society, my friends. The times have changed.

When did it become acceptable for people to spout their own uninformed views and opinions through social media and pass them off as fact? Seriously, people, do your homework before you take to the cyber networks and make a fool out of yourself and all of those who follow you.

When did it become okay to blame someone else for your problems?

Seriously. If something isn't right in your life, then you need to do something about it. Yes, there is no question that it takes less effort to sit back and point your finger at someone else than it is to take some initiative to do the work for yourself. However, you'll often find that making a positive contribution is much more rewarding than complaining, even if it does take some effort.

When did vehicles entering Highway 103 (or any highway, for that matter) have more right of way than vehicles presently on the road? Wait. That's not how it works. Safety first, please.

When did Canadians lose their compassion for those in need? This blanket statement obviously doesn't apply to every Canadian, but I find it disturbing when I hear people complaining about the government's plans to welcome displaced Syrian refugees into our vast and rich nation. There is no doubt that many Canadians have their own problems, and we must do better by them, but surely, we can still find it in ourselves to help those who are desperate and are literally fleeing for their lives. Canadians can and must do better than turn a blind eye to the humanitarian crises currently unfolding in Syria and Europe.

When did Nova Scotians develop such a negative view of immigration? After all, isn't Pier 21, once the beacon of hope and freedom for so many people fleeing oppression and searching for a new beginning, located in Halifax? And isn't Pier 21 the place through which more than one million immigrants entered Canada between 1928 and 1971? I believe it is. Now, isn't it ironic that, in this day and age of worldwide unrest, so many Nova Scotians have such a fear of immigrants when the Canadian Museum of Immigration is located in our province?

When the world seems like a dark and bleak place and we face issues for which we're seeking answers, sometimes all you have to do is ask the question, or at least that's the view from here.

Lessons from a road trip

August 10, 2016

I am a huge Toronto Blue Jays fan and I have wanted to see a live game at Roger's Centre for as long back as I can remember.

And for as long as I can remember, my two sons and I have been talking about travelling to Toronto to take in a game or two. Sadly, we just never got around to doing it. For one reason (excuse) or another, we just kept putting it off.

Well, this spring my older son said that if we were going to do it, we should just do it. And I, in my infinite wisdom, suggested that if we were going to Toronto, then we should make a road trip out of it.

We all agreed that driving for 18 or 19 hours to Toronto in the middle of summer sounded like a good idea.

In the end, I'm happy to say, it turned out to be a good idea. We had a wonderful time and made many precious memories that I'll cherish forever, but I've also learned a few things from the recent trip that I'd like to share with you.

First, let me state that while I have been to Pearson airport many times, this recent excursion marked the first time that I have ever driven to Toronto. With those hundreds of kilometres now behind me, I can say from first-hand experience that Canada is one heck of a big place. It's also a beautiful country.

One of the things that impressed me the most is the vastness of the region and the large, unspoiled areas that exist within the four provinces through which we travelled. The views were spectacular and the sheer size of the landscape left me in awe. Canada truly is a wonderful country, and taking a road trip is probably one of the best ways to appreciate the scope of this place we call home.

It's best to drive through the northern part of New Brunswick at night, as there isn't much to see there except trees, more trees and then, more trees. At least in the dark, everything looks the same.

I've also learned that when it comes to signage, the provinces of Quebec and Ontario leave a great deal to be desired. In fact, directional and speed limit signs are at a premium, so it's best to map out your route before setting out on your trip. Once there, pay attention for those elusive speed signs lest you run the risk of suffering the consequences, as the police are everywhere.

While one might think that driving from Nova Scotia to Ontario might pose some problems, I will say that I was definitely impressed with the ease in which one can map out the route. The roads were great, with few delays except the occasional construction zone, but even at that, we continued to move along at a steady pace.

I was pleasantly surprised that, considering the volume of traffic one would expect to encounter on the twinned Trans-Canada Highway, drivers were, for the most part, well behaved and considerate. Of course, you can expect to encounter the occasional yahoo who defies logic, but I will admit that while I was apprehensive about driving through Quebec and Ontario, it really wasn't any different than driving through Nova Scotia. Sometimes thinking about something is worse than actually doing it. Lesson learned.

On another positive note, I was impressed with the number of roadside stops all along the Trans Canada. Seeing as I had never made this trip before, I admit that I was a bit apprehensive about finding service should we need it, but we should have guessed that entrepreneurs have long ago recognized an opportunity to cash in on the travelling public.

However, it is comforting to know that, should you need to make a pit stop anywhere along the route, you don't usually have to travel far before you'll find a service station, convenience store, a wide variety of eating establishments and fast-food joints or just a place to pull over and rest.

When you are taking a long road trip, like we did, always leave yourself extra time to get from Point A to Point B, primarily so that you don't have to rush. I know that's just simple common sense but as we were driving along, soaking up the sights, I came to appreciate how nice it was not to have a tight schedule to follow. That flexibility gave us the time to move along at a steady, but leisurely, pace and that was relaxing, indeed.

On the trip back, however, all we wanted to do was to get home, so my advice to anyone contemplating such a road trip is to always make sure you have some sort of diversion built into your route because, invariably, it always seems like it takes longer to get home than it does to reach your destination.

Regrettably, the boys and I didn't do that, because all we wanted was to reach Nova Scotia, but I do think a diversion would be helpful to reduce the stress. Not sure what that would be, but I would encourage you to come up with something.

If you like listening to a certain kind of music during a long drive, make sure you have some selections recorded on a CD or some other device because, honestly, your choice of radio stations through northern New Brunswick and Quebec are…well, let's just say they didn't appeal much to our tastes. When you're making such a long drive, music certainly does make the trip go more smoothly, so plan accordingly.

If your vehicle or phone is not equipped with a GPS tracking device, then I highly recommend that you invest in one before embarking on a road trip, as this marvel of modern technology can save you a whole lot of headaches. I know I sometimes put out the impression that I'm against all the techno gadgets that have invaded our lives over the past two decades, but this one, my friends, not only puts you on the right track from the very start but can help to put you back on the right track if you get turned around. See, not all technology is bad.

Here's the most important lesson of all. Taking a long road trip gives you the opportunity to spend quality time with your companions, so it's important to travel with people you like. Seriously, who would want to spend 18 hours cooped up in a vehicle with someone you don't like? That would be one heck of a drive. I had the best companions anyone could hope for.

When we decided to take this long road trip in the heat of summer, many people asked why we would do such a thing when it would be quicker and easier to just hop on a plane. We'd be there in a few hours and then we could enjoy the city, these people pointed out.

This is true, of course, but besides being less expensive than flying, the road trip to Toronto also gave us the opportunity to see some of the beautiful countryside we call Canada. More importantly, it allowed me to spend some quality time with my boys, and that was the most important part of the entire trip.

There was a time, not too many years ago, when I would never even have contemplated taking such a trip. I was too busy or I couldn't find a way to make it fit into my schedule, I'd reason. Now, though, I've come to realize that doing these things is important to one's quality of life, or at least that's the view from here.

Pondering some of life's greatest mysteries

August 30, 2017

So, here I sit on this rainy Sunday morning trying to find a topic to address in this week's column and it seems that I'm being bombarded by a series of silly and not-so-important questions. Then I wonder, why not make that the focus this week?

I discovered a long time ago that when you're doing a column on a weekly basis, it's important to sometimes mix in the fun and whimsical with the heavy and thought-provoking issues.

I hope you will agree that, in this world of today, it's even more important to hit the pause button and take a walk on the lighter side of life. So, this week, take a deep breath and let's ponder some of life's great mysteries.

And just a word of caution: if you're expecting to find hard-hitting, politically-charged commentary in this material, you likely won't find it here this week. Just some fun.

With that being cleared up, here goes. These are just a few of the things I'm wondering about today:

- Did they ever find who let the dogs out? And if they did, why haven't they ever told us?
- What's with camouflaged underwear? Who goes hunting in their skivvies?
- With all the technology and smarts that exist in the world today, why hasn't someone invented a resealable cereal bag? Don't you find it aggravating that once you rip or cut open the bag inside the box, there's no easy way to reseal the bag and the cereal often gets stale? Can't be that complicated to come up with a better way, can it?
- Why is it that the warranty always runs out just a few days before your appliance decides to break down? Now *that*, my friends, is a conspiracy worthy of an FBI investigation.

- Why is it that grocery stores always seem to pull a product from its shelf just after you discovered that you really like it?
- Who taught U.S. President Donald Trump how to tie a tie? Doesn't his tie get in the way when he uses the urinal?
- Here's another question about Trump. Does he really think he's the greatest president in U.S. history? Oh, wait a minute. He's the guy who believes that if you repeat the lie often enough—no matter how far-fetched it is—people will eventually come to believe it.
- Speaking of world leaders, is Justin Trudeau's thick hair naturally curly, or does he have a monthly perm?
- Here's another one that has always bugged me. When I hear people say they have the life of Riley, I always wonder, just who is this Riley? And how did he or she have such an easy life? Perhaps he or she could share their secrets of life.
- Whenever we talk about something strange that may have occurred and I hear someone refer to it as an old wives' tale, I always wonder just who were those old wives? How did they become so wise and why should we listen to them?
- I wonder the same thing whenever I hear someone say "they" won't allow this or "they" prevented something from happening in our town. I have two questions related to this — who is "they" and how come "they" know so much?
- The other day, I heard someone say time was really flying by. It sure seems that way, doesn't it, but how can time fly? Does it have wings? Does it take a plane? Does it use a glider? Does it have superpowers?
- And again, I ask, who thought it was a good idea to put relish in a squeeze bottle? Ketchup, yes. Mustard, yes. Relish, no. Absolutely not. No way.
- Why is that some people, who are obviously old enough to purchase a coffee or hamburger, will walk right up to a trash receptacle but still toss their garbage onto the ground? I just don't get it.
- Is this not the year 2017? So when we look at the news coming out of the U.S. in recent weeks, why does it seem like we're back in the mid 1950s and 1960s? I know we, as a collective society, can be naive at times, but it seems painfully clear, based on what has been going on in the U.S., that hatred, bigotry and intolerance have brutally trampled tolerance, acceptance and understanding.

And no, it's not fair to include all Americans in that statement because I think, by and large, the majority loathe what is happening in their country. It's certainly a sad, sad, state of affairs.

- In this day of mass communication, why do some businesses make it so difficult to find their contact information on their web pages? It doesn't make sense to me. If you go through all the expense and effort to create a page, why not make it more accessible to users?
- So, we've all probably heard the phrase "Bob's your uncle." You've heard that, right? But I can't help wondering if Bob really is your uncle? I, for one, don't have an uncle Bob. Huh. Go figure.
- Is it just me, or does it always seem that weekends go faster than weekdays?
- Why is that when the lights turn green, some motorists are slow to take off? I have a suggestion. Put your phone down and pay attention to the traffic lights. When the light turns green, put your foot on the accelerator. It's really that simple.
- Why does Tim Horton's still insist on using pennies in their prices when you pay with your debit card? Pennies haven't been in circulation for several years now. Just round it off to the nearest nickel. They do that when you pay cash.
- Why does Facebook keep asking me what's on my mind? Does it really care? Seems like a less than sincere question coming from a computer program, but then again, the computer asks more often than anyone—or anything—else I know. People, we have to talk more.
- Speaking of Facebook, why don't they have a "Don't Like" option? There's a pretty good chance you don't want to "Like" everything that's posted on Facebook. I'm just saying that a second option would be good.
- Do you think if the U.S. election was held today, the outcome would be the same as it was last November? Boggles the mind, doesn't it?
- Do you really think an apple a day keeps the doctor away? Sometimes, it really is just the little things that amuse me.
- What's up with the pop-up ads on my computer screen asking me if I get annoyed by pop-up ads popping up? Don't they see the irony in that?

I know. Silly right? Well of course it is, but in light of what's happening around the world, I say it's time to lighten up a bit, or at least that's the view from here?

That moment when ...

September 17, 2017

The world is a serious place these days. Between a growing threat of possible nuclear annihilation with the U.S. and North Korea on the brink of war, political and social unrest south of the border, and natural disasters leaving a swath of death and destruction in their paths, it's no wonder most of us are wondering what the future holds.

To escape from these oppressive, sometimes smothering topics, every now and then I like to throw in a fun column just as a diversion and to break up the serious talk. For instance, just the other day while I was having a conversation with a friend about those little things in our lives that sometimes cause us big embarrassment, I thought, what a terrific idea for a column. So here you have it.

I call them some of life's most embarrassing and frustrating moments, but I'm sure we've all experienced that certain moment when...

You're driving along the highway on a hot, sunny day with the window down just minding your own business and enjoying the cool air on your face when you feel something fly through the window and hit you in the head. A few minutes later, when you just happen to look down, you see that a bee has come to rest on your crotch. What do you do? Do not panic. Your first instinct is to swat it away, but then you remember you're driving, and this may not end well.

You get stopped at an RCMP road check and you suddenly realize you have left your wallet at home, meaning your driver's license is also at home. All you can do is hope for a forgiving officer, plead forgiveness and promise it will never, ever happen again.

You go to pay for your goods at the grocery store, only you don't have enough money in your pocket. It's been a while since that's happened, but can you say embarrassing?

You meet someone on the street, and they immediately start talking to you as though you are a long-lost friend, and they very well could be. However, try as hard as you might, you just can't remember their name. Can you say bad memory?

You're sitting in a busy restaurant, talking to a friend, when you knock over your cup of coffee and the hot liquid spills all over your lap. Can you say very unpleasant experience?

You're eating in a restaurant and, as you squeeze ketchup over your fries, you miss your plate and the thick, red liquid lands on the front of your light-coloured shirt. Since you're out of town and don't have a spare shirt in your car, you quickly wipe away the ketchup and hope no one will notice the red stain that's left behind.

You're standing in front of a group of people when you realize your shirt is buttoned improperly. You just hope no one notices, but then you realize they can't help but see it. When that happens, just ignore it and move on. Besides, it could always be worse, right? You could discover that your fly is open or that you had a piece of spinach stuck in your front teeth.

After you rush and practically kill yourself to get to your appointment on time (because you can't stand to be late), when you get there you find out that your appointment isn't until the next day. Can you say, stressed out?

You think you have enough time to make it through the intersection before the yellow light turns to red, but you were wrong. Remember, yellow means slow down. It does not mean speed up.

You hit the send button on the e-mail and then immediately regret that you sent the nasty message. Piece of advice here—be absolutely positive that you want to send the message before you hit send, as there's no taking it back once it's gone. The cyber world is very unforgiving that way.

That moment when the person you just called answers the phone and you immediately forget who you called. Does it get any more embarrassing than that? Well, in fact, yes it does.

You push on the door and try to walk through it at the same time, only the door doesn't push in, it pulls out.

After you've just washed your hands in a public washroom, you realize that not only does the hot air blower not work but there isn't any paper towel either. This is a conundrum, especially if you're at a formal function. Who wants to shake hands with someone who has wet hands? I hate it when that happens.

Speaking of washrooms. That moment when you're standing at the urinal and hear someone talking to you and you answer. Only, seconds later, you realize they aren't talking to you at all. In fact, they are talking to someone through their Bluetooth connection. You can chalk that one up as another of life's most embarrassing moments.

You've just realized that you've walked out of the washroom with a piece of toilet tissue stuck to the bottom of your shoe. Here's a piece of simple advice: check your shoes before leaving the washroom.

Worse still, you've walked into a crowded room with your fly open. Now, don't deny it guys, we've all done it at some point in our lives.

You drop a glass jar in the supermarket, and it shatters into a thousand pieces, making a mess for someone else to clean up. It was an accident. Honestly!

You've argued with your wife that you can't find (insert whatever item you want here), and she walks into the room and puts her hand on it in less than a minute flat. Awkward for sure, but all you can say is, "Sorry, honey," and insist that it wasn't there just the minute before because you looked for it. Really! Hold your ground. It wasn't there.

You've burped (or worse) in a public place, much to the chagrin of your spouse. Admit it. I know you've done it at least once.

You immediately know you've said something in a crowded room that you shouldn't have said, but once it's left your lips, you can't take it back.

That moment when you are talking about something or someone, perhaps not in a flattering way, and you suddenly realize you are talking to someone who is actually related to the subject of the conversation. The message here is two-fold—always be aware of your surroundings and always know to whom you are speaking. Better still, don't talk about other people and then you won't find yourself in this situation.

That moment when you read something you've written for the first time in print and you immediately think, darn it, that's not what I meant to say. I think every writer has, at some point in his or her career, experienced that embarrassment. Here's hoping that I don't experience that feeling when I read this week's column.

Okay, so, as I've said, we all have these moments when we wish we could snap our fingers and be somewhere else, but when life throws you an embarrassing curve ball, all you can do is shrug it off and accept it because, once it's done, it's done. The best solution is just to laugh about it, or at least that's the view from here.

20 things that really peeve me off

November 29, 2017

Okay, time to vent.

Every so often, it's healthy to cut loose with those things that bother you or that get under your skin, so this week I'm going to talk about twenty things that really peeve me. You know, they're the little things that happen, it seems, and while they are nothing more than common annoyances sometimes, they're just enough to spoil your day.

You know what I'm talking about, I'm sure. Let's get after it.

1. People who post on Facebook the outcomes or ending of a television show right after it airs. What about those people who may not have seen it yet, but have it recorded and plan on watching it when they can? Talk about spoilers.
2. Same with a movie. Don't ruin it for everyone else who wants to see it, and if you have to talk about it on social media, at least let people know you're going to post spoilers. Please be considerate of your fellow movie watchers.
3. When the television show I taped ends prematurely because the DVR only recorded part of the program. That happens when the program starts later than its scheduled time because something before it (usually football or golf) runs late. When my DVR is set to begin taping at a given time, it doesn't know what it's taping. It just starts and stops as it's programmed to. You'd think with modern technology we could address this problem. Thank goodness for TV on demand.
4. Donald Trump. Period. What else is there to say?
5. People who toss lit cigarette butts out their vehicle windows. Yes, it's hard to believe that anyone would still be doing something so careless, but it happens a lot. In fact, it happened to me not too long ago and the butt actually hit my windshield. Can you say, not a happy camper? Yup. That would be me.

6. Drivers who speed past me and then slow down once they're in front of me. Really. How rude. Why would you do that? Do you have something against following another vehicle?

7. Also, in the same vein, drivers who speed up when I'm trying to pass them really irk me. Come on. That's not only unlawful, but it's also not safe.

8. Drivers who don't pull over or even slow down when they see emergency vehicles approaching really peeve me off. I do believe that, by law, you are required to yield the right of way to any emergency vehicle. Every driver should know that.

9. Another issue that really peeves me are drivers who do not use signal lights when making a turn. It's a basic rule of the road, so try following it.

10. And finally, drivers who pass me and then five minutes later down the road, take the next exit. Really! What's the rush?

11. Okay, so maybe that wasn't my last complaint about drivers. Is there anything that peeves you more than tailgaters? Perhaps that's the worst driving infraction of them all. And don't even get me started on nighttime tailgaters who keep their headlights on high.

12. People who are quick to shoot down someone's new idea simply because they don't like it or because they have already determined it won't work for whatever reason really irk me. Can't you at least give it a chance before you poo-poo an idea? Perhaps it will surprise you.

13. People who spit their gum on the sidewalks really peeve me. That's just nasty and uncalled for.

14. Shoppers who don't bother to put their carts back in the corral when they're finished with them, but instead leave them to sit in parking spaces where someone else can hit them with their vehicle, really peeve me off. That's what those structures were built for. How about we all try using them?

15. I get really frustrated when I'm sitting in the lineup at the gas pumps and motorists who have already pumped their gas are standing around chatting and holding up the line. That is very inconsiderate. Come on, guy, just move along and let someone else have access to the pump.

16. People who bathe in perfume before going out in public really peeve me off. Please be aware that many people are sensitive to

strong perfume smells, and just because it smells nice to you doesn't mean it's nice for others.

17. People who talk in movie theatres really irk me. I paid good money to see the movie and I would also like to hear it.

18. Those who know me will know that I do not care for winter (let's be honest, I hate it) so it should come as no surprise that one of my biggest pet peeves is having to scrape the car windows in the morning. Yes, I know I could turn the car on and let the windows defrost, but is that really any way to treat the environment? The good thing is that spring is only four months away. See, now that's the positive side of this one.

19. I get really peeved off when I think about the growing disparity between the haves and the have-nots in our society. One would think that in a country as great as ours, with so many riches, the gap would be shrinking, but instead, it seems to be expanding. There is no excuse for this divide. We must do better to ensure every citizen of this nation has all the basic needs to live at least a comfortable life, one without poverty and violence.

20. And finally, one thing that really irks me is when people make a commitment to do something by a certain time—it's called a deadline for a reason—and then fail to deliver. I'm not going to name names here, but you know who you are and shame on you.

There. Now I feel a whole lot better now that I've vented.

Sometimes it's the little things in life that really gnaw at you, and when that happens, you just must get them off your chest, or at least that's the view from here.

25 silly questions that may or may not boggle the mind

April 18, 2018

We live in tumultuous times and, as regular readers of my column will know, I occasionally like to deviate from seriousness and take a walk on the lighter side.

In recent weeks, as I was preparing to take a trip with my wife to celebrate our 30th wedding anniversary, it became increasingly more difficult to focus on anything poignant, so, thinking it must time for a diversion, I turned to a tried-and-true formula to lighten the mood.

In that vein then, I present 25 silly questions that may or may not boggle the mind but have absolutely nothing to do with world peace, the environment, poverty, disease, natural disaster or the future of human life on this planet we call Earth. If they accomplish nothing but to make you chuckle a few times, then I have achieved my goal. Here goes:

1. In a major windstorm, whose hair do you think would stand up the longest, Justin Trudeau's or Donald Trump's?
2. How did people watch TV before they could binge watch their favourite shows on Netflix?
3. Is this the season that the Leafs finally win the cup or is the team just teasing their fans?
4. Which really is tastier, the Whopper from Burger King or the Big Mac from McDonalds?
5. Who is the more powerful superhero, Spiderman or Superman? As a side note, if Batman doesn't have superpowers how can he be considered a superhero?
6. Which kind of peanut butter do you prefer, smooth or crunchy?
7. Do you eat bread with the crust on or with it cut off?
8. Does the toilet paper go over or under on the roller?
9. When did the words "Bomb Cyclone" become a real thing? In all

101

my 56 years on this plant, it has only been the past year that I've heard those words used together to describe a major weather event. According to Google, it's a real weather phenomenon. Who knew?

10. Speaking of weather, is it really smart for television reporters to stand out in the middle of strong winds and driving rains to report that the winds are "really powerful" and "the rain is coming down hard"?

11. If I leave my shopping cart in the middle of the parking lot, will it miraculously find its way to the cart corral? Apparently, some people think so, as this continues to be a problem.

12. Is a bird in the hand really worth more than two in the bush? Who decides such things?

13. Is Donald Trump's skin really orange? Ewwww! It can't be natural, can it?

14. What genius thought it was a good idea to eat Tide pods or to snort condoms? Yes, shake your head. Can't even imagine the thought process that would have gone into that.

15. If you find poutine disgusting, does that mean you are less Canadian that someone who loves it?

16. Just have to ask again, how can you text and drive at the same time? Does that make you talented or stupid? It surely makes you dangerous, let's be clear about that.

17. What do you do when the power goes off and you have no television to watch or computer to play on because the Internet is down? It's a dilemma that has defied the ages. Seriously, though, have you heard of reading a book or playing a board game?

18. And is it just me, or do we seem to have more power outages these days than we had in the past? There was a time when a power outage was a rare occurrence, but today it seems like we have them with even the most minor windstorm. What gives?

19. If someone puts something on Facebook and I want to acknowledge it but don't want to hit "like" because I don't like it, what do I use? Why don't they create a "don't like" option or an "I'm thinking about it" option?

20. Who would have thought that something called a fidget spinner would be so freaking entertaining and addictive? What's that they say about small things?

21. Why don't people say goodbye when they are talking on the

phone on TV or in the movies? They just cut off the conversation and hang up. That's pretty rude.

22. With all the technology in the world today, why hasn't someone invented a way to get the last of the toothpaste out of the tube? Just asking.

23. Has technology gone too far? I recently saw an advertisement on television for an app that can tell you where your dog has pooped. All I can say is, huh? Do we really need to know that? Someone has way too much time on his or her hands.

24. How did people build homes or cook meals before the age of HGTV and the Food Network, with their home and cooking shows? I never knew that watching someone drive a nail into a board or boil an egg could be so entertaining, but you know what? It really is.

25. Where did Shubenacadie Sam study meteorology? Someone ought to tear up his weather-forecasting papers, 'cause he surely messed up this spring.

I know some of you are probably saying, What's wrong with this guy? Why do such little things seem to bother him so much?

All I can say is that sometimes distractions are good. I believe it's healthy to look at the world we live in and question what's going on, even if it is simple and mundane things, or at least that's the view from here.

Let's talk about stuff

April 18, 2018

We live in a throwaway society filled with all kinds of stuff.

We see people's stuff every spring and fall, when mountains of it are piled along the roadside waiting for pickup, its ultimate destination being the already-overflowing landfills and illegal dumps that litter the countryside.

I'm amazed and sometimes even repulsed when I observe this twice-annual ritual, in which people throw away stuff they no longer need or want as they've moved on to newer and upgraded stuff, complete with all the bells and whistles.

There is ample proof that we live in a materialistic world filled with stuff. There's stuff here. Stuff there. Stuff everywhere. Our world is literally bursting at the seams with stuff.

Yard sales and second-hand stores are now popular as we sell our old stuff to get money to buy new stuff that we may or may not need. There's stuff stacked on shelves and stuff hanging on racks, stuff that someone thought might fetch them a few dollars.

At least if this stuff is repurposed, it won't end up in the dump. That's a good thing, though, as our stuff is given a second life when someone else buys it from us.

When you go to these places, you see bags of stuff and boxes filled to overflowing with stuff.

There are piles and stacks of stuff—literally mountains of stuff just waiting for someone to take it to a new home or, if not, to the landfill.

It seems no one is immune to the lure of this stuff.

As I look around my home, the two storage sheds in my backyard and in our attic, I see we have way too much stuff.

I'm especially guilty of hanging onto stuff. I'm not a hoarder by definition, but I am definitely a pack rat, as my wife would surely agree. It's stuff that I thought I wanted to keep for whatever reason that I can't even remember now.

There are stacks and piles of stuff that has sentimental value.

Stuff that may have monetary value...to someone, I suppose.

Stuff that has historical value, or at least family heritage value.

And then there's lots of stuff that I'm sure has no value whatsoever, but it's stuff that I just can't find the courage or heart to throw away.

I am not alone with my obsession with stuff. Our society is built to accumulate stuff.

I defy you to walk through any retail outlet these days and not be overwhelmed with the overabundance of stuff you'll find there.

There's stuff stacked in the aisles and piled ceiling high on the shelves, sometimes so high you can't even reach it, which poses another problem altogether.

In these marketplaces, there's stuff strategically placed for you to see and stuff that's put at a low eye level for youngsters to see because retail marketers and merchandisers know that children like stuff, and sellers know that if they place the stuff in just the right location, the children will see it and demand that their parents buy the stuff for them.

And most parents will buy the stuff because, in many cases, when you're tired and hurrying through a busy department store, it's easier to buy the stuff for your children than to stand your ground while saying no.

It's not easy telling your child he or she doesn't need any more stuff as his or her room is already filled to overflowing with stuff that they never use, stuff they cried for but never played with once they got it home.

In the end, most parents will relent, buy the stuff, take it home and add it the growing mountain of stuff their children have already accumulated.

But we can't only blame the children. Adults are often more demanding and wasteful than children because, in our case, the stuff we covet costs more and adds to the ever-growing environmental catastrophe that's sweeping the globe.

Our world is fuelled by electronics and computers, stuff that's expensive, usually has a short life span and isn't easy to dispose of. Yet we all collect this stuff at an alarming rate.

For instance, most homes today have a television in every room—including the kitchen and bathrooms. Most homes also have more than one computer and most family members, no matter their age, have a cellphone or IPad, stuff that we all claim we can't live without, although earlier generations somehow managed to get by without this stuff.

But when it comes right down to it, at their very core, all these electronic gadgets are basically still stuff. It's stuff that accumulates at alarming rates and stuff that's difficult to dispose of once it's outlived its usefulness or isn't wanted anymore. The sad part is that some of this stuff could still be useful to someone.

When we decide it's time to get rid of some of our stuff, we usually try to find a way to repurpose it. We used to have yard sales but now we usually just give our stuff to the Salvation Army thrift store. At least by giving our stuff to a worthy charity, we hope it will once again become useful while at the same time generating a few dollars for an important cause.

But stuff is like that. We see it. We want it. We may use it for a while and then, when we long for something new, we discard the old stuff for something newer. That's just the nature of stuff and, like it or not, stuff has become an important part of our society.

We simply have too much stuff cluttering up our world, or at least that's the view from here through all my stuff.

Patience. Got to get me some

July 25, 2018

Anyone who knows me will know that patience is not exactly my middle name. While patience may be a virtue, I'll admit it's not one of my best qualities and, without question, it is something I have to work on.

People like me don't do well in this fast-paced world. This hurry up and wait society in which we are forced to function often causes me great angst because I simply do not like to wait. Instead, I'm all about just getting there, getting it done and then moving on. In other words, don't keeping me hanging.

In fact, I'm the one who usually shows up twenty minutes before the scheduled time of whatever appointment I'm supposed to attend, be it a meeting, social function, something work related or even a doctor's appointment. Doesn't matter what it is. I'm mostly early and often the first one there, sitting around waiting for things to get started.

I know. It drives other people crazy, but it's my thing. Besides, I would rather be early than late, but that's another story altogether. Don't even get me started on that issue.

I am sure my wife will confirm that patience is not my strong suit. You can imagine how well I cope when my everyday routine runs into a delay, such as being forced to sit in a string of traffic at construction sites, just sitting waiting for that bloody "follow me" truck.

I know. We complain when the roads are bad, and we complain when they fix them. I get it. I understand that the work must get done when weather conditions allow for it, but is it really necessary to make us wait so long at each stop? The wait times have gotten shorter in recent weeks, but it's still difficult for people like me to remain idle when we have things to do.

Even standing in a lineup at the supermarket or waiting at the drive-thru while someone gets his or her special order can push me over the deep end. I know, I should just park my car, get out and go inside. It would be better for the environment and for me, but sometimes it seems the drive-thru would be the faster alternative; often it isn't.

Simple things such as sitting in the theatre waiting for the movie to start cause me great frustration if it's five minutes late, and waiting for the traffic light to turn green sometimes tests my patience. And don't get me started on how much I grumble when the light turns green, and the cars don't move.

I know, I shouldn't sweat the little stuff, but come on already. When the light turns green, it means you're supposed to move, not sit there and gawk around or talk to someone in your vehicle. Put the phone down and put your foot on the gas pedal.

No, there's not a chance that anyone could ever accuse me of being a patient person, and I know I'm not alone. It's just that many of you won't admit your failings.

However, as a friend recently pointed out, there are times when we should all exercise some patience. He rightly noted that while we have all likely blown our horns, shaken our fists, grumbled under our breaths or even cursed out loud at strangers in our communities for causing delays or getting in our way, we ought to be more considerate to those who are visiting.

Furthermore, when we are about to lose our patience and blow our tops at that person who seems to be wandering aimlessly across the street in search of some elusive treasure that we can't see, or that driver in the vehicle with the out-of-province license plate who appears to have no idea where he's going, we should consider the positive impact these tourists have on our communities.

Let's consider this argument more closely.

Even if these visitors have inconvenienced you, anyone who lives on the South Shore must agree that the tourism industry is an important component of this region's economy that injects millions of dollars into the local marketplace. In turn, that money supports our businesses and creates jobs.

If you agree with that—and you should—then it behooves us to welcome these visitors to our communities with open arms. If you don't agree, then it's time to become educated on the facts.

Believe me, I know how frustrating and aggravating it is to be stuck behind someone who doesn't seem to have any idea where they are going. However, when you get frustrated over such things, try to remember the last time you were in a strange place and had no idea where you were heading. Would you appreciate being yelled at, berated or being on the receiving end of the finger?

Not likely, but this isn't about your personal feelings. The issue runs deeper than that.

Think of all the tourism-related businesses that exist in our communities and benefit from the tourist trade, and then think of all the jobs these businesses create. Think of the dollars that pass from the hands of these visitors and maybe even end up in your bank account where you, in turn, hand them over to other businesses. It's an economic cycle that's important to our region, especially now that many of our traditional industries have fallen on hard times.

It may be difficult to guess at the rate of impact one visitor can have on our community, but we can assume it's significant and, if that's the case, then we aren't doing ourselves any favours when we lose our patience with these strangers.

The next time you grumble and growl about a stranger getting in your way, think of the important role that visitor plays in our economy. That tourist may be helping to give you, or maybe someone else in your family, a job.

As we build our tourism infrastructure and help our industry grow, it's important that we all become good ambassadors. No matter how inconvenient it may seem to have to slow down to allow a stranger to cross the street and no matter how much a lost driver may frustrate us as he or she navigates our roads, it would be more beneficial to offer a helping hand than to grumble and complain about it. And I certainly include myself in that group, as I've lost my patience more than once.

Sometimes, it's not easy for impatient people (yes, just like me) to slow down and give people an extra five minutes to get their bearings, but let's all promise to do better in the future. We want people to visit our communities and so, when they get here, let's make them feel welcome.

Let's not blow the horn, yell, shake our fists or make obscene gestures at them. Instead, let's greet them with a smile and offer a helping hand. In doing that, we'll be making a positive impact on our community, or at least that's the view from here.

When technology becomes old or obsolete

March 20, 2019

The one thing we know for sure about technology is that, no matter how innovative and cutting-edge it may be today, eventually it will become outdated and obsolete, destined for the scrap heap.

And the rate at which these so-called advances have occurred over the past half-century boggles the mind. I say so-called because in some cases I'm not really convinced that all technology has advanced humankind.

But the world has certainly changed over the past 50 years. Today, almost every home has at least one computer, if not two or three. And practically everyone you know has a cellphone of some type and is connected to the Internet. Even the world of entertainment has changed dramatically in the past couple of decades, with streaming services opening up more viewing opportunities than one could have ever imagined. Coupled with the arrival of digital and smart televisions, and hand-held devices, there are limitless entertainment possibilities.

But seriously, have our lives really improved because of video games, television programs and cellphones? Perhaps it has in some ways. However, there are many negatives to such technology, but that's an argument best left for another day. Right now, I want to talk about what we do with the equipment once it becomes obsolete.

What do we do with the computers, cellphones, tablets and televisions that have outlived their often all-too-short lives? In some cases, no sooner do you buy an "upgrade" than it's practically obsolete the minute you leave the store or it arrives on your doorstep, if you shop on line.

It's a conspiracy, don't you know? It's an elaborate plot designed by multi-billion-dollar corporations to perpetuate the buying cycle, thus filling their bank accounts to overflowing and the landfills with electronic devices that probably had a few more good years left in them but were tossed away because someone somewhere needed the latest gadget.

There are government-funded programs and private initiatives designed to divert these devices from landfills and trash heaps, but the advances and production of new gadgets are happening far too quickly for these efforts to keep up. This buy-discard cycle happens around the world as advancing technology makes it necessary for us to buy into the upgraded equipment when our older equipment becomes unable to adapt to the changes.

Usually, you have no choice but to play their game. Either you upgrade your equipment, or you risk becoming disconnected. The bottom line is that we have been caught in the web of technology, and in this ever-advancing world there is no way out.

Look around your home. I bet many of you have old cellphones in a drawer or box that you no longer use because you just had to have the upgraded version. Truth be told, you could still be using that old phone, but we consumers have been brainwashed into believing that it is necessary to upgrade every couple of years, even if you really don't have to.

In some cases, though, some equipment just becomes obsolete. Take VCRs. This is an excellent example of how advancing technology with DVD players has rendered obsolete a device that was once widely used by millions of people.

I remember in the late 1980s when VCRs first arrived on the scene. Home entertainment would never be the same. As a movie fanatic, I was on cloud nine. I paid $600 for my first VCR (yes, I really did). I just had to have one in my home because the device not only allowed me to rent movies that I could not get to the theatre to enjoy, but I could also buy them and watch them again whenever I wanted.

Today, we have several VCRs in the house that are just gathering dust, along with boxes and boxes of VHS movies that haven't been viewed in years and are never likely to be viewed again. What a shame and what a waste. When I think of the hundreds of dollars we spent over the years adding to our collection of movies only to have them become obsolete, it makes me cringe.

It also makes me sad because eventually we will have to find a way to get rid of them, and at the end of the day maybe they will end up in the garbage, as the equipment to play them is mostly no longer available.

Old analog television sets are in the same boat. What does one do with a perfectly good television set that was loved and well taken care of until it was pushed aside into the spare room after our new flat screen arrived? It's time to clean house, and the old television must go.

It seems like such a waste to add it to the recycling pile, but it appears there are few other options. You can't sell it. Heck, you can't even give it away. If you know of someone who could use a perfectly good television, albeit an old-fashioned model, please let me know and he or she can have it for free.

Now don't get me wrong. I'm not totally against technology. I enjoy my digital television as much as the next person and we have several computers in the house. Every member of our family has a cellphone, but we don't upgrade every year or two just for the sake of having the latest gadget with all the newest bells and whistles.

In fact, I'm still using an iPhone 4, which in cellphone years is several generations removed and almost ancient. But it serves my purposes, and I don't feel the need to upgrade just for the sake of upgrading. As long as it continues doing everything that I need it to do, I'm perfectly content to keep on using it.

Advancing technology is a beautiful thing when it enhances our lives, but we should always be wary of buying into the upgrade mode just for the sake of having something shiny and new, or at least that's view from here.

So, I was just wondering

May 8, 2019

I've always considered myself to be a naturally curious person, and sometimes my mind works in mysterious ways, as we have established in earlier columns. As I'm sitting here, contemplating my next column, these random thoughts just popped into my head.

So, I was just wondering ...

If a tree falls in the forest, does anyone hear? So, by the same token, if millions of voters tell their elected representatives they don't want (place your favourite issue here) do those politicians really hear? Furthermore, do they really care what the citizens think?

Do April showers really bring mayflowers?

Does the early bird really get the worm?

Does the springtime ritual of burning grass really serve some purpose, like making your grass greener, or is the practice nothing more than a dangerous myth?

Did you know there is a federal election coming this October? If not, you should be ashamed of yourself and you should be paying attention so that you can make an informed decision on election day. No matter which party you support, you owe it to yourself to become informed and then, most importantly, to vote.

So, which is more harmful to the environment—tossing a dirty tin can into the recycling bag or using several gallons of hot water to rinse out the can?

By the same token, how do you get all the peanut butter out of the empty jar? It's really not that easy.

Is it time to revert to the good old days of horse and wagon? With the rising cost of gasoline, that might be a more affordable option. Yikes!

Is it just me, or have drivers forgotten that they must dim their lights when driving at night and when approaching an on-coming vehicle? This is not only annoying, but it's also very dangerous.

What's up with the messed-up weather patterns and major storm events we've been experiencing in recent years? Is it global warming or a natural environmental cycle? If it's global warming, is it too late to correct it? And if it's too late, then what?

Why does it seem that, as one gets older, it's harder for one to lose weight?

Why do some of us take for granted the simple things in life, the things that are free such as a child's laughter, the ability to put one foot ahead of the other, the feel of the spring breeze on our skin, the beauty of a sunset, the touch of a loved one, and so on?

What's the first thing you make for when you return to Canada after travelling abroad? Let me guess. A Tim Horton's double-double, right?

Tell me this, how is it that major airlines can get away with charging customers $25 for a piece of luggage? It is skyway robbery, I tell you. Considering how much it costs to fly, at least the first suitcase should be free.

What are you supposed to think when the flight attendant on the plane you're travelling in ends her safety demonstration with the phrase "good luck"?

How can we convince people to stop using the word "retarded" when referring to individuals with special abilities? (It is easily one of the most offensive words in the English language and I cringe just writing it, but how else will you know what I'm talking about?) This word should be banned and never uttered again by anyone.

Why does Facebook ask what's on my mind more often than another human being?

Here's one of the biggest mysteries in the universe—will the Toronto Maple Leafs ever win another Stanley Cup?

And here's another hockey related question. If I'm not a lover of hockey, Canada's national pastime, does that make me any less Canadian? On the other hand, I am a huge Blue Jays fan, so that must count for something, right?

What says Canada more loudly? Hockey? The maple leaf? Back bacon? William Shatner? Peace? Or poutine?

Who really thinks that Kraft Dinner is real food?

Why are people so resistant to change when it is painfully clear that the status quo is not working?

Likewise, why are some people more inclined to espouse negative thoughts than something positive?

Is it really possible that someday people won't use verbal dialogue whatsoever? Instead, they'll rely on texting to communicate.

Time to settle this age-old argument. Who's the biggest, baddest superhero of them all — Batman, Superman, Captain America or Spider-Man?

How can two people hear the same weather forecast and take away two different opinions of what they just heard?

How can there be so much poverty in a country as rich as Canada?

If the products we buy are new and improved, what does that say about old and experienced or tried and true?

The answer to this age-old mystery still eludes me: how can you put two socks into the laundry and end up with one missing? Is there a sock-eating monster hiding in the washer or dryer?

I know there is some serious business going on in the world right now, with many issues that require our attention, but sometimes you just have to have a little fun, or at least that's the view from here.

30 burning questions just screaming to be answered

March 11, 2020

I think it has been well established over the years that I am a naturally curious person. In fact, I'll admit that I'm downright nosy and as such I have a lot of burning questions that need to be answered.

This week, I'm just going to put some burning questions out there to see if any of you good readers have answers that will satisfy my curiosity.

In no particular order then, I'm just wondering:

1. Will they ever solve the mystery of Oak Island? What's really buried in that famous Money Pit?
2. Why is it that drivers continue to exit and enter at intersections on controlled access highways like the 103, when it is clearly marked that no turns are permitted? Are these drivers above the law?
3. Has it ever gotten so hot that you could actually fry an egg on the pavement? I'd like to see that.
4. Has anyone ever seen it rain cats and dogs?
5. Will the federal Liberal minority government survive a full year until its first anniversary in October, or will it fall early with a non-confidence vote?
6. Will the Yarmouth to Maine ferry really sail this year?
7. Will they ever come up with a formula to create a pavement strong enough to defy potholes?
8. How much money is floating around the world on gift cards that have not been fully used? A few cents here and a few cents there and they all add up to a lot of dollars.
9. Will the crevice (which is actually more like a canyon) between the haves and the have-nots ever be narrowed?
10. Did they ever figure out how they got the caramel in a Caramilk

bar?

11. Why does so much poverty still exist in a nation as rich as Canada?

12. Will we ever put a person on Mars?

13. Have we passed the point of no return to save the planet from the devastation that is global warming?

14. Is it really bad luck when the 13th day of the month falls on a Friday? I ask because, this Friday is, coincidentally, the 13th of March.

15. Will this finally be the year that the Toronto Maple Leafs win all the marbles? It has been 53 years since the Leafs lifted Lord Stanley's cup in victory. That would have been in 1967, Canada's 100th birthday. A fitting celebration, to be sure, but another win is long overdue, or so Leaf fans would surely say.

16. Will the twains ever meet?

17. Do you really have an Uncle Bob?

18. Will we ever be able to train some people to stop littering? It's not that hard, folks. Just take your garbage home with you.

19. If a hamburger is made out of a plant-based "meat" product, can it really be sold as a hamburger?

20. Why is it when my wife asks me to find something I can never locate it, but then she goes right behind me and puts her hands on the object? Does she have a sixth sense or is it magic?

21. Will humans ever figure out a way to get along regardless of our race, culture, religion affiliation, age or sexual orientation? This is the year 2020. Let's all just promise to do better moving forward.

22. Can someone please invent signal lights that come on automatically? Please? Surely, we have the technology to do this and it's something we desperately need, as it's painfully obvious that many drivers on our roads do not know how to turn them on manually.

23. Have our electronic devices permanently and irrevocably supplanted the fine art of face-to-face conversation? (Excuse me a second. Just got a text.)

24. So, have you noticed that more and more people start their sentences with the word "so" these days or is it just that I'm noticing it more? So, I'm just asking.

25. How soon until self-driving cars are travelling the highways of

Nova Scotia? It will happen. It's just a matter of time. The bigger question is, are we ready for it?

26. Is it time to start charging consumers a tax on disposable cups? Or would offering an incentive to bring in reusable cups do the trick? Would it really reduce the amount of litter destroying our land-scape, if people had to pay a five-cent deposit on every throwaway cup they use?

27. Will people ever get it in their heads that using cellphones while driving is not safe? Apparently not. RCMP recently reported that they issued 1,547 tickets for driving with a cellphone in hand in 2019. The numbers do not lie folks. Smarten up.

28. Is it just me or do we seem to lose power more often these days than in the past? Is it that the storms are more severe or is it that infrastructure of Nova Scotia Power has become so weak that it cannot withstand the elements?

29. Is it time to stop the clock on Daylight Saving Time? I could use that extra hour.

30. Is this column the real thing, or is it fake news?

Questions, questions, questions. So many questions. If you can answer any of these questions, I'd love to hear from you. Until next week, that's the view from here.

Kids these days

May 5, 2021

"Do you think you had a better childhood without the cell phones, tablets and social media that our younger generations have today?"

That's a pretty deep question and I'll admit that when it popped up in my Facebook feed, it caused me to pause and think about what it was asking. My first instinct, as it may have been for the countless number of other people who saw the same post, was to answer in the affirmative.

Yes, I thought, indeed I did have a better childhood without all the electronic gadgets and gizmos than younger people have today. But then I found myself second-guessing my answer. We senior folk always seem to lament the younger generations and their new-fangled technologies, which some of us don't even understand, but is that really fair?

Think about it. Did people of my age (I'm almost 60) really have a better childhood or was it just different from what younger generations experience today?

I would speculate that most people in my generation would argue that we had it better, and I would agree with that observation on many levels. For one thing, people like me who grew up 60 years ago were often left to our own devices to come up with games and activities to keep us occupied instead of relying on technology to fill our spare time.

We didn't have electronic devices that could keep us entertained for hours nor did we have hand-held gadgets that we could take with us anywhere we went to keep us distracted. Instead, we had to rely on our own ingenuity and that of our friends to keep us busy.

Furthermore, some would argue that people from my generation also spent more time outside playing with our friends than inside the house glued to a computer screen, which made us more active and, as result, healthier. I would generally concur with that sentiment. As children, we proudly point out, we spent many hours outside in the fresh air, playing tag, hide and seek, kick the can and a long list of other activities. And we did it no matter the season.

Given the chance, people from my generation wax poetic about how great it was to grow up in a time when children talked to one another and played with each other in person rather than being linked by Wi-Fi through their devices, as most young people are today. And while I would also agree with that point, I would note that interacting face to face wasn't always what it was cracked up to be.

There were certainly lots of good times to be had while playing outside with our friends, but there were also many rough times where we didn't always get along. I guess if we learned anything from these early scraps it was how to resolve our differences and come to terms with whatever caused the strife in the first place. That's a life skill that you can't learn in front of a screen.

Our childhoods weren't all about play. It was the step toward maturity and adulthood. The good times and the bad times were part of growing up and I have often thought that I wouldn't trade my childhood for that experienced by younger generations.

Now, I am not dismissing any of the modern technologies that appear, on the surface, to have given younger generations opportunities that we couldn't even imagine when we were children. In truth, I often cringe when I hear someone say that today's younger generation have it so much easier than the generations that came before them.

I think, do they? Do they really?

While they have a different experience than we had, I would also point out that they don't have it easier.

As the father of two young men who grew up in the midst of the electronic explosion, I would agree that our children had so many different experiences than I had as a kid, that I can't even compare my childhood to what they went through. There really is no way to draw a correlation because it was a different time and a different era.

It's like saying oranges are better than apples, even though they are totally different. And to say which is better depends entirely on one's personal perspective and individual taste.

Regardless of what devices we provided our children, however, I would never say they had it easier than I did as a child. In fact, this modern era of mass and instant communication, in which you can connect with someone else in the blink of an eye no matter where they are in the world, opens up a list of opportunities and challenges that we could never have imagined when we were youngsters.

Sometimes, for people of my generation and older, it's hard to wrap our heads around just how much things have changed. It's mind-numbing.

But it hasn't always made life easier for the younger generations, as this new technology has come with its own issues, including cyber bullying and around-the-clock peer pressure. Then there are the financial pressures that many parents experience when they can't provide their children with the same devices that other children may have.

These challenges are real for many people, so while I agree the lives of younger generations have changed over the decades, I would not agree that their childhoods are better.

Every senior generation laments about the younger generations coming up behind them. It's the natural order of evolution. I recall many times when my parents would say something like, "When we were kids…" or, "You kids have it so easy today." Or how about this gem: "Kids today don't know what hard work is."

Kind of sounds like something people from my generation might say to a young person today, don't you think?

It's easy to make a blanket statement like "young people have it so much better today than we had it when we are kids," but unless you're in that moment with those youngsters, you can't really understand their perspective, and that's the view from here.

Some things are just meant to happen

July 7, 2021

You know how they say that some things are just meant to happen and there's nothing you can do to change that fact?

That's exactly the situation my wife and I encountered a few weeks ago. Allow me to set the scene for you.

The story takes place on a sunny Saturday morning, June 19. It was the kind of day that compels you to get out for a drive, especially after having spent more than a month in almost total lock down. Since we had some errands to run in Bridgewater and because we just wanted to get out for a well-deserved break, we decided it was a good time for a quick jaunt, so off we went.

We spent a couple of productive hours there and took care of our business, then it was off to home. As we headed back toward Liverpool, we talked about our plans for the rest of the day and weekend. Since Sunday was Father's Day and we were having company, there was a lot to do.

Then fate intervened, as it has a way of doing.

The traffic was flowing smoothly along Highway 103 until, just past the Camperdown exit, my wife said "deer" and the next thing I know this huge animal bounced right across in front of us.

Yes, you guessed correctly. It was too late. It was nothing more than a quick blur of brown. I hadn't seen it and I did not have time to react.

In hindsight, it's probably a good thing that I hadn't reacted as there was an 18-wheeler right behind us, and if I had slammed on the brakes, like you would instinctively do, the truck would have slammed right into us as the driver would not have had time to slow down. Who knows how that would have ended? I cringe at the thought.

I know it happens all the time, but in all my years of travelling the highways along the South Shore and throughout Nova Scotia, I had never

119

hit a deer. I've seen dozens of them on the roads and I've had a few close calls along the way but, luckily, I had avoided a mishap. Regrettably, that was not the case on this particular day.

As the deer crossed in front of my vehicle I hit the large animal, causing extensive damage to our Volkswagen Tiguan, the SUV we had only just purchased less than a month earlier.

I have to tell you that the thud of animal flesh and bone connecting with the metal of our vehicle was one the most sickening sounds I have ever heard in my life. It was over in only a matter of seconds, but it made my stomach churn and, once I came to my senses and I could safely pull off the road, I brought the vehicle to a complete stop.

The transport truck that was on our tail swerved around us and kept right on going, as did the vehicles that had been approaching from the other direction, but that's another issue.

However, there were some very kind and caring people who, once they saw us stranded on the side of the road, stopped and checked to see if Nancy and I were okay. In particular, we want to extend a special thanks to Andrea, Jack, Maude and Clarance. Your thoughtfulness and generosity meant the world to us, but I am getting ahead of myself.

Once Nancy and I assured each other that we were okay, we got out to assess the damage. We were heart-broken, both for our vehicle and for the poor animal that had caused such extensive damage.

We didn't blame the deer, for it was only reacting as animals typically react. Considering the amount of broken and twisted metal that lay before us, we were sure the animal must be seriously injured; but, miraculously, the deer had kept on going and, even though we looked, we could not find it anywhere.

We then turned our attention to our personal plight. We called a tow truck, which eventually arrived and moved the Tiguan to a body shop in Liverpool. We were well shaken from the ordeal, but several hours later, after calls to the insurance company and RCMP, we were home and trying to calm our nerves, just thankful that the situation hadn't been any worse.

Things were bad enough, but we know that we were lucky, indeed, that we had not been injured or even killed, which would have most likely been the case if that large truck had collided with us. So, while we were upset and stressed over the situation, we also knew that the vehicle would either be fixed or replaced. Thank goodness for insurance.

And I do hope the poor deer is okay. We hit hard and, in light of the damage it caused, I still cannot even imagine how the animal continued to be mobile, but clearly it was a resilient beast.

I know in the overall scheme of things, with the challenges being what they are in the world right now, my personal dramas may seem inconsequential to some people, but it feels good to talk about it. I think getting these things off one's chest is good medicine.

It's good for the soul, and I believe we all need to talk more. Imagine how much better everyone would feel about things if we just talked with one another. Expressing our thoughts and views in a cordial and non-confrontational manner could resolve a lot of differences and maybe even cure a lot of headaches. Give it a try.

So back to my story: I will simply end by saying that there are many things in life that we cannot control, and clearly this situation was one of them. Deer and vehicle collisions happen far too often on our highways, but the reality is that in most cases there simply is no way to avoid it.

After all the second-guessing, the 'what if we had left Bridgewater at a different time?', 'what if we hadn't stopped here or there?', 'what if we had taken a different route home?' or 'what if we hadn't been on the road at all that morning?', we can't change anything.

The bottom line is: we were there at that precise moment and the collision between animal and machine happened. Complete stop. That is the simple, unbridled reality.

You can call it fate or whatever you want to call it, but clearly some things are just meant to be and that's the view from here.

Vernon Oickle

The view from here on

The news of the day

Vernon Oickle

A simple 'thank you' will do

June 25, 2014

We take them for granted. We bitch and complain about them, and we even blame them when they catch us doing something wrong, such as speeding or using a cellphone while driving, but police officers deserve our utmost respect and deepest appreciation for the jobs they do.

Without law enforcement personnel, who risk their lives every time they put on their uniforms, our society would disintegrate into chaos and disorder. Without the dedicated men and women who protect our communities, there would be pure pandemonium and mayhem.

Most of us go about our daily routines oblivious to the turmoil that bubbles below the surface. However, as we've seen, that serenity and security can be shattered in just a matter of seconds.

In recent weeks, following the brutal slayings of three RCMP officers and the wounding of two others in Moncton by a well-armed gunman whose motives still remain a mystery, our senses of insecurity and vulnerability have been heightened to a level we seldom experience in this part of the world, where things like this aren't supposed to happen.

The trio of Mounties were shot and killed June 4 while responding to reports of a man roaming a residential area heavily armed and dressed in camouflage. Parts of the city of Moncton were on lockdown for nearly thirty hours as the shooter remained at large.

The siege eventually ended with the arrest of a twenty-four-year-old suspect, who is now in custody. He faces three counts of murder and two of attempted murder.

In what can best be described as a senseless act of violence, it appears the gunman methodically hunted and shot the officers with little care for the consequences of his actions. In the wake of his shooting spree that reminded us that such brutality can happen even in our serene Maritime communities, he left behind a trail of broken families and a community struggling to come to grips with questions that defy logic. They are questions that may never be answered yet we ask them anyway.

Who was Justin Bourque? Where did he get the weapons? Why did he target the police? Could he have been stopped? Why didn't someone see the warning signs and intervene? Do we do enough to help identify and help those struggling with mental or emotional disorders? Are our gun laws tough enough? How could such violence happen in a Maritime community known for its friendliness? Will it happen again?

So many questions...so few answers.

At the core of this tragedy is the reality that police officers often plunge headfirst into situations that present risks to themselves. When they pull over a vehicle for a traffic violation or respond to a domestic violence dispute or answer a call like the one in Moncton, they have no idea what dangers they could be facing, yet they do it because it's what they've sworn to do.

It's not just a job for these dedicated men and women. Their sense of responsibility compels them to rush into potentially-deadly situations. They do it because it's their duty and they've committed their lives to the service of protecting their communities and fellow citizens. If that doesn't make them heroes, then I don't know what does.

As I watched the regimental funerals for the three fallen Moncton officers on June 10, memories of another tragedy closer to home, in which a dedicated RCMP officer was senselessly gunned down in the execution of his duty, rushed to the foreground. I shivered with the reality that such violence knows no geographical boundaries.

When Sgt. Derek Burkholder was shot and killed on June 14, 1996, while investigating a domestic dispute at Maders Cove, Lunenburg County, he was the 190th RCMP officer killed in Canada in the line of active duty.

I remember the day very well and it gives me goosebumps, as I can still hear the urgent RCMP transmissions that spilled from the scanner in the newsroom where I was working at the time. The death of Derek Burkholder shook the entire province because it was the first time in the history of Nova Scotia that a Mountie had been murdered.

Just like a few weeks ago in Moncton, the raw emotions resulting from the death of Sgt. Burkholder were palpable as his friends and colleagues in the force, his family who were suddenly thrust into the national limelight as they mourned his passing, and, in fact, the entire community where he lived and worked, struggled to deal with the horrors of such an extreme act of violence.

And just like in Moncton, there were no simple answers to satisfy everyone's questions or to quell their emotional suffering, but it reminded us just how vulnerable these brave officers become each and every time they don their uniforms.

In the days, weeks and months that follow, the people of Moncton—and, indeed, many Canadians—will go through a litany of emotions that come with the grieving and healing process, but any effort to make some sense of the recent tragedy will prove to be futile, as we know from previous examples that such violence defies logic; such violence can never be easily explained.

Life is filled with ironies and, in a way, society itself is a bit of an oxymoron. We need police to help keep the peace and preserve our safety, but it was that violence that ultimately took these lives. There is simply no way to explain or make reason out of such a confluence of circumstances. In the end, all we can do is accept it and hope that we, as a collective society, learn from these events. We can also pray that the day will come when such violence is no longer an everyday occurrence.

Until that day, however, we will continue to depend on the dedicated police officers to keep the peace and they will answer the call to serve, sometimes even at their own peril, as this recent tragedy clearly illustrates. That is simply society as we know it, and those brave men and women expect nothing more from us than just a simple show of respect.

Ultimately, a simple "thank you" is all that most law enforcement officers need, and such a show of gratitude is the least we can do. We can also vow to be better citizens and to appreciate the police officers who lay their lives on the line each and every day they answer the call to serve, or at least that's the view from here.

What happens when you fall off the grid?

July 23, 2014

If we've learned one thing from the recent power outages that resulted from post-tropical-storm Arthur's assault on the Maritimes, it's that our world revolves around electricity, and we've evolved (or perhaps devolved) to the point that we can't function well without it. Without electricity our lives practically stand still.

The storm that ravaged Nova Scotia, New Brunswick and Prince Edward Island on July 5 and 6 left tens of thousands of homes without service for several days and, in some cases, as long as a week.

That is simply unacceptable in a world powered by electricity, and it's encouraging that our government has initiated a full review of what went wrong. After we have the facts, we must take steps not only to mitigate the damage caused by this storm, but to also prevent a repeat of the circumstances that created this recipe for disaster in the first place.

Let's not crap on the front-line workers who struggled around the clock to restore the electricity. There's no doubt they did their best to keep up with the disaster. Instead, let's get to the root of the problem and take steps to make sure the issues are addressed before another major storm, which, based on weather trends over the past few decades, is surely going to happen again.

In Nova Scotia, where high winds and leaf-heavy trees combined to wreak havoc on the power lines and other utility infrastructure, work crews simply could not keep up with the demand. In recent years, Emera, the parent company of Nova Scotia Power, has reduced the number of available line crews throughout the province and we need to know if such reductions have resulted in slower reaction times during emergencies.

On-going line maintenance and vegetation management are key elements to preventing a repeat of this recent mess. Improved communication during such a disaster is also essential to mitigating the human suffering that results from an extended power outage. After all, considering the high fees that customers pay for electricity, no one deserves to be without power for an extended period, yet it happens far too often. That is simply not acceptable.

But that's the politics of a power outage. We all want answers to what went wrong during this recent storm, and, more importantly, we want to know that such circumstances won't be repeated. Perhaps the outcome of the government's review will lead to such improvements. However, there's another pressing question that demands an answer: what do you do with yourself if you lose power for an extended period of time?

It's true that our world revolves around electricity (and gasoline, but that's another story). Next to the need for a hot shower and coffee, one of the most common comments I heard throughout this recent ordeal was that people don't know how to entertain themselves when they don't have electricity.

In a society that's dominated by electronic gadgets, devices and gizmos, people have lost their ability to entertain themselves in more traditional ways. It's more difficult to entertain oneself during a power outage when it occurs in the wintertime, but I heard many people bemoaning their predicament during this recent interruption simply because they didn't know what to do, as their daily routine is clearly dependent upon electrical devices.

It says a lot about society that emergency centres also now include "charging" stations in their services. Seriously, though, how difficult can it be to find something to do during the summer that does not require electricity?

Shouldn't be too difficult, or so you'd think. Apparently, though, some people have lost their creativity. Heaven forbid that we have a repeat of this recent storm, but in the event that we do, I've come up with this handy-dandy list of activities for everyone's use. Feel free to clip and save to use as a reference.

In the event that a power outage occurs in the future you could:

> Spend some quality time with your family and talk to one another.
> Play cards or a board game. They were invented well before video games came along.
> Read a book.
> Take a walk or go for a run.
> Have a game of catch with your children.
> Go for a swim.
> Find out which coffee shops are open and meet a friend at the one of your choice.
> Go exploring in your neighbourhood.
> Plan a barbecue dinner.
> If you have a battery-powered radio, listen to some music. (Also good for updates on the outages.)
> Mow the lawn (providing you have a gas mower, and your lawn isn't littered with debris).
> Hang out the clothes (providing you can find a washing machine that works).
> Go for a bike ride.
> Go on a family picnic.
> Clean the house.
> Write some letters the old-fashioned way—with pen and paper.
> Go fishing.
> Build a tree house for your children or grandchildren.
> Weed the garden. (If you don't have one, you can weed my

garden.)

Organize a street hockey tournament.

Have your children put on a talent show.

Pull out the craft supplies and help your children make something artsy.

Colouring books and crayons have been entertaining children for generations. Why not get them out of the closet and show your children how well you can keep within the lines?

Do those odd jobs you've been putting off, such as cleaning out the garage or basement.

Go golfing, if the golf course is open.

Meditate.

Exercise.

Pull out those old family photo albums that have been gathering dust and show your children what "real" photos were like before the age of digital photography.

Help your children build a fort out of pillows and blankets.

Wash and wax your vehicle.

Clean out your closet and get rid of all those clothes you haven't worn since the 1980s.

Trim your hedge (unless your trimmer runs on electricity).

Visit with your neighbour. You know, the one who's upset that you haven't trimmed your hedge in a while.

Write your memoirs.

Or, as a last resort visit a close friend or family member who has power and reconnect to the grid, but whatever you do, don't complain about the front-line crews who worked around the clock to restore your power. They aren't responsible for the mess, so they don't deserve the grief, or at least that's the view from here.

Can we talk?

August 27, 2014

People don't talk any more. In fact, there is indisputable proof that the art of face-to-face conversation is quickly becoming extinct, thanks to the arrival of social media and hand-held computers that are with us 24-7.

This point was recently driven home to me while I was sitting in a local office and, honestly, I find the trend extremely disheartening and a little scary.

Perhaps it's because of my profession, but I watch people's behaviour. When I'm sitting in a room full of people, I like to talk. To me, striking up a casual conservation about any possible topic is part of the human experience. It's what I like to do, and I also find these impromptu discussions help to pass the time, especially when you know you're there for the long haul, as the person you are waiting to see is running late.

So it was with great interest that I scanned the room that day, looking for someone to chat with. However, to my dismay, everyone was too preoccupied with his or her compact computerized gadget to acknowledge my interest or, for that matter, even notice that I existed let alone that I was in the room.

There were six other people present, including a younger couple, a man and a woman, whose eyes were glued to the cell phones they were each holding. I have no idea what they were doing on those devices, but whatever it was, they were each caught up in their own little worlds that existed on those tiny screens. Maybe they were texting their friends, playing a game or doing their banking, but clearly, they were too preoccupied to talk, not even to each other, so I moved on.

Next, my attention was drawn to a young girl who was, I'd guess, somewhere in her mid-teens, and while I was sure I knew her from some of my previous experiences in the local schools, I was unable to strike up a conversation with her because, like the earlier couple, she too was more interested in whatever was happening on her cell phone than anything happening in the room.

Unlike the previous woman and man, however, the teenager did briefly glance up from the palm-sized screen and smile at me. I guess that was a brief reprieve of sorts, as at least she acknowledged my existence, confirming I wasn't invisible.

From there, my attention moved to a woman and a young boy, whom I concluded was most likely her son and, based on his size, maybe four or five years of age. I have two children of my own, which means I had spent many hours over the years with them in similar circumstances, so I could certainly commiserate with this woman as she tried to keep the young boy occupied.

I could see this little guy was one of those youngsters who could easily be distracted, as he was clearly struggling to sit still in his chair. Anyone who has ever been in a similar position will understand this woman's struggle, but when she pulled what looked like an iPad from her bag and handed it to her son, he immediately settled down and went to work on whatever was on the screen. I assumed it was a game or something like that, and I could see the relief wash over the woman's face. Clearly, in this case, technology had found its place.

I said something like, "Thank God for computers and the internet." She smiled and replied, "For sure," then she promptly pulled out her phone and began texting.

I shrugged and thought, so much for conversation.

So now what, I wondered? I scanned the room once more and was immediately relieved to find an elderly woman sitting across the room, smiling at me. I couldn't help but think she was actually bemused with my reaction to all this wizardry of modern technology.

"You don't text?" I said with a smile.

"Wouldn't know the first thing about it," she answered. And I got the feeling that she was grateful that, in a room full of people, another human was talking to her.

"Honestly," I confessed, "neither do I." However, I quickly added, "I think it's high time for me to learn. It's become clear to me that if I want to have a conversation with anyone in this 'modern' era, then I have to get with the program."

She chuckled. "I'm too old to learn something like that."

"Not likely," I assured her, adding that if I can learn all this new-fangled technology, then anyone can adapt, because I'm not known for my prowess around anything remotely connected to these new devices. My wife and children, and most of my friends and colleagues, are connected, but me? Not so much.

She laughed again and told me that a while ago her daughter tried to show her how to use a computer so she could talk to her granddaughter out in Alberta, but she admitted she became too flustered and gave up. She pointed out that she got lost when her daughter tried telling her about something called "Sky" or "Skip" or something like that.

"Was it Skype?" I asked.

"That sounds about right," the woman replied. She pointed out she had no idea what it was or how it worked, but added that, once her daughter got it up and running, it was nice to be able to see her granddaughter as she talked to her over the computer.

"Technology does have some good points," I agreed, while at the same time glancing around the waiting room again and thinking that it also has its bad points. "But I do like talking to people and I actually miss it."

"Conversation is a dying art," the woman said. "Sad, really."

"It certainly is," I agreed.

In the interest of full disclosure, I will confess I do have a cell phone and I could text on it, but I've never tried. However, this recent experience has proven to me that it's high time I learned how to use it. Clearly, if you can't beat 'em, you've got to join 'em, or at least that's the view from here.

Is this really Canada's new normal?

November 5, 2014

Like most Canadians, the news left me numb.

October 22 started like any typical fall day, but by noontime I found myself glued to the television screen and searching the Internet, looking for any little piece of information I could find about the incident. I couldn't believe what I was hearing. The first newscasts out of Ottawa didn't tell the whole story, as it was initially reported that a gunman had opened fire in the nation's capital and at least one soldier had been wounded.

How could something like this happen in Canada? A huge question with few answers. But that wasn't the worst of it.

As the day wore on, the news became grim. We learned that the young soldier shot while standing guard in front of the National War Memorial, twenty-four-year-old Corporal Nathan Cirillo, a reservist from Ontario, had, in fact, died from his wounds. We also learned that the gunman had also laid siege to Parliament, the seat of this country's democracy, leaving the nation's capital in chaos.

The attack was an affront on the Canadian way of life, the very principles, rights and freedoms on which our society is built.

Sadly, this despicable attack of violence has left many citizens wondering if the country we've known for generations has changed forever, as it emphasized the dangerous times in which we live. The country is now teetering on a precipice, dangerously close to falling into a dark void unlike anything we've previously experienced in Canada.

Our lawmakers and authorities now face the ultimate test. There is no doubt that they will want to protect Canadians from coast to coast to coast, as they should. However, we must exercise caution, and therein lies the conundrum.

In wanting to protect Canadians, those in charge must not overreact. We must guard against any intrusion into our rights and freedoms. It will surely be a delicate balancing act, as our security has been rocked to the core, but it's still not clear how far the threat reaches or how deep it has penetrated the country.

For the past decade and a half, the world has been engaged in a conflict unlike those seen by other generations, and for the first time in our country's history, the war on terrorism has spilled Canadian blood on Canadian soil.

Surely, we would be naïve to think, considering our involvement in the international coalition of nations that appears united in an effort to stamp out terrorist groups around the world, that the battle wouldn't someday find its way back to our own doorstep. It has and it will continue to intensify.

Even if those engaged in the recent attacks were not directly supported by or linked to militant terrorist groups, we must accept that their actions were done out of sympathy for those causes. Directly or indirectly, the attack on our military personnel and house of government was just the latest salvo in this escalating war.

The question remains, will we allow these acts to change how we live in a free society? Has the violence that has erupted in the streets of our communities changed how we function as a democratic nation, a country where citizens' rights must remain a top priority?

In truth, while we may like to tell ourselves that we will not allow fear to influence our existence or to infiltrate our security, it most surely will. Our government will take action to clamp down on suspected militants. Government will likely enact rules and regulations that will slow down and restrict our movements even within our own country. However, while we take steps to protect our safety, we must also guard against government over-reaction to such possible threats.

In fact, as Prime Minister Stephen Harper stood before the nation on the evening of October 22 and expressed the country's resolve to fight terrorism at home and abroad, I couldn't miss the irony that, as stunned Canadians were trying to come to grips with the reality of such an attack, during the past ten months we have been observing the 100th anniversary of the start of the First World War.

It's also sadly ironic that these attacks against our military and democracy came only weeks before we mark Remembrance Day, a time devoted to honouring the heroes of past conflicts, those who fought and died for our freedom.

It's likely that the timing of these attacks is more symbolic to observers such as you and me, but it makes me shiver to think that, as we prepare to remember the sacrifices of so many men and women from past conflicts, a new war has been declared. I wish we lived in a different world where war and terrorism did not exist, a world where we all got along and where peace reigned supreme, but clearly that is not to be.

How should Canada respond to these recent attacks? Well, that's the real question, isn't it? Clearly, this war has been boiling inside our nation for some time. So then, how our politicians and authorities respond to this burgeoning threat will set the course for Canadians in the coming years.

Based on the actions earlier this year, when three RCMP officers were mercilessly gunned down in Moncton, and now this brutal attack in Ottawa, it is clear that terrorism is alive and well in our country. No matter how you slice it, such brutal acts of extreme violence, even if they are perpetrated by a loner, are terrorism, pure and simple.

The threat is real and, while every act of violence that occurs is not considered terrorism as it is defined today, it's also true that when armed gunmen roam our streets, targeting the brave men and women who are the visible symbols of our democratic society, then such attacks are beyond the scope of anything we've seen in the past.

When the blood of our police officers and soldiers is being spilled in our streets, then it's clear we are at war, and that, in fact, is the new normal in Canada, but it doesn't mean we have to allow it to control our lives.

No matter how horrific these attacks are, we cannot let these incidents to control our lives or to handcuff our democracy, because once we start down that slippery slope, there is no telling where we'll end up.

We must be vigilant, yes; but we can't let these attacks define who we are as Canadians, or at least that's the view from here.

Sears closing marks end of an era

September 6, 2017

First it was Zellers and now it's Sears.

The closure or impending closure of many Sears outlets across the country signals the loss of another iconic Canadian retail giant. How many other Canadian retail icons are on the chopping block?

That Sears—once the giant in catalogue merchandising and sales—has fallen on hard financial times is a grim reminder that the retail world has undergone a major metamorphosis, leaving traditional operations struggling to keep a foothold on the marketplace.

The impending closure of Sears outlets causes me to think of my childhood in Liverpool and to reflect upon the changing retail hub in our rural town. Fifty-odd years ago, Liverpool, and most other similar sized communities, had at least one general department store and, in some cases, two and maybe even three or four.

When I was growing up, our town had three department stores—Stedmans, Peoples and the Metropolitan, which eventually was shortened to The Met. In time, those stores disappeared from our shopping districts, pushed out by larger chains. Zellers, K-Mart and Woolco moved in to swallow the market by luring customers to regionalized shopping districts. It was basically the survival of the largest, not necessarily the fittest.

As the competition increased, smaller businesses could not survive the onslaught, so they closed, leaving voids in rural communities, many holes in their shopping districts that remain gaping to this very day.

In time, those mid-sized operations also faced stiff competition and they too were eventually pushed out when larger conglomerates such as

Wal-Mart came along and consolidated the marketplace even further. We saw that happen in Bridgewater, as Zellers was eventually wiped off the retail map.

Now we're losing Sears, the once-proud Canadian retail icon. But Sears' predicament is notably different from that of the Zellers' experience. It used to be that Sears had cornered the market on catalogue shopping. Years earlier, there was also Eaton's, but that company phased out its catalogue operations decades ago, leaving Sears with the monopoly on that portion of the Canadian market.

Sears had its niche and, with it, the company hummed along for several decades, raking in huge profits, until one day that so-called Internet thing arrived, essentially changing the face of retail shopping.

Today, competition from on-line shopping poses the biggest threat to the traditional retail model. Where customers were once obligated to visit the brick-and-mortar structures that warehoused the goods, today, the Internet allows shoppers to remain in the comfort of their homes and browse the websites of savvy retailers, such as eBay and Amazon, that have figured out how to capitalize on the digital marketplace.

For shoppers, it's more convenient to order on-line and have the goods delivered right to their front doors. In many cases, it's also cheaper, as these on-line operations have products in such large quantities that they can offer the items at greatly reduced rates, leaving established businesses at a considerable disadvantage. All of this adds up to tough competition for traditional retailers.

We can't blame the shopper. Technology has provided this means and the consumer has taken advantage of the opportunity, and why shouldn't they? But that shift has had major negative impacts on the traditional shopping experience, changes that have led to shopping districts, especially in rural communities, struggling to survive.

It is a challenge, but those communities that are now flourishing (and there are several in Nova Scotia, some right here on the South Shore) are doing it without the presence of what we consider mid-sized department stores. Mahone Bay and Lunenburg are two prime examples of this model.

But what they do offer in their shopping core is a unique experience featuring an eclectic mix of shops, specialty stores and boutiques.

I understand the tendency to hang onto things that we know. I recall what Liverpool's shopping core was like when I was a youngster. Heck, I can remember when the Sears store was in two other locations, one of which was right on Main Street. But, as Bob Dylan once said, the times they are a-changing.

The challenge is to embrace the change and find a way through it so that we, as a community, become stronger. It can be done.

We'll miss the traditions, that's for sure. We'll certainly miss the Sears Christmas Wish Book. In our house, when I was a kid, that was part of the excitement and build up to Christmas. I remember the thrill of flipping through the Wish Book and dog-earing the pages that featured the items I was wishing for. I have fond memories of circling the items so that my parents could easily find the things I wanted that Christmas.

It was the same when my own children were growing up. It was like the arrival of the Christmas Wish book unofficially signalled the start of the holiday season, even if it was in September. But the sad reality is that, with people shopping on their computers these days, the Sears catalogues are no longer needed nor, in many cases, are they wanted.

The catalogue model also faced growing challenges on the environmental front, as savvy consumers, concerned about their world, chose to use the digital versions instead of the older paper model. The truth of the matter is that the Sears' way of shopping is now gone and, with that loss, away went the chain's one piece of leverage that once made it a powerhouse in the Canadian retail market.

I'm sure there are other financial factors that contributed to the collapse of the company, issues that I don't know and probably wouldn't understand, but the shift of consumer patterns obviously played a large role in its demise. The larger question for some communities is, how do they cope with the loss of another retail outlet.

I am thankful that, here in Liverpool, the phased-out Sears outlet will become the location for a new store selling appliances and furniture. Thank you to the business owner, who has the experience, resources and business acumen to push through this challenge instead of folding up shop altogether.

I hope the void left by the departure of Sears outlets across the country will quickly be filled with other shopping opportunities, because the last thing these communities need is another empty storefront.

Those traditional operations, that were once the anchor for most main streets and shopping districts, are mostly relics of history. The challenge for us is to stop dwelling in the past and stop hanging onto things that we once had. We must adapt to the quickly-changing and ever-evolving marketplace, or at least that's the view from here.

Newspapers still have their place

June 27, 2018

There was a time when community papers kept everyone connected, and informed about what was happening right in their own and also in their neighbour's backyard.

A community paper recorded both hard news events such as crime, politics, business activity, and tragedies, right alongside the softer news of church teas, suppers, card parties, ox pulls and, at one time, even livestock sales and auctions.

Those days are now part of our collective history, largely replaced by the Internet and social media sites. The rise of computer technology over the past two decades also means societal needs have changed, as, have reading patterns and habits. People have become more and more dependent upon these sites for their immediate news updates.

These changes have had a profound impact on the traditional media, but that's all right. It's called evolution. You can put computers right up there alongside other great game-changers such as the printing press, electricity, the automobile and the telephone.

These inventions have caused societal shifts throughout the course of history, because as technology changes, our needs and demands evolve right along with it. Unfortunately, as these shifts occur, they cause ripple effects that may negatively impact how we're used to doing things.

There can be many reasons why a traditional newspaper closes or merges with another entity, including a dwindling population, erosion of the marketplace and the emergence of new technology. As a result of these changes, decisions must be made that often result in a reimagining of how a community newspaper will look, or if in fact it will continue at all.

Such is the case with the Queens County *Advance*, which after 140 years of serving its community will cease publication with its June 27th issue.

While I understand and appreciate the realities behind such a decision, and while many people have told me over the past month since the closure was announced that they weren't surprised to hear the news, it's still

139

a difficult thing for me to wrap my head around.

I spent 13 wonderful years at *The Advance* between 1980 to 1994. Sometimes challenging but always rewarding, that period represented some of the best years of my journalism career.

Call me a hopeless romantic if you will, but being given the opportunity to work for my hometown community newspaper was a major accomplishment for me. I will be forever grateful that Jock Inglis, the publisher and editor of *The Advance* back then, took a chance on a fledgling reporter fresh out of journalism school.

I may have still been wet behind the ears, but I was full of vim and vigour, and what I lacked in experience, I made up for with enthusiasm and determination. I was always willing to tackle a story, no matter how big or how small the assignment.

I cut my journalistic teeth at *The Advance*, chasing down stories that were sometimes difficult to pursue and working hard to capture my hometown community as it was in the 1980s and 90s.

When I graduated with an honours diploma in journalism in the spring of 1982, I had no idea where I was going. But because I had worked summers and Christmas holidays at *The Advance*, Jock asked me to come to work there for the summer. I was ready for the challenge. In the end, as I've said, that summer turned into 13 rewarding years.

It was a time when local residents would line up at the office door early every Wednesday morning to get their paper because, in Queens County in that era, Wednesdays were "Advance Day" and people couldn't wait to get their hands on the paper.

Seeing that response from the community was confirmation to me that I had chosen wisely when I decided to stay and work at my hometown paper.

I was proud to work there. I was offered jobs in other communities over the years, but Liverpool is my home and so, too, was *The Advance*. I liked every aspect of the business, from collecting the news (both the hard and softer varieties), to photography, to laying out the pages, to waiting on customers at the front counter, to taking classified ads over the phone. All of these tasks were important to putting out a good paper.

I especially liked writing stories about the people who lived and worked in our community, people who had achieved success or who had done something noteworthy. These people inspired me to get into journalism in the first place and I found it deeply gratifying that they would welcome me into their homes. It meant a great deal that they trusted me to tell me their stories. It was also humbling to be given such a responsibility, and I never took the assignment lightly.

Through my job at the paper, I felt a special connection with the community in which I was born and grew up. It's a bond that I feel even to this day.

When I left *The Advance* in 1994, it was a difficult decision, but there comes a point when you know it is time to move on, and, for me, that was the time. But even though I went to a new job, I never stopped caring about my hometown paper.

Don't get me wrong. Those days at *The Advance* weren't all sunshine and roses. There were difficult times, especially when it came to writing about tragic events that rocked the community. While people may remember these hard news stories because of their sensational nature, I remember them because I felt I was recording those events for history.

When people would ask how I could write about tragedy, I would explain that it is the newspaper's job to mirror what happens in the community, not to sugar-coat the news, even the hard stuff. It's not the media's job to cherry pick what we feel people should know or serve up only the things that we feel they can handle.

It was, and still is, a newspaper's job to collect the data and preserve it for future generations. The method of delivery may be evolving, but the mandate is the same: gather the facts and convey them in an accurate, clear and concise manner, without prejudice or bias. The reader will judge how well we do.

It isn't an easy task. Reporting for your hometown paper—or any paper, for that matter—has its rewards, but it also has its difficulties, and I can remember occasions when I was attacked, both verbally and physically, for doing my job.

But I understood that emotions were sometimes raw, and that people reacted as you would expect them to react under such circumstances. I carried on and did my job to the best of my abilities. All reporters, no matter which medium they are working for, do that.

Times have changed since 1980, when I first walked into *The Advance* office and sat across the desk from Jock. Even though I lived through the changes, I still find myself shaking my head and marvelling at the speed at which change has come about. But be that as it may, the community was well-served in the past by *The Advance*, and it will be well-served in the future as *The Breaker* assumes the mantle as the community's paper.

So, while it is with some sadness that we bid adieu to *The Advance*, the simple fact remains that, no matter how much we may wish for it, nothing stays the same forever, at least that's the view from here.

Vernon Oickle

Riding out a major hurricane

September 18, 2019

Okay, I'll admit it. By the time Friday, September 6 rolled around, I was freaking out.

Seriously, anyone who had followed the devastating progress of Hurricane Dorian, the killer storm bashing and grinding its way through the Bahamas, up the American eastern seaboard and then making a beeline to Nova Scotia, had every reason to be nervous.

The swath of death and destruction the storm left in its wake had reached catastrophic proportions in the South Atlantic, and now our province lay squarely in its path. Anyone who said they weren't intimidated by the massive storm was not being truthful, or they were very naïve, as all signs indicated this was going to be a massive storm that would still pack a punch by the time it reached us...and it did; well beyond anything we could have imagined.

I know we've endured major storms in the past and it's also true that storm warnings have become an all-too-familiar occurrence in this era of global warming, but it was clear that Dorian, packing winds that had previously reached Category 5 level strength, was going to match, if not surpass, the fury of other massive storms that have hit our region, even the most recent killer, Hurricane Juan from 16 years earlier.

Following the news coverage of the death, destruction and absolute devastation that Dorian delivered to the Bahamas, all we could do was hope and pray that the storm would be well spent when—not if—it made its way north.

By earlier in the month, it had become painfully clear that the hurricane was targeting the Maritimes. All the models indicated that the storm had set its sights squarely on Nova Scotia.

For the first time in my memory, officials issued a hurricane warning for the entire province, while decision-makers in Halifax Regional Municipality called for a voluntary evacuation of residents living in coastal regions. This was scary stuff, folks.

There was enough data to suggest there was reason to be alarmed and that a threat was imminent. Fortunately, the early warnings gave people the chance to be prepared for the worst.

Something about this approaching storm made people sit up and take notice, as they should whenever such warnings are issued. Thanks to the twenty-four-hour news channels and social media platforms, it's easy to become jaded, complacent and dismissive about these warnings, as they seem to happen at regular intervals these days.

However, I would rather be forewarned of possible danger to be prepared in the event of a major storm than to be caught off guard. And that's exactly what Dorian was—a powerful and destructive storm, one that had to be reckoned with.

It appeared that most Nova Scotians paid attention to the warnings and prepared for the worst, as best they could. By the evening of September 6, many businesses throughout the province had announced they would remain closed the next day—the date of Dorian's predicted arrival—for the safety and wellbeing of their customers and staff.

Likewise, many community groups and organizations either postponed or cancelled their events for the same reasons. Good for them. With a possible Category 2 hurricane zeroing in on us, it was the smart move.

When was the last time you heard of a major resort like White Point Beach cancelling reservations and shutting down overnight for the safety of guests and staff?

When was last time that you heard that Kejimkujik National Park had asked campers to leave so they could close down operations?

When was the last time that all provincial parks, campgrounds and beaches were closed?

When was the last time that major commercial outlets and shopping malls in metro and other centres around the province closed even before the storm hit?

Service stations across Nova Scotia ran out of gasoline and grocery store shelves were picked clean as Nova Scotians filled up and stocked up on essentials. The message had been sent and received. Dorian was not a storm to be taken lightly. In fact, by the evening of September 6, you could sense that there was something serious in the air.

By Friday night, Dorian had been upgraded to a Category 2 hurricane, with Nova Scotia sitting smack-dab in its path. It was like a monster moving in the dreary darkness, a cunning menace that had methodically zeroed in on its prey, that being all of us in this beautiful province.

There were many tense hours in the last day leading up to Dorian's arrival. And when it ultimately arrived on September 7 with all its breath-taking fury and anger, there were many more nerve-wrecking hours.

Hurricanes are among the most powerful forces in nature and, even though by the time Dorian hit our shores it had been downgraded again to a still-powerful Category 1, this was not a storm to take lightly.

Riding out the fury of a raging hurricane is not a fun experience, nor is it for the faint of heart. While in the past we may have taken some comfort in the fact these monstrous weather events were a very rare occurrence in this part of the world, we can no longer be complacent about that, for it appears we live with a new reality, one in which these storms will hit with more regularity.

If we are to believe—and we absolutely should—the indisputable scientific facts that the earth's surface is heating up, then such storms will become more common. In truth, we ignore the signs and warnings at our own peril, and that's the view from here.

20 wishes for the year 2020

December 31, 2019

As we close the door not only on another year, but also on an entire decade, we may be tempted to dwell in the events from the past. But let's not do that this week. Instead, let us look ahead at the coming twelve months with optimism and faith that the New Year will be filled with opportunity, prosperity and success.

Doing just that, here are my twenty wishes for the year 2020.

1. That we will find a way to eradicate hatred, bigotry, intolerance and violence at home and around the world.
2. That we will accept all people are equal, regardless of the colour of their skin, age, race, religious beliefs, political affiliation, physical or mental abilities, societal standing, how much money they have or their sexual orientation.
3. That we accept that people with physical and mental challenges have a right to be treated just as everyone else is treated, and that

they can do great things in achieving their greatest potential.

4. That poverty will be wiped out and that every person will have equal and easy access to the basic needs of life.

5. That politicians will find the wisdom, courage and fortitude to make decisions that not only enhance the lives of their current constituents, but also ensure that future generations will have a world in which to grow up in.

6. That humans everywhere will become better stewards of the world we inhabit and that we will finally realize our actions impact not only us but all living creatures on the planet.

7. That the gap between the haves and the have-nots will finally be closed.

8. That the sick will find access to speedy, high-quality health care.

9. That all forms of injustice and prejudice will be stopped cold in their hate-filled tracks.

10. That we will lend a helping hand to our neighbours in their time of need.

11. That we will accept that others will often have different opinions and beliefs than our own, and that we will find a way to live in harmony with them and embrace those differences.

12. That Canada will continue to be a beacon of hope for those seeking shelter from oppressive regimes, those who are looking to find a tolerant and just society to create a home where they can live free and follow their dreams.

13. That bullying will be recognized as the scourge that it is and be wiped out in its entirety.

14. That those who wish to work can find meaningful and gainful employment in satisfying jobs so that they can afford a good quality of life and can pay for their needs.

15. That scientists and politicians will get on the same page when it comes to global warming so that we can get on with fixing the problem instead of debating whether it's real or if it's a hoax.

16. That we find a way to help every hungry person in Canada find food to feed themselves and their families and also that every homeless person in our country finds shelter from the elements.

17. That every person struggling with mental illness finds the help he or she so desperately needs.

18. That we continue to enjoy and celebrate the freedoms that a democratic society provides for us and that we never take those freedoms for granted.

19. That my family, friends and readers enjoy good health and unbridled happiness in the coming year and into the future.
20. That you all have a happy and prosperous New Year, and that all your hopes and aspirations become reality.

I know these are tall orders, but do you think I am so naïve to believe these twenty wishes can be realized in one year?

No, I'm a realist and I recognize there's a lot of work to be done, but I do believe that, if we all make an effort, then we can live in a world where we can all get along and everyone can reach their full potential, or at least that's the view from here.

It's just a beard, folks

January 22, 2020

Earlier this month, Prime Minister Justin Trudeau caused quite a commotion, setting the social media world on fire and creating a national buzz filled with tales of high intrigue, nefarious schemes and undercover conspiracies.

And what was the root cause of all this speculation and fuss?

It had nothing to do with managing the country's affairs or the climate crisis that's threatening to destroy the planet or the fact that the world is teetering ever so precariously on the brink of another major war that would surely cost untold death and destruction.

Instead, we were fixated on the prime minister's new beard, that suddenly showed up on the man's face in a photograph that was released around the dawn of the New Year. It was a hairy growth that prompted many conspiracy theorists to ponder, "What's Trudeau hiding?" or, "What's he up to?"

Some of the most profound thinkers even ventured to explain that the prime minister must dye his hair because his beard has streaks of grey running through it.

It must surely be a slow news day when the prime minister's beard becomes fodder for debate amongst friends, causes arguments to erupt, makes national headlines, leads newscasts and generates inches of copy in newspapers (yes, just like the one you're reading).

Yikes.

Yes, folks. This is the world in which we live.

I know I'm not the prime minister, but I must be perfectly honest and come clean with all of you, lest I be accused of being biased—I've had a beard for the past forty years. Now, *that's* a headline.

That's right. I started growing my beard when I was eighteen years of age, and I haven't shaved it since. In fact, my wife and I have been married for thirty-two years and she has never seen me with a cleanly-shaven face. Not sure what that says about my face, but she has threatened to leave me if I ever remove the beard.

But I digress. This isn't about my beard and, in truth, it shouldn't be about Trudeau's, either.

In all honestly, we should be thinking about the many serious issues that threaten our very existence, like the fact that U.S. President Donald Trump continues to play a dangerous game of cat and mouse with the powers in the Middle East. The decision to take out a powerful Iranian general two weeks ago pushed the world closer to the eruption of global war than it has been in many years, yet we've burned up precious hours talking about Trudeau's salt-and-pepper beard.

We should also be thinking about the catastrophic wildfires that have scorched eighteen million acres of land in Australia, razed more than 2000 homes and businesses, displaced thousands of residents, wiped out millions of animals and killed nearly thirty people. These unprecedented fires have been burning for months and, by all accounts, will continue to rage out of control for many more months, fuelled by record-breaking temperatures caused by global warming. Yet we became fixated on Trudeau's facial hair.

And we should be thinking about the 176 innocent souls who perished on January 8, when their plane crashed at the Tehran, Iran airport. Among the deceased were sixty-three Canadians, all of them immigrants, who died when the plane was shot from the sky by a surface-to-air missile launched as a result of the U.S.-Iranian military stand-off, yet through all this tragedy Trudeau's beard continued to receive attention.

I honestly don't know what all the fuss is about over Trudeau's beard. He is not the first Canadian prime minister to sport facial hair. In fact, based in images found on the Internet that look like official portraits, several leaders in our nation's history have had beards. Most notably, Alexander Mackenzie and Sir Mackenzie Bowell had thick facial growths.

And while Sir Robert Borden didn't have a full beard, he did have quite the impressive moustache that would be the pride and possibly even the envy of most men. Prime Minister Louis St. Laurent also sported a minor cookie duster, albeit not in the same league as Borden's outstanding 'stache.

Let's be real here, folks. It's time to get our priorities straight. When I consider the attention Trudeau's beard garnered over the past couple of weeks, I'm reminded of that old saying, "Nero fiddled while Rome burned," only we're fixated on facial hair while the world burns.

It's time to get over it and move on. If there's some sort of nefarious conspiracy behind Trudeau's beard, I'm sure we'll learn about it in due course, but I suspect the prime minister's decision to grow a beard—which is actually a pretty common thing for Canadian men to do in the wintertime—was more about wanting to change his proverbial image than taking our minds off of the business of the day as if he had something to hide, as many have suggested.

It's a distraction, to be sure, but a distraction of whose making?

We live in serious times, with many issues like war, climate change, global warming, hunger, poverty, disease, and freshwater shortages that deserve our undivided attention. These are the issues on which we should be focused, not a few sprigs of silver and black hair on the face of our prime minister, and that's the view from here.

The good, the bad and the ugly of social media

October 20, 2021

Over the past two decades, Facebook and other social media platforms have changed the way we see the world. The changes have been so substantial and profound that they are difficult to put into words but rest assured that the changes are not all for the better.

The spin-off effects of social media have dramatically reshaped our society and contributed to the public discourse which currently embroils most of us. Even those who don't follow social media are affected by its reach, as it has infiltrated our daily lives like some insidious monster consuming the very air we breathe.

In one way or another, social media influences our opinions on most topics and issues that concern the general population. Sometimes this is done in a good way, but often it's in a bad way, leading to arguments and disagreements based on half-truths, innuendo and misinformation that fractures our society in ways that have not been previously seen.

The good news is that, because of social media platforms, everyone has a voice.

The bad news is that because of social media platforms, everyone has a voice.

There is a strong argument that social media is good for society, that it opens the whole wide world to global communication, that it lifts the dark veil of secrecy that far too often enveloped important decisions that affect our lives and that it allows people to reach out and connect in a way that wasn't even imagined just a few decades ago.

But there is also an argument that social media platforms have driven a sharp wedge between people of opposing opinions, that it allows people to launch faceless attacks on others, that it contributes to the moral decay of society and that it allows people with nefarious motives to instigate deception that leads to turmoil and distrust within the general population.

No matter which side of the argument you come down on, I am sure we will all agree that social media has become a mainstay in our daily routines and, for better or worse, it has become part of our very fabric, almost consuming us and distracting us from real life experiences.

Have you noticed how many people walk around carrying their phones with them? They are practically glued to our hands. You should need no more proof than that.

In recent years, however, social media platforms—in particular Facebook and Twitter—have fallen under scrutiny as some begin to question our reliance and dependence on such digital forms of communication, especially the role they have played in spreading misinformation about elections, the COVID pandemic, global warming and a growing list of other important topics that shape the public psyche.

Now, don't get me wrong. There's a lot I like about Facebook. I like being connected and the feeling of being in touch with others and seeing what my friends, family and neighbours are up to. I like being informed about things in my community and beyond.

But I don't like the vitriol and anger that's so prevalent in social media these days. I don't like the rifts that social media has manifested or how it has created factions in our society, people who are so polarized in their differing views that they cannot or will not see an opposing perspective. This isn't healthy for us as individuals or for us, collectively, as a society.

It's a no-win situation, and sometimes it's really not a nice place to visit or spend time with. Furthermore, it has become clear that harmony on social media is not tenable, as current trends suggest that its major objective is to divide society into opposing forces. Many special interest groups, governments and individuals have weaponized social media in a way that traditional media could never have been used, and that's a scary proposition, indeed.

For one thing, while the effort has been ramped up in recent years (or at least they tell us it has been stepped up), there is no one out there policing or vetting what people post on their platforms. Some very dangerous and destructive information has infiltrated our thinking, driving the public debate. And even if these malicious posts are eventually revealed for the propaganda that they are, it's often too late to reverse the damage that has been caused.

We need to look no further than what has happened with information surrounding COVID, in particular the use of masks and vaccinations. Now I am not going to debate any of those topics right here today, but it is painfully clear that social media, with its barrage of so-called facts, has created such a divide in our society that the damage may never be reversed.

I am all for informed decision making, no matter which side you come down on. I am all for sharing information and having open discussion on the issues. Sharing information has been my work for more than forty years. However, I am against the spreading of misinformation, half-truths and lies, as these deceptions can have serious and dangerous implications, as we have seen in the past year and a half.

Sadly, social media has become the vehicle through which this type of propaganda is disseminated for public consumption, and, because of its global reach, campaigns of misinformation have spread like malignant tumours until they have finally metastasized into a killer disease.

I will admit that, outside of Facebook, I am not a huge follower of any other social media platforms, but unless I've missed something, I'm pretty sure they all accomplish the same thing, and they all have a massive reach. I will also admit that I use Facebook a lot. I like some of what I see, but I also hate just as much of what I see, especially the nastiness that fuels the discussion.

When Facebook first started, way back in the early 2000s, I came late to the party, and I came grudgingly. In fact, I initially dismissed Facebook as some sort of fad that would eventually die off much like pet rocks, mood rings and Snuggies, as people moved onto something new.

Boy, was I wrong.

Now, the U.S. Congress, thanks to a whistleblower, is threatening to tighten the reins on Facebook and most other platforms, so perhaps things will change. But there is also a good chance that nothing will change, as there have been other recent murmurs of stronger restrictions on social media, but the status quo remains.

It's clear that Facebook and other social media platforms are here to stay, as they are such a large part of our lives that it would be impossible now to pull the plug on them. However, it is also painfully clear that if we hope to maintain our civility, we have to do a much better job in controlling the content and that's the view from here.

Hello, this is the Grim Reaper calling

October 12, 2022

Hey, you.

Yes, you.

I am talking to you.

You need to pay close attention and listen very carefully to what I am about to say.

You thought you got away with it, didn't you? You thought that you could use your cellphone while you were driving down the highway the other day and that no one would notice, didn't you?

Guess what? You weren't so smart. Someone did see you breaking the law and putting the lives of everyone else on the road in danger. That someone was me.

And I know you do it all the time. Do you think you're invincible? Do you think you're Superman? Do you think you are special and can do whatever you bloody well like and there will be no consequences?

What you are doing is extremely dangerous.

What do I have to do or say to make you understand just how danger-ous it is for you to use your cellphone while you are operating a motor vehicle?

With all the stories in the news these days about how dangerous the roads are, why can't you get it through your thick skull that when you talk on the phone while driving, you not only risk your own life but also the lives of everyone else you meet?

This must stop, while you still have a chance.

You may have been lucky so far, but others have not been as fortunate. Believe me. Someday, I will catch up with you, and when that happens, it will be too late. So, heed my warning.

We know accidents happen. Statistics confirm that fact, but they also confirm that many mishaps happen because of driver inattention or carelessness. Most of these collisions could have been prevented, but for someone doing something they ought not be doing...such as using a cell-phone while driving.

Just the other day I watched as two vehicles came dangerously close to colliding on that strip of highway just outside of Bridgewater, where the 90 km zone transitions into a 100 km zone. Why? Because the driver en-tering the highway at that gas station was on his cellphone and didn't see the other car quickly approaching.

It was a near miss, and this could have been a serious tragedy. I held my breath as the driver who was not on the phone just managed to squeak past the other guy. Seriously! What is wrong with people?

Close calls happen more times that we care to admit. There was an-other recent incident when I observed a young woman with two small children in tow enter a crosswalk in downtown Liverpool, and this car, driven by another woman, just sped through the intersection without even slowing down.

It was a close call...too close. I cringed and closed my eyes as I seriously thought there was going to be a tragedy, but instead I witnessed a miracle, as the woman and her two children were spared.

Clearly, the woman behind the wheel of the car had not seen the ped-estrians. Why? I'll tell you why. Because she was on her cellphone and wasn't paying attention.

What could possibly have been so important that this driver just had to be on her phone at that moment? What business could have been so pressing that she could have killed a mother and her two small children in order to conduct it?

Clearly, some people have no common sense.

I shouldn't have to remind people of the dangers of driving while using your phone. Is it just plain stupidity or do some people think they are above the law, or they are immortal? Do they think that nothing bad will happen to them, or do they just not care that they could die or kill someone else?

How could they live with themselves knowing they killed someone simply because they couldn't wait another five minutes to make a phone call or send a text?

It happens all the time. No, I am not exaggerating. This type of thing happens every day, more often than I care to admit, and in my line of business, that is really saying something.

I feel like I'm preaching to the converted here. Those who agree with me will read this note and, well, agree with me. While I am grateful for the moral support, it's you, the driver who ignores safety concerns and disobeys the laws, who may read this, shrug your shoulders and think, "So what?"

You're the ones I'm really trying to reach, so listen up, folks.

When you get behind the wheel of your vehicle, you need to remember the power that has been entrusted to you. In the wrong hands a vehicle, even when moving slowly, can be a dangerous weapon. If you are driving, it is your responsibility to follow the laws, obey the rules of the road and put down that bloody phone before it's too late.

If you don't heed my warnings, I will be seeing you soon, and that is the view from here (the other side) this week.

Let's talk technology

May 3, 2023

I was shocked to read the results of a recent survey that revealed that more than 50% of today's teenagers admit they are addicted to their handheld electronic devices.

That's a scary statistic, indeed, but today's youth are not alone in their technological dependency as more than 30% of parents interviewed as part of this same survey admit that they, too, are addicted to their devices.

Considering the explosion of technology that has dominated society over the past two decades, I suppose we shouldn't be surprised that today's younger generation is growing up with such a dependency on it, nor should we be surprised that adults are likewise attracted to such devices. What surprises me, however, is the rate at which the technology has evolved in recent years.

While reflecting upon the results of this survey, I couldn't help but flash back over my lifetime and think about my own exposure to advancing technology. It's laughable, really, as the technology from my youth certainly pales in comparison to today's high-tech devices that are in the hands of just about every youngster I know.

If my aging and somewhat sketchy memory is to be trusted, my first brush with anything that could be considered even remotely high tech came when I was still a child and I received a digital watch for Christmas. I believe I was seven or eight, and I remember thinking how cool it was that the watch told time in numbers instead of the old traditional minute and second hands. To top it off, the bluish numbers even glowed in the dark. Now *that* was high tech to be sure.

My next memorable encounter with technology came when I was in Grade 7 or 8 and hand-held calculators arrived on the scene. Today, calculators are commonplace in homes, schools and businesses, but I can remember the outcry that erupted when they were introduced, five decades ago.

We may scoff at such a notion, but fifty years ago the fear was very real and palpable that these handheld devices were going to destroy people's ability to do math. Unlike today, when calculators are actually mandatory in some classes, they were the subjects of much debate when I was a student.

I'm not sure if the fears were founded, but the concern was so profound that calculators were banned from many schools.

Considering the technology that we deal with today and how schools have embraced it, such outrage hardly seems logical, but we lived in a different time and era. It was a time when things such as cellphones that can take pictures and create videos, computers that can fit into the palm of your hand, and the instant connection to the entire world were only the stuff of good science fiction.

Those of us who were born before the technological explosion will recall how we thought things like Atari, Pong and Space Invaders were the height of human ingenuity. To us, it was cutting edge stuff.

We were so naïve.

It may now seem like the Stone Age, but seriously, it was amazing to witness the birth of this technological generation in which we carry computers in our back pockets and hold them in our hands. Only those who were alive during that time can appreciate what I'm saying.

The rapidly expanding technology has impacted every facet of our lives, from our homes to our leisure time and entertainment, to our work, to our travel and even to our social interactions. I'm willing to bet that just about every home today has at least one computer in it, and most homes are likely to have more than one.

Just imagine doing your work without the use of computers and the Internet. Just imagine staying in touch without Facebook and texting. Just imagine watching some of your favourite shows without being able to stream them on your computer. Let's face it, our modern world revolves around technology.

Speaking from personal experience, technology has had no greater impact on any profession than on my chosen career. I started working full-time in community newspapers upon my graduation from journalism school in 1982, at a time when newspapers were still printed on paper. There was no Internet, World Wide Web or social media and our computers were as large as a table. We had not heard of texting, skyping, Zooming, face time, Facebook, tweeting or any of the modern gadgets and programs that have become such an integral part of our lives.

Heck, when I started in the business, our newspaper office in Liverpool didn't even have a fax machine. In fact, I can remember that when fax machines first arrived on the scene, we thought we had finally gone high-tech.

Our newspaper office was one of two locations in town where you could go to fax or receive a document. I remember that we charged ten cents to send a fax and twenty-five cents to receive a message, since we were using our paper to print it. My, how times have changed. Today, fax machines are practically obsolete, and in the Maritimes they're mostly used as boat anchors.

All kidding aside, however, technology has evolved, and we've had to adapt right along with it, but sometimes I wonder if all these new-fangled toys have been a blessing or a curse. We've seen the good and the bad of modern technology, but I think the good far outweighs the bad. We just have to be mindful that, in the wrong hands, technology can be very harmful.

I know that today some people from my generation and those who are older still tend to rebuff the technology explosion, but really, it's time to accept that the world as we once knew it is gone. The advancements in technology have seen to that.

I'm not saying that we have to become totally dependent on technology —although some people already are, so it may be too late for them—but I am saying that we have to accept this new world and work with it, while at the same time trying to maintain some perspective.

I remember when the Internet and World Wide Web arrived. Some people (including yours truly) thought it was a fad that would quickly disappear. Obviously, anyone who thought such a thing was out of touch with the facts. Could we have been more wrong about anything?

We've come a long way since those first calculators arrived on the scene some fifty years ago and the bottom line is simple—either you adapt or you get left behind, or least that's the view from here.

There, but for the grace of God

June 21, 2023

When we hear news about a major tragedy unfolding some place far re-moved from our own communities, our first instinct is to feel empathy toward those impacted by such horrific events.

Our second instinct is to expel a sigh of relief as we appreciate how lucky we are that the tragedy occurred someplace else. However, as we've recently been reminded, the stark reality is that disaster can strike any-where and without warning.

As major forest fires were raging throughout the South Shore region earlier this month, we were reminded that tragedy knows no geographical boundaries or borders. In fact, we were also reminded that by the grace of God, we have been fortunate that our part of the world has been relatively unscathed in our times.

However, as the recent events in the Shelburne and Halifax regions have proven, things can change quickly. If we haven't given it much thought in the past, it should now be painfully clear that we must all be prepared, because disaster can be waiting just around the corner.

The unprecedented fires that destroyed thousands of hectares of forest, reduced hundreds of homes to ash, displaced countless Nova Scotians and drove wildlife from its natural habitat has put us all on notice that we must always be prepared because, as we've seen, the unimaginable can happen.

It's hard to think of anything positive to say about such a catastrophe, but there are some things that are deserving of praise.

Even in the darkest of hours, when we were bombarded by the dreadful news that comes with such tragic events, the human spirit of survival and compassion broke through the heavy smoke and persevered. Like a bright beacon on a dark, foggy night, that spirit shone brightly in the darkness.

Even the smallest gestures such as a word of compassion, a bottle of water, a cup of coffee, a free haircut, a homemade meal or baked goods, a gift of personal items, a donation of cash or gift cards, a room in which to find shelter in the storm of embers, or a place to shower and rest made the difference to those immediately impacted by the massive fires.

It may be an old adage that Nova Scotians are some of the kindest, most generous and caring people in the world but, once again during these horrific fires, the people of the South Shore and, indeed, throughout this entire province answered the call to help those directly impacted.

In the midst of all the destruction, the chaos and the loss, and all the suffering, Nova Scotians found it in their hearts—and in their pocketbooks —to help those who have been directly impacted by the fires. To see such generosity is, indeed, heart-warming and inspiring.

There are many people deserving recognition and praise for the work they did during these disasters, but we would be remiss if we did not single out the brave fire fighters, first responders and emergency personnel who answered the numerous calls for help. To say they all went above and beyond the call of duty is truly an understatement.

But people in general provided exceptional support to their neighbours and fellow Nova Scotians during their most desperate hours. There are many who donated food and water, made meals and provided sustenance to the first responders and those who were fighting the fires.

Some donated money to help their fellow Nova Scotians who lost everything to the flames, and others not only opened their hearts but also their homes and cottages, or provided campers to those displaced by the raging fires. Still others helped locate, shelter and feed lost animals, something many of us without pets may not even think about.

You are all to be commended for stepping up because, when the situation was dire, you answered the call.

It is true that the material things such as buildings, furniture and vehicles that have been lost in these fires can be replaced, but the emotional impacts of such a disaster will be difficult to overcome.

For instance, while a house can be rebuilt, the memories that are made in a home can never be replaced. It's also a sad reality that the scars that result from such a loss will last forever.

These have been difficult times for many Nova Scotians, and the impacts of the fires will be felt for years to come, but let this serve as a stark reminder that no one or no place is immune from disaster, and that's the view from here.

Expect the unexpected

August 16, 2023

Here we are, halfway through the summer of 2023, and what an eventful summer it has been. We've seen more than our fair share of unusual weather events leading to several major disasters that have tested our collective resolve to persevere.

As of the end of July, we've suffered through extreme heat and drought that left the land parched and the forests tinder dry. As a result, in late May and early June we witnessed major wildfires in the region that levelled homes and shattered the lives of many people.

It is going to take many years for some people to recover from that disaster, as they lost everything in the fires. Truthfully, some people may never get back to normal, whatever normal is these days.

Then, as if destructive wildfires were not enough to contend with, near the end of July the province was hit by unprecedented, record-breaking, torrential rainfalls that swamped many parts of the province, wiping out roads and infrastructure, destroying homes and leading to four heart-breaking deaths, including those of two young children who were swept away by the raging waters.

Nova Scotia is not immune to natural disasters and catastrophes. We've witnessed other tragedies throughout the province's history, but we have rarely seen anything quite like this in such a short period of time, with back-to-back destructive events. Something has changed, throwing off the natural scheme of things.

Even though some people refuse to accept the science or choose to label it as a conspiracy, the evidence is mounting that global warming is real and is having a serious impact on the world's climate. Sadly, that same science suggests that what we are now experiencing is likely to become the new normal for us here in Nova Scotia.

Timothy Halman, Nova Scotia's Minister of Environment and Climate Change, said in a recent news release, "Climate change is the most pressing global emergency, and this past year has been a pivotal moment, both in the impacts we are witnessing and experiencing from storms, flooding, heat, rainfall, wildfires and more."

The catastrophic threat that climate change poses to our world and the potential disaster it means to us is not to be shrugged off or taken lightly. No one wants to think about our situation getting worse, but I fear we must brace for that possibility. The prospects are frightening, as was driven home to me during the recent floods.

My family and I live in Liverpool and our home is not far from the picturesque Mersey River. We can see it from our front yard. It's a beautiful location and, on most days, I wouldn't want to be anywhere else. However, despite its beauty, we also know the river could pose a real threat to our future wellbeing.

The Mersey River has played a major part in the community's existence throughout its history. From shipbuilding and lumber mills to the Bowater Mersey Paper Mill, the river has been an important economic driver for the entire region. It has also played an intricate role in the town's social and recreational lives since its early days and continues to be a vital component of our tourism infrastructure.

However, as we've just witnessed, in addition to all the positive spin-offs associated with the river, it can also pose a major risk, especially during these changing weather patterns that result in extreme storms, such as the one we experienced a few weeks ago. During the recent floods, residents along the river were put on alert of a possible breach at one of the hydroelectric dams that are located further up the river.

Those who have ever received an emergency alert on their phones know how scary that situation can be. I've lived here my entire life, and I do not ever recall ever before being told to prepare for an emergency evacuation as fears that the inordinate amount of water building up be-hind the dam was threatening to swamp the homes along the river.

We have been fortunate, indeed, that such a catastrophe did not come to pass. But will that luck continue?

What a breach of that magnitude would have meant to our community is frightening. It would surely have been a disaster. However, we now know the possibilities are real and that the new reality must serve as a wakeup call that we can no longer take comfort in the status quo. We must take steps now to mitigate the threat, but is it already too late?

Recent events have been a lot to deal with and, dare we tempt fate, the year is only half over. Who knows what awaits us before the end of 2023 and beyond, but one thing is for certain, these disasters have proven that the world is changing.

It's also shown us that we must all expect the unexpected and that's the view from here.

The Amazing Race: South Shore version

August 23, 2023

I have been watching *The Amazing Race Canada* ever since it premiered in the summer of 2013, and I mostly still enjoy the show.

But as I've been watching this summer, I've been thinking why couldn't we do our own version of the race right here in our region? With our rich and diverse history, culture, food and natural resources, this seems very doable to me. And it would be a whole lot of fun.

With that in mind, welcome to *The Amazing Race: South Shore*. In this version, eight teams of two will start in Lunenburg County and travel throughout the region performing a list of twenty-five tasks and chal-lenges designed to reflect the area's unique attributes. The race will end in Yarmouth County.

On your mark. Get set. Go!

1. In Hubbards, teams must learn the words to the first verse of *Barrett's Privateers* and perform it on stage at the historic Shore Club. When you sing the entire verse with no errors, you will receive your next clue.
2. Next, go to Chester and take part in a sailing race. Remember to keep the wind in your sails.
3. Participate in a treasure hunt on the world-famous Oak Island to find the next clue.
4. In Mahone Bay with its rich ship building history, follow simple instructions on how to build and race a cardboard boat. When you cross the finish line, you will get your next clue.
5. In Lunenburg, teams will learn how to shuck scallops, a local tradition, and then take part in a timed contest to see who can shuck the most scallops in three minutes.
6. Find one of the eight dimes hidden onboard Nova Scotia's famed sailing ambassador, *Bluenose II*.
7. With the dime, teams must "purchase" a dory and compete in dory races in Lunenburg Harbour in order to advance.
8. Next, teams must pan for gold at the Ovens Natural Park, just like they did in the 1860s.
9. From there, teams travel to the Wile Carding Mill in Bridgewater, where they must search through barrels of wool to locate the clue that will give them directions to their next challenge. This clue will be in the form of a picture—a sandcastle.
10. Take part in a sandcastle building contest at Rissers Beach Provincial Park. Teams must recreate the sample sandcastle in their picture to the satisfaction of the judges in order to proceed.
11. Entering Queens County, teams go to Greenfield and compete in a lumberjack event consisting of log rolling, axe throwing, and a Swede saw race.
12. In Liverpool, go to the Fort Point Lighthouse Museum and dress in period King's Orange Ranger uniforms. There, teams must defend Liverpool against the invading American privateers by finding the enemy soldier hidden somewhere within the "battle" zone. He will give teams their next clue.
13. Next, teams go to White Point Beach Lodge, where they learn to surf and prove to the instructor that they can stand upright on the board for three minutes without falling into the waves.
14. Carters Beach is known for its abundance of sand dollars. Racers

must locate one of the six painted sand dollars buried here.

15. In Shelburne County, teams must find the three Canadian $50 bills hidden on Crescent Beach at Lockeport.

16. In the town of Shelburne, racers will see who can be the quickest to build a barrel at the historic Barrel Factory.

17. Next, find ten specific whirligigs strategically located throughout the town of Shelburne, and hidden among numerous decoy whir-ligigs.

18. Teams must now race to Barrington, where they will select a lobster from the tank, build a fire on the beach and then cook and clean the lobster to the chef's satisfaction before receiving their next clue.

19. In Clark's Harbour, teams must learn how to row the world famous "Cape Islander" and use the boat to complete an obstacle course in the allotted amount of time.

20. At Shag Harbour, the site of one this country's most famous UFO incidents, racers must search for the three aliens that have crash-landed there.

21. In Yarmouth County, go to Pubnico and learn how to prepare a traditional Rappie pie, the well-loved traditional Acadian dish made from a delicious mix of potatoes and chicken. Make six pies in order to move onto the next leg of the race.

22. In Tusket, go the Argyle Township Court House & Gaol, the oldest courthouse in Canada, and participate in a mock trial. Teams must correctly answer six questions about the South Shore or go to jail, where they must serve their one-hour sentence before proceeding onto the next challenge.

23. At the Firefighters' Museum in the town of Yarmouth, dress in period turnout gear and complete a series of challenges related to fighting fires.

24. Go to the W. Laurence Sweeney Fisheries Museum and learn how to properly repair your ship. Your repairs must be carried out to the satisfaction of the expert on hand before you can receive your next clue.

25. At the end of the race, climb Cape Forchu lighthouse, the tallest lighthouse in Nova Scotia that is open to public tours to the lantern room, and search for the finish line.

I apologize for all those places I missed along the way, but I'm hoping the producers of *The Amazing Race Canada* will see this list and decide to do their next show right here in this region. Regardless, this exercise provided an opportunity to highlight some of the many unique cultural attributes of the beautiful South Shore. That's what's important, and that's the view from here.

End of an era

April 19, 2024

In an era of immense economic, societal and technological change and upheaval, many smaller rural communities across North America are struggling to maintain their base. Facing the current pressures, survival is their priority.

With a shifting thrust to how consumers conduct business, recent decades have not been kind to many communities, especially those places where resource-based industries have been curtailed for various reasons.

The realities of the modern marketplace, combined with the unequalled advancements in technology, have resulted in the changing makeup of local commercial districts and main streets, leading to business closures, shutdowns, and mergers.

For instance, this year numerous smaller towns throughout Atlantic Canada, including two right here on the South Shore, are among more than a dozen rural communities that are suffering the ill effects of such changes. This month, the Liverpool branch of the Bank of Nova Scotia is permanently closing its doors, while the Shelburne branch is being shuttered in May.

Not only does this move displace employees, but it also causes hardships for thousands of clients who must adjust their banking needs, either by going digital or by moving their business to a new bank altogether.

Switching can be difficult for some people, as many communities only have one bank and if that closes, then customers are forced to either do their banking on computers or travel to another, larger community where in-person banking services are still available. People who can't easily travel to another community have fewer options.

These South Shore branches are not facing this fate alone, as banks in other Nova Scotian communities, including Annapolis Royal, Bridgetown, Glace Bay and New Waterford, are also facing closure. Some may have already been closed. According to information from the bank, these smaller branches are being consolidated with larger branches because more customers are choosing digital options.

It may be true that a growing number of customers prefer to do their banking online, but it is also true that many, many clients still prefer to do their business in person at a physical structure where they can work with service providers on a face-to-face basis.

As they say, nothing beats dealing with a "real" person; and let's clear up one misconception: this is true of people of varying ages, not just the elderly, as we incorrectly assume.

The loss of local banking—or the closure of any business, for that matter—represents the continued erosion of rural commercial districts, but such a loss also has serious historical implications.

Take the Liverpool branch. Its roots reach back more than a century to the Bank of Liverpool, which operated from 1871 to 1879. Yes, Liverpool had its own bank at that time, complete with its own currency.

The Bank of Liverpool had its office in a large frame building on Liverpool's Main Street at the northwest corner of Gorham Street, the road that today runs past the current town hall structure which also houses the historical Astor Theatre.

Records indicate that when the Bank of Nova Scotia took over the meagre assets of the Bank of Liverpool in 1874 and started its long and ruthless campaign to recover its debt from shareholders under the "Double Liability" clause, its Liverpool agent took over the Bank of Liverpool office.

Subsequently, this location became the Liverpool branch of the Bank of Nova Scotia. It operated locally until this year. When the local branch of the Bank of Nova Scotia shuts its doors for the last time this month, it will be closing the page on a significant piece of Liverpool history. That's a loss, to be sure.

Luckily for local clients who do not want to travel outside of town for their banking services or do their banking online, Liverpool also has branches of the Bank of Montreal and the Royal Bank of Canada, which are ready to welcome new customers.

Those in many communities, however, are not as lucky, as the local branch of the Bank of Nova Scotia represented the only financial institution in town. There are rumours that the bank will continue to offer an ATM in some locations, but an ATM is not a brick-and-mortar building with real people. But it could be an option, nonetheless.

There is no denying the times they are changing, like it or not. We have no choice but to meet the changes and adapt or be left behind, and that's the view from here.

The day Donald Sutherland called

July 10, 2024

The news that legendary actor Donald Sutherland died a few weeks ago made me very sad, but, as a film buff, I appreciate his legacy.

Not only was he an iconic Canadian, but he also had ties right here to the South Shore, having spent his formative teenage years in Bridgewater, and going to work at radio station CKBW at age fourteen. As someone who is very proud of my roots and where I grew up, I was always impressed that we could lay claim to someone so distinguished as Mr. Sutherland.

Beyond his connection to Bridgewater, however, I recently learned that Mr. Sutherland also has family ties to Shelburne County. According to a recent Facebook post, his paternal grandfather, Frederick Winslow Sutherland, was born in Lockeport. The post also explained that Mr. Sutherland's paternal grandmother, Louisa/Louise Condon Day, was also born in Lockeport.

When I heard the news that Mr. Sutherland had died at the age of eighty-eight, it made me very sad, but it also made me smile as I was reminded of the day, several years ago when he called me out of the blue. Here's how it came about.

In my previous life as a newspaper reporter, whenever I heard that a film or TV production was coming to the South Shore, I would pursue every possible lead I could think of not only to get on the set to observe the cast and crew in action, but also, I hoped, to score an interview with the actors. Sometimes those efforts proved successful, but most often, they proved futile as these productions are usually locked down pretty tight, which I totally understood.

165

I was excited whenever I was able to chat with some major stars, but the one who caused me the greatest disappointment was Mr. Sutherland. Not only did I appreciate his work, but I believed that, as someone who had such strong ties to the South Shore, he should make an effort to speak with the local press.

Now, I know when these actors are here for a production, they come to work, and there are many demands put on their time. The fact is, Mr. Sutherland didn't owe me anything, but I just felt it would have been the courteous thing to do, all things considered.

Mr. Sutherland had come to work in the region on several occasions during my tenure at the local newspapers, but each time I was told by production publicists that he would not be doing any interviews. And I would write in my articles, that efforts to speak with Mr. Sutherland had been unsuccessful.

It appears I may have done that one too many times, because somehow in 2009, when Mr. Sutherland was in the area to film *Moby Dick*, he learned of my efforts and of my great disappointment at not being able to speak with him. Apparently, my words had such an impact that one day I received an unexpected phone call.

As the editor of a large newspaper, I received a lot of phone calls on any given day, but imagine my surprise when I answered and the man on the other end said, "Hello, Vernon. This is Donald Sutherland. I understand you want to speak with me."

I recognized his distinguished voice right away and, after I got over my immediate shock, we proceeded to have a most enjoyable chat. He was calling from Montreal and was on his way to catch a plane.

We covered a lot of territory during that ten-minute phone call, including his work, his family, his memories of growing up in the area, and some of his favourite roles, including the recent one he had just wrapped up on the South Shore.

To this day, I have no idea who shared my articles that talked about my efforts to speak with Mr. Sutherland, but I knew he had many friends and connections in the region. Truthfully, though, I am forever grateful to whomever it was, because that conversation was one of the highlights of my journalism career.

Donald Sutherland was a singular talent. There will never be another like him. That he would go out of his way to reach out to a reporter at a weekly newspaper on the South Shore of Nova Scotia speaks volumes to the calibre of person that he was, and that's the view from here.

The view from here on

Special occasions

Vernon Oickle

Every birthday is a gift

September 3, 2014

Every time I hear someone bemoaning another birthday, I quickly point out that instead of complaining about turning another year older, why not count your blessings and be thankful that you've been given such a wonderful gift?

After all, there are many who aren't as fortunate.

I've known many people who died way too young. To honour and remember those I've lost, I thought I'd have some fun on this, the occasion of my 53rd birthday. (Yes, I am turning another year older as of September 3, and I know how fortunate I am to be doing so.)

To salute my birthday, then, let's talk about all those things that remind us we're getting older. For instance, you know you're getting older when:

1. You start sounding like your parents when you're giving advice to your children.
2. Songs you were listening to as a teenager are now considered "golden oldies."
3. Movies you enjoyed as a teenager are now considered classics and, in fact, are now being remade for a new generation of viewers.
4. Television shows you watched in your youth are now considered the golden age of TV.
5. People you run into on the street look familiar, but you can't remember their names.
6. You can't get through eight straight hours of sleep without getting up at least once to have a pee.
7. Going to bed at 10 p.m. is considered late while getting up before 5 a.m. is considered the norm.
8. You can remember cooking without using microwave ovens.
9. You know what a "Walkman" is.

10. You can remember when the first fax machine arrived in town.
11. You remember that, during long drives with your parents, you actually played car games.
12. You can remember a world without the Internet and the World Wide Web.
13. You can remember a time when there was no such thing as "texting" and people actually talked to each other.
14. You can remember when people sent letters through the mail.
15. You can remember when calculators were considered "high tech" equipment.
16. You remember buying your first VCR machine and actually renting VHS movies from the local corner store.
17. Furthermore, you can remember when there was a video store on just about every corner of town.
18. You can remember when it would take an entire room to hold a computer.
19. You can remember when cell phones were the size of a shoe.
20. You've actually been inside a phone booth.
21. You can remember when 25 cents would buy you a bag of potato chips and a chocolate bar. There was even a time when you would have change left over!
22. You can remember a time when children had to use their imaginations.
23. You remember a time when hanging out with your childhood buddies actually meant playing outside.
24. You remember when bell-bottom jeans, Fry boots and water buffaloes were actually in style.
25. You remember using encyclopedias to do research.
26. You remember when music was available on vinyl LPs, 45 records, 8-track tapes and cassettes.
27. You can remember when the Lighthouse Route was considered the main road to Halifax.
28. You can remember when every vehicle came equipped with a push-in cigarette lighter.
29. You can remember a time when you could smoke inside any building (not a good thing).
30. You remember what life was like when you had to make your own coffee or tea at home.

31. You can remember when service station attendants pumped your gas, checked your oil and cleaned your windshield. They'd even put air in your tires if you needed it.
32. You can remember when a clerk would not only bag your groceries but would also carry the bags from the check-out to your car.
33. You can remember when pictures were made on film with an actual camera, not digitally on your phone.
34. You can remember playing with Stretch Armstrong and Big Jim's Sports Camper. Actually, I think I could still find them in my attic.
35. You can remember when the word "selfie" didn't exist.
36. You can remember a time when your television set only had two channels and you had to actually walk across the room to change the channel.
37. You can remember when you watched your favourite TV shows in black and white because technicolor hadn't arrived yet.
38. You can also remember a time when rabbit ears weren't necessarily referring to the ears on a cute little cuddly animal.
39. You can remember getting on an airplane without being "goosed."
40. You can remember when there were two major league baseball teams in Canada.
41. You remember when a phone was a phone, and a camera was a camera.
42. You can sing all the words to the theme songs from "Gilligan's Island" and "The Beverley Hillbillies."
43. You remember when you'd call a business and actually talk to a real live person.
44. You can remember when you could listen to your transistor radio on the AM dial.
45. You can remember when gas sold for less than $1 per litre.
46. You remember when you only had to use five numbers to make a local phone call.
47. You remember a time before Facebook, Twitter and Instagram, when you kept your private and personal information private and personal.

Seriously, though, it doesn't matter what you can or can't remember as you get older. The important thing is that we keep our lives in perspective and be thankful for what we have because every birthday is a gift, or least that's the view from here.

Be thankful

October 8, 2014

This weekend, Canadians will gather in their homes, around the dining room table or in front of the television, to celebrate Thanksgiving.

Traditionally, it's a long weekend filled with feasting, relaxing, quality family time, putting away any last reminders of summer, such as the bar-becue and lawn chairs, completing yard work in preparation for the coming winter months, watching sports on television or perhaps even playing a game yourself.

However, Thanksgiving should be about more than that. While we are fortunate that the South Shore is immune to much of the tragedy, strife and human suffering that often grip other parts of the world, we know that poverty, disease and crime do exist here.

We would be naïve to think otherwise.

Despite the darkness that has rocked the world in recent times, there is still much for which we should be thankful, and we should reflect upon our blessings every day. Thanksgiving affords us an excellent opportunity to take stock of those positive things in our lives.

For starters, be thankful you woke up this morning.

If you're in good health, be thankful for that.

If you are ill, be thankful that you can access free medical care. Yes, the system is not perfect, but it's better than what is available in most other countries.

If you got out of bed this morning and went about your business on your own steam, then be thankful for that.

If you opened your eyes this morning and marvelled at the wondrous colours of autumn or looked into the faces of your loved ones, be thankful that you can see.

If you awoke to the sounds of that annoying alarm going off, be thankful you could hear it.

Be thankful that you have family around you.

If you are a parent, be thankful for your children and take the time to let them know how you feel about them. Tell them you love them every day.

Surely you must have someone you call a friend or, if you're really lucky, a group of people you call friends. Be thankful for them.

Here in Nova Scotia, we live in relative safety away from the wanton destruction of war and terrorist attacks. Be thankful for that.

In this part of the world, we should also be thankful that we enjoy a comparatively low crime rate, making our rural communities wonderful places to work and raise our families.

We also live in a place where neighbours still extend a helping hand without expecting anything in return. Be thankful for that.

There are still places in the area where you can go away and leave your doors unlocked. That's something to be thankful for.

We should also be thankful that we live in communities where we can go for a walk after dark if we want to and still feel safe.

With the world's environment continuing to deteriorate at an alarming rate, be thankful our little piece of paradise is still relatively clean and pristine.

You might also be thankful you live in a place where, if you step out on your front lawn, you can still see the stars at night and the sun in the daytime, and where you can breathe smog-free air.

When you turn on the tap and lift that glass to your lips, be thankful you have a supply of fresh, clean water.

Considering the oppression suffered by so many people in other countries by powerful regimes that have little or no regard for humanity, be thankful that we enjoy democratic freedoms here in Canada.

Be thankful that if you don't agree with any political leader, you have the freedom to stand up and say so.

In fact, we enjoy many freedoms in Canada such as the freedom of movement and the freedom to follow whatever career path we choose. We should be thankful we live in such a country.

Let's also be thankful that we live in a mostly-tolerant society where you can be who you are and follow your own lifestyle.

If you are a religious person, you must be thankful that you live in a country that allows you to practice the religion of your choice.

If you don't observe a religion, then be thankful you have the freedom to follow your own path.

If you have a job you enjoy, or maybe even one that you don't enjoy so much, be thankful anyway that you have a means to provide for yourself and your family.

If you are going home tonight to your house, be thankful that you have shelter.

If you had breakfast this morning and will have dinner (or supper) tonight be thankful for the food on your table and in your belly.

No matter how tired you may be this evening, be thankful that your child needs help with his or her homework or wants to play.

Be even more thankful that your son, but particularly your daughter, lives in a place that allows both genders to attend school and to learn.

Be thankful as well that you live in a neighbourhood where you can let your children go outside to play without fear of them being gunned down.

If you can read this column, then be thankful that someone, perhaps many years ago, taught you to read.

If someone is reading this to you, be thankful that someone cares enough to do it for you.

As you sit down to your Thanksgiving meal this coming weekend, be thankful for the fellowship and food that you're about to share.

And finally, as you turn out the lights and fall asleep tonight, be thankful that you do not hear the sounds of bombs and gunfire outside your home. From all of this you can see that, indeed, we have much for which we should be thankful. It's just that many of us don't stop and count our blessings. Perhaps it's time we did, or at least that's the view from here.

My favourite Christmas memories

December 24, 2014

Someone recently asked me what stands out as my most favourite Christmas memory, and I couldn't give him one specific answer. While my response may have been viewed as a cop-out, it was honest and sincere.

When I think back over my lifetime, I find it's a difficult challenge to pinpoint one event and say definitively that's my favourite Christmas memory. Over 53 years, there have been so many events and special occasions that stand out as cherished memories that I would have to say they are all equally special and important to me.

One of my earliest Christmas memories is of the year when I may have been four or five and my grandparents gave me a red racing car for a gift. Compared to today's high-tech toys and remote-controlled vehicles that cost hundreds of dollars, there was nothing particularly special about this die-cast metal car, except that it came from my grandparents.

I remember how excited I was on Christmas morning when I opened that present and saw the car for the first time. In fact, the car was such a special present that I still have it packed away in the attic.

Another special memory from my childhood occurred when I was six or seven and my older sister, Heather, woke me early on Christmas morning to tell me Santa had been there.

Now when I say early, I'm talking three or four in the morning, but time held no meaning for two excited children on Christmas morning and so, with my sister's urging, we got out of bed and opened all the presents under the tree. And when I say everything, I mean everything including the gifts that were for our mom and dad.

After all the gifts were opened and the living room was a sea of brightly-coloured paper, boxes, ribbons and bows, we went back to bed and fell asleep. Not surprisingly, our mom and dad were none too impressed when they got up a few hours later and discovered the mess we had made under the tree.

However, like all innocent children before us and all those who have come after us, we blamed the situation on Santa, insisting it must have been someone else because we hadn't been out of bed the entire night.

We weren't punished for our behaviour, as our parents embraced the Christmas spirit. Coincidentally, however, the next year, I remember that our parents had seemingly made no Christmas preparations and, in fact, when my sister and I went to bed on Christmas Eve, we didn't even have a tree as our parents had told us that, if we were good and did as we were told, Santa would bring gifts and he would even trim the tree, but we had to promise that we would stay in bed until the next morning, waiting for our mom and dad to get us up.

Thinking that maybe Santa was still upset with us for the previous year's actions, we did just as our parents had made us promise and, to our pleasant surprise, we found the next morning that we had gifts and even a tree.

Indeed, Santa had done a wonderful job the night before, but my sister and I couldn't understand why our mom and dad seemed so tired all the next day. Needless to say, that was the one and only year Santa trimmed the tree on Christmas Eve. Clearly, it was too much work for him.

As I got older and travelled to Alberta to study journalism, some of my favourite Christmas memories are from those years I returned home for the holidays. In fact, it was during my first year in college, in 1980, that I flew for the first time, making the plane trip from Calgary to Halifax for Christmas. Now, *that* was an experience, let me tell you.

Since I had taken the train out to Alberta when I left for college the previous summer, not only had I never flown before, but on this particular trip I was travelling alone and didn't have the first clue about what to do. However, I made it home safe and sound, and I remember having a wonderful holiday with my family.

Being away from home for the first time had given me an entirely new perspective on what it meant to spend that special time of year with family.

Years later, after I had become settled into my career, I was fortunate to meet my future wife, Nancy. The Christmas that she and I became engaged obviously has deep meaning for me.

As the years have unfolded, we've built many wonderful holiday memories together, such as the first Christmas we spent in our first tiny apartment. It was small and extremely tight when we added the Christmas tree, but we made it work.

A few years later, we celebrated our first Christmas in our new home, and we've been here ever since. We've made many wonderful memories in this house, including our sons' first Christmases here and the great Christmas Eve gatherings we had with family and friends who would drop by for refreshments and fellowship. They are great memories, indeed.

In time, these celebrations have changed and some of my most cherished memories are of the last Christmases we had with my parents and with Nancy's dad. They may be gone now, but they are still an important part of our holiday traditions as we hold their love in our hearts and recall all those wonderful years we had with them.

In recent years, as we've lost family members through death or by circumstances such as those who moved away, our Christmas celebrations have evolved as we've had to embrace the changes that come with the passage of time, but the important thing for us is to be with those who are still important in our lives.

When someone asks me about my favourite memories, I tell them it's important to embrace the season and enjoy the holiday. Spend time with your loved ones and make memories that you can hold into the future, but, above all, celebrate the fellowship, peace and joy of this special time of year.

Christmas really isn't about what's under the tree, it's about who's around the tree, or at least that's the view from here.

We will remember them

November 11, 2015

They shall grow not old, as we that are left grow old:
Age shall not weary them, nor the years condemn.
At the going down of the sun and in the morning
We will remember them.

These lines of the poem 'For the Fallen', by Laurence Binyon, will be familiar to anyone who attends Remembrance Day ceremonies such as those being held across Canada today, November 11; but do we really understand their deep meaning?

I find its reading is one of the most sombre moments of any Remembrance Day ceremony, as these words are a stark reminder of the hundreds of thousands of Canadian men and women who have made—and who continue to make—the ultimate sacrifice in wars and conflicts both past and present so that you and I can enjoy the freedoms we take for granted each and every day.

This year's remembrances are especially poignant because, coming as they do following the recent federal election, we have just experienced one of the greatest gifts our heroes have given us: the right to vote.

I've heard these words a great deal over the years as I've attended Remembrance Day ceremonies and I've marvelled at the powerful message contained in these four short lines. Since Canadians pause each November 11 to remember their fallen heroes and to honour those who are still with us, I thought it appropriate to take a closer look at these words.

While they are the most familiar lines, the above stanza is, in fact, only a portion of Binyon's best-known poem, but they have become the lasting symbol of remembrance. For those of you who don't know the story, Binyon composed the poem while sitting on a cliff-top, looking out to sea from the dramatic scenery of the north Cornish coastline at Pentire Point, north of Polzeath.

According to a website dedicated to Binyon, he wrote the poem in mid-September, 1914, a few weeks after the outbreak of the First World War. During these weeks, the British Expeditionary Force had suffered casualties following its first encounter with the Imperial German Army at the Battle of Mons on August 23, its rearguard action during the retreat from Mons in late August and the Battle of Le Cateau on August 26, and its participation with the French Army in holding up the German Army at the First Battle of the Marne between September 5 and 9.

Binyon said in 1939 that the four lines of the fourth stanza (quoted above) came to him first. These words have become especially familiar and famous, having been adopted by the Royal British Legion as an Exhortation for ceremonies of Remembrance to commemorate fallen servicemen and women.

Like our British friends, Canadian Legions have also adopted the poem, which will be repeated hundreds of times today across this country. It saddens me, however, to think that, while many Canadians will pause to honour our war heroes during these Remembrance Day services, some Canadians look at November 11 as just another holiday.

I was recently reminded of this reality when I overheard two people in their 20s or 30s talking about how many holidays there are between Labour Day and Christmas. It was their cavalier attitude toward November 11 that struck me the most when I heard one of them say they look forward to these days to get caught up on their sleep.

Seriously? I thought, resisting the urge to break into their conversation and remind them of the importance of Remembrance Day. In hindsight, perhaps I should have done so, but I'm sure my attempt to educate these two young men would have been soundly rejected and I suppose that in a free country—one of the very things we give thanks for on Remembrance Day—they have the right to use their "day off" any way they see fit.

But November 11 is not just another "day off" for sleeping in or partying. In fact, November 11 is a day to say thank you and to remember all those Canadians who have made the ultimate sacrifice so that our generation will not suffer the oppression and horrors of war.

For the record, here are the numbers of Canadian military personnel killed while serving their country just in the past hundred years:

First World War	66,665
Second World War	46,998
Korea	516
peacekeeping postings	121
Afghanistan	157

When I attend a Remembrance Day service and hear the names of those who died, perhaps alone and terrified, in some far-off land away from their loved ones, it causes me to shiver. I cannot even begin to imagine the horrors of war, but I am thankful for those who paid the ultimate price so that I can enjoy the life I lead today.

While November 11 is set aside every year to remember the past sacrifices so many have made, it's also a good time to wonder what our world would be like if war and strife did not exist.

In an ideal world, with no wars, our brave men and women would not have to put themselves in harm's way. However, as history has shown us, this is not a perfect world. War has existed for centuries and, sadly, it appears as though it will be with us well into the future.

Our world would be a lot different today were it not for the brave men and women who stood up to those who would do us harm. Surely, we can all set aside a few hours one day of the year to say thank you for their sacrifices.

Too many fought and died for us to ever forget. Sacrifices made by those Canadians must not be forgotten or at least that's the view from here.

A visit from the Christmas Spirit

December 23, 2015

So here I sit, staring at the blank computer screen and contemplating what to write, but nothing comes. It's as if the words are blocked and refuse to find their way from my fingertips to the keyboard, but I feel the pressure to come up with something.

Deadline approaches and will be upon me before I know it. What to do?

Writing a weekly column can sometimes be a challenge, especially during the holidays when you feel compelled to produce something insightful and inspirational. This year, though, those thoughts remain elusive, buried under piles of recent news events that have shocked and saddened the masses.

It's the morning of December 3, the day after the senseless and tragic mass shooting in a San Bernardino, California community centre that left 14 people dead and 21 others wounded, many of them clinging to life. It was a horrific act of violence that left us saddened and, in some ways, feeling vulnerable.

I get it that Christmas is upon us, but how can we talk about being happy and joyful when there is so much pain and sorrow in the world? How can we find happiness and peace when there are people among us who would bring so much horror and violence into the lives of innocent people?

These are the questions I ponder as I sit in front of the blank computer screen in my home office on this early December morning, trying to collect my thoughts and put them into some kind of positive, uplifting message that will inspire and enlighten my readers.

The house is quiet and the world is still this morning, with few distractions. It is usually a good time to write, but I remain stymied on this day. *What I need is a hot cup of tea*, I tell myself. That will get the creative juice flowing, as caffeine is always a good remedy for writer's block.

Making my way through the darkened house to the kitchen, I gaze out into the neighbourhood and decide that I am fortunate to live in such a wonderful place where peace and quiet are usually the norm.

I am not naïve. I know that tragedy can arrive unannounced and at any time. I also know that no community, no matter how big or how small, and regardless of its location, is immune to crime and violence. It can and does happen all around us and comes when we least expect it.

However, for the most part, I'm thankful that the wonderful communities here on the South Shore are typically peaceful and safe, so as I go about the business of making my cup of tea, taking extra precautions to remain quiet so that I do not disturb anyone else, I ponder my current conundrum—what shall I write for my Christmas column?

I'm lost deep in my own thoughts while waiting for the kettle to boil when I suddenly hear the commotion back in my office. I'm convinced that it sounds like someone tapping away on my keyboard. *But how can that be?* I wonder.

I know everyone else in the house is sound asleep and should remain snuggled comfortably in his or her bed for at least another hour, so there's no reasonable explanation for the noise coming from the room that's located next to the dining room.

My first thought is burglars, but I immediately dismiss that possibility.

That's ridiculous, I tell myself. If someone had broken into my home, I would have surely seen the intruder before now. Besides, burglars don't typically stop and write on computers, do they?

Cautiously tiptoeing toward my office and slowly poking my head through the door, I'm startled to see a stout, elderly gentleman working away on my laptop.

"Who are you?" I ask the bald man with a thick, white beard who somehow seems oddly familiar. Swallowing hard, I continue, "How did you get in here?"

"That's not important," the old fellow quickly replies, glancing up from the keyboard and smiling slyly at me, instantly putting me at ease. I'm convinced I've seen this man somewhere before, but I just can't figure out where.

Then suddenly, he tells me, "I'm here to help you."

"Help me?" I manage to ask, wondering if I should pinch myself to wake me from this dream I must surely be having. "Help me with what?"

"I understand you're struggling to find an appropriate topic to write about," he answers, turning his eyes back to the computer. "I simply don't understand why you should be having such a problem. It's Christmas, which means there are lots of topics to tackle. You could write about how generous and caring people are this time of year or you could write about all those people who go out of their way to help others in the community during the holidays. There's no shortage of ideas, my friend."

I think his attitude is rather stuffy and presumptuous, so I take up the challenge.

"Yes," I answer purposefully, with an air of cockiness and arrogance. "But the world seems like such a dark and depressing place these days. It's a challenge to write about bright lights, decorations and festive tidings when so many people are hurting and just struggling to hang on."

"Don't you get it?" the old man fires back.

"Get what?" I ask, somewhat sheepishly, for I anticipate a lecture is at hand.

"Don't you understand that when times are tough and people are at their lowest, that's when they need to hear words of inspiration and hope," he tells me.

Turning his head to look me squarely in the eyes, he smiles and continues, "Yes, there are tragedy and sorrow in the world, but as a writer it's your responsibility to dig deep and to find those words of enlightenment."

I nod. "I suppose it is, but it's difficult to do that when we're constantly bombarded with so much darkness, such as the mass shootings that have just taken place."

"The world is filled with sorrow, but that's why this season is important to us," the visitor explains. "This season is about hope and overcoming tragedy."

"I don't think everyone understands that," I reply.

"Perhaps, but the holidays aren't about the number of gifts under the tree, who spent the most money to celebrate, who threw the biggest party or who has the most decorations on their house," the mysterious old man continues. "It's about family and helping others. And in these dark times, we value reminders that we need each other and that we should be counting our blessings, not dwelling on the tragedies. There will always be darkness in the world, but during Christmas we're reminded there is also light."

I still have no idea who this man is, but he is certainly making a lot of sense and in the process giving me some serious food for thought. "I could not agree more."

"Think you can handle this now?" he asks, rising from the chair.

"Yes," I answer with a nod. "I think I can."

"Then I must be going."

"Will you at least tell me who you are before you go?"

"That's not important," he answers as I watch him fade away. "Remember the task at hand."

And that's it. In an instant the old man is gone, and I still have no idea who he was.

Quickly moving behind my computer and glancing toward the screen, I am pleasantly surprised to see these words written there:

'Tis the season for peace, love and hope, or at least that's the view from here.

Life just happens

May 4, 2016

Letting go of a loved one or close friend is one of the most difficult things we will ever have to face in our lives, but it is also one of the most natural and, if you can believe it, sometimes even one of the most beautiful experiences you may ever have.

Looking into the face of death can be a powerful, life-changing experience that many of us may find overwhelming, as it reminds us of our own fate. Accepting the death of a loved one is also accepting our own mortality because in life, death is the only thing that comes with a 100% guarantee.

However, depending on your personal and religious beliefs, you may also see death as a new beginning, a time of renewal and hope, and a release from the bonds of this mortal existence. This is especially true for those who are in pain from a serious or debilitating illness. Even those who are not particularly religious may find comfort in knowing that death can be a humane escape from the agony that some people must endure.

However, despite all this reasoning, accepting that someone you love is gone can be a tough reality to embrace. In recent years, it seems I've come face to face with this reality more times than I care to remember, but as we grow older, we must understand that's how life happens.

We must accept that as senior generations grow older, death will inevitably become a more common occurrence. It's the river of life, its ebb and flow carrying us from one generation to the next. It is a stark dose of reality that is often hard to embrace, and one of the most difficult aspects of that reality is facing the death of a parent.

I had to deal with this truth ten years ago, when I lost my father to lung cancer. It was a difficult journey as we watched him struggle and cling to life through some very emotional and painful times. He fought valiantly and remained strong throughout the ten-month ordeal, but the dreadful disease was just too strong and finally, on January 17, 2006, he peacefully slipped away.

While we grieved our loss, we also accepted that he was no longer living with the pain that had consumed his body in the months leading up to the end, though at times, I will confess, it was often a struggle to carry on without him.

After all, how do you fill the void that is created with the loss of a parent? It isn't easy, but somehow, we soldiered on and, in time, the wonderful memories we have of him when he wasn't in pain filled that emptiness. He set a fine example for his family, and those are the images we cling to.

As we look forward to Mother's Day this coming Sunday, I am reminded that, three years later, I found myself dealing once again with many of the same emotions I had faced following the death of my father.

In a remarkable and somewhat unsettling twist of fate, on the third anniversary of my father's passing, my mother slipped quietly into the great unknown, finally giving up her own valiant struggle for life.

Death came slowly to my mother on January 17, 2009, creeping up on her like a predator stalking its prey, and then finally enveloping her in its dark cloak.

For several years, we watched as my mother clung to life, refusing to give in to the pain and suffering she most certainly was enduring. She didn't go easily, her steely will to live putting up a brave defence against some very tough odds posed by diabetes and a variety of other illnesses.

Many times during those years, doctors told us to brace for the end, that her body could not take much more, but despite their warnings, miraculously, she kept coming back to us.

I think it was pure willpower that kept her going, but at some point, the body and mind know when the battle is lost and I truly believe that, while she wanted desperately to live and used every ounce of strength she could muster, subconsciously she accepted the inevitable. At that point she was at peace with her fate.

With her journey here on earth over, we took comfort in knowing that her pain and suffering had ended and that, if there is some place beyond these earthly confines, then that's where she is.

I confess that I do not consider myself to be a particularly religious man, but I do like to think that there is more to life than what we have here in this world.

Is there a heaven or paradise? I don't know, but it is comforting to think that my parents have gone to some place better, some place where there is no more sickness or illness, no more pain and suffering, only sunshine and health and happiness.

Accepting the possibility that there is such a place allows us to cope and, having been present at the death of both parents, I can say without hesitation that it did appear as though they were drifting off to some place better than the existence they were leaving.

Perhaps religion or science can explain such a phenomenon, but it was clear to me as I watched them each draw their last breaths that in death, life just happens. And it was comforting to know at that very moment when their lives here ended, their suffering stopped as well.

No one wants to let go of a loved one, but who are we to question the way nature works? We can't stop death, so we better find a way to come to terms with it. Both my parents went peacefully and quietly to whatever awaited them on the other side of death and, in drawing upon that reality, we say Godspeed to them.

As you celebrate this special day on Sunday with your mothers and all the other women who are just like your mothers, take the time to tell them how much they mean to you because, just like that, life happens and they could be gone, and that's the view from here.

A Husband's Handy Holiday Shopping Guide

December 6, 2018

Husbands, beware. As of today, it's just under a month until Christmas. But I'm sure you've all begun shopping for that special someone in your life.

Yeah, right! I know better.

With that reality in mind, I've written *A Husband's Handy Holiday Shopping Guide* to help husbands get through this busy season. I thought I'd prepare a few tips to help you guys out. After all, compatriots, we're all in this together and, I'd do anything I can to help my brethren.

I get it that you consider Christmas shopping to be one of the most painful, excruciating and time-sucking experiences in your whole life (much akin to passing a kidney stone or walking over burning coals in your bare feet), but, my friends, it's time to accept the reality—it's got to be done.

Your first mistake is thinking you've got lots of time. You don't. In fact, before you know it, December 24 will be here, and if you keep procrastinating, you still won't have anything for your wife or partner.

If you're smart—as I know you are—you will not wait until the last minute, as you've done every other year. If you start now, you just may beat the rush and there'll still be a good selection of items from which to choose. If you put it off until the day before Christmas, as I know most of you do, then everything will be picked over, and if you don't get what she *really* wants, there could be trouble in paradise on Christmas morning.

To aid my fellow man here's *A Husband's Handy Holiday Shopping Guide*

> **Tip #1.** Stop living in denial. This holiday arrives every year on the same day of the same month, so there really is no excuse for leaving your shopping until the last minute. You know when it's coming, so embrace it, relish it, become one with the idea—accept it. Stop dragging your feet, get into your happy place and just go with it. Honestly, it's all about your mindset.
>
> **Tip #2.** Make it a point to start your shopping no later than the first of December (earlier if you're a real keener, but don't overexert yourself). Force yourself to hit the stores at least once every week in December. The more you get done early on, the less you will have to worry about when the stores are crammed full of sweaty, hateful customers pushing and shoving to get the few remaining items on the shelves.
>
> **Tip #3.** Listen for clues. It's a cop-out for any man to say he didn't know what to buy his spouse or partner because, without a doubt, she's been telling you for weeks what she wants. I know it's hard for most men, as you're genetically programmed to tune out your wife when she speaks, but start paying attention when she's talking. Listen carefully and I promise you'll pick up a few suggestions of what she wants to find under the tree. And if you're especially coy about it, you could score a few brownie points in the process.
>
> **Tip #4.** Pay particular attention to key phrases such as "What I really need" or "I'd like to have" or "Wouldn't it be nice to have (insert whatever here)?" Invariably your wife will provide you with more than enough suggestions to stuff her stocking, but it's up to you to be smart enough to pick up on the hints. Caution: Stay on your toes. Be sure to decipher the clues properly, as sometimes she'll say one thing and mean something completely different. I

know you ultimately want to fulfill her wishes, and these clues are vital components of successfully completing that mission.

Tip #5. If you've listened for hints and you're still not picking up the vibes, then it's time to send in the troops. If you have children, have them pump their mother for ideas on what she'd like for Christmas. In order to preserve the surprise, though, encourage them to be sneaky, as their mother will quickly catch on if they're too obvious. Kids can make excellent spies, so use these reinforcements wisely.

Tip #6. Ask the mother-in-law for ideas. You can bet that at some point your spouse has said to her mother, "I hope Earl gets me that new reciprocating saw I've been eyeing down at the hardware store," or "I could really use a new tool belt." If there's one person in the world who knows what your wife wants for Christmas, it's her mother. A word of advice, though, don't get her new oven mitts if what she really wants is new work gloves to match her steel-toed boots. The devil is in the details.

Tip #7. Drop the macho façade. You know Christmas is coming and you've got to get something for your spouse, so accept the challenge. It's time to man up. Get out there and shop till you drop. You can take solace in knowing that millions of other men around the world share your pain. And one more thing: it's cheating to get your wife's best friend or sister to shop for you. The gift will mean more to your spouse if it comes from your heart, not her best buddy.

Tip #8. Keep a list. If you've been paying attention, then you should have a well-composed inventory of what she's been dreaming of. Never, never go into the stores unarmed. Your list will be your best friend this holiday season. Once you buy something, be sure to cross it off that list. You're doing this for two reasons. First, to avoid duplication. Second, to make sure you don't forget something she really wanted, like that new hammer.

Tip #9. Don't wait until Christmas Eve to unpack the bags and wrap your gifts. Imagine your angry surprise and frustration if you wait until the last minute and then you discover that something you thought you bought two weeks ago didn't get put into the bags at the checkout. It happens, so be sure to double-check when you get home.

Tip #10. Don't cave to last-minute flip-flops. Once you've made your list and done your shopping, don't rush out the week before

Christmas to pick up something new she may have suddenly decided she'd like to have. Resist the urge to get it unless you really, really, really want to score brownie points with her; then by all means go and get whatever it is she wants. The sky's the limit in that case.

Tip #11. Save all cash register slips. This is the cardinal rule of Christmas shopping for your wife or partner, because you know that, sure as you're likely to overindulge during the holidays, something will have to be returned because you've bought it in the wrong size, wrong colour or wrong style. Or she's decided it's not really what she wanted after all.

Tip #12. Make sure you have a wonderful holiday season with your wife or partner and your family because, despite all the gifts under the tree, Christmas isn't about that.

And remember, guys, it is better to make the effort at shopping and fail than to make no effort at all, and that's the view from here.

An ode to fathers everywhere

June 12, 2019

With Father's Day being celebrated this coming Sunday, June 16, I find myself thinking of my own dad, whom we lost in January, 2006 following a courageous battle with lung cancer.

The thing about fathers and mothers is that when you are a youngster you think your parents are immortal and that they will always be there for you. But the cold, hard truth is that they are only humans, and the day will come when you will no longer have them to reach out to or to lean on.

As we celebrate fathers everywhere this Sunday, I'll be thinking about my father, who valiantly fought the ravages of lung cancer for nine months from his diagnosis in the spring of 2005 until the dreaded disease eventually took him. During that time, we constantly lived under the shadow of death, knowing that his prognosis was not good, but always remaining hopeful that a miracle would occur.

Anyone who has watched a loved one suffer from cancer, or who has personally fought cancer, will know the challenges, stress and heartache of such a journey.

From the beginning, doctors said we should not expect him to live more than six months. They said he would not live to see Christmas that year. He proved them wrong. Defying the odds, he did survive to see the holidays, and it was wonderful having him around for one more Christmas.

But then, on January 17 of 2006, following a brave but often painful struggle, my father lost his battle. When the end finally arrived, he passed quietly and peacefully into whatever hereafter awaits all of us.

No matter how much wealth we accumulate or how much power we amass, death is the one thing we all have in common. We can't escape it. We can all be sure our life's journey here on earth will meet with the same ending. Sometimes death comes without warning, leaving survivors stunned. Other times, it comes slowly in the form of a disease that leaves the body nothing more than a shell of its former self.

To be there when death arrives is an awe-inspiring experience. It is sad, to be sure, as one's emotions are laid open like a fresh wound. But it is also fulfilling in a way that defies explanation. In escaping the mortal confines of a body ravaged by a dreadful disease, my father became free of the pain and suffering he had endured for so long. We found comfort in that.

To witness the death of a family member, close friend or another loved one is not an easy thing, but sometimes a certain amount of closure and relief comes with the loss. We all struggle to understand and come to grips with our own mortality, but in the end, we discover there are no easy answers, only hopes and assurances that we go to a better place where pain and suffering no longer exist.

Now, on the eve of Father's Day, I remember my dad's life and the time he spent with his family, his most important possession. I consider myself lucky to have known such a man. He taught me a great deal over the years.

My father always put family first and, though of modest means, we were never in want of anything. He made many sacrifices for us, but that's what a husband, father and grandfather does, and he did so without regret.

It isn't easy to deal with the loss of a parent, but during his battle in those last nine months, my father taught me the true meaning of courage, and I will remember those life lessons.

In the face of terrible news—that he had terminal lung cancer—I never heard him complain about his fate. He faced it on his own terms. He was aware of the struggle that lay before him, but he met it head-on. He often said he had nothing to complain about, that at the age of 76 he had lived a long life and his struggle was part of the bigger plan. And, he pointed out, there was no use in complaining as such things were out of anyone's control.

Sure, he grumped and took issue with the health care system for the long wait times to see doctors and undergo tests. He wasn't alone there, as many people face the same hurdles.

And he often became frustrated when he believed he was falling through the cracks, as would anyone in his position. But in facing his own death, my father came to terms with that reality rather quickly.

The doctors had told my dad early on that there was little hope for treatment, and as the months slipped by and he grew increasingly frailer, he accepted that his end was near. Through all of that, however, he maintained a certain and unbendable resolve to rise above the pain and keep his dignity. In truth, he worried more about his family than the state of his own declining health.

Dealing with such a reality is no easy feat. It takes great strength, courage and faith, traits he displayed on a daily basis and right up to the end. When he became confined to hospital several months before his death, he rose to that challenge as well and made the most of it.

The staff, particularly the nurses at Queens General Hospital, became more like friends than caregivers. They always demonstrated compassion and understanding, and as family members watching one of our own slipping away, they became our support system. For that we will be forever grateful.

There's an old belief that people nearing death know they are about to pass on. Perhaps that's an old wives' tale, but in Dad's case, it certainly seemed that way.

Only a day before he died, he told us matter-of-factly that he was near the end. It had been a long journey, but it was as if he knew it was just about over.

I remember at one point asking him why he had to go and get sick. His answer was short and to the point. He simply looked at me and said, without hesitation, "That's just the way it is."

Throughout his ordeal, my father was a portrait of strength, courage and dignity. If he had lived, he would have turned 90 years old last month, but it just wasn't meant to be.

On Sunday, then, as you celebrate the love and warmth of your dad, remember to tell him how much he means to you. Take it from someone who has lost both parents: cherish those moments you have with them as you never know what the future has in store, and that's the view from here.

Dear Santa...

December 25, 2019

Here we are again, smack-dab in the middle of another Christmas season.

Can you believe it? Well, yes, of course you can. After all, this is the busiest time of year for you. I know you've spent the past several months making your lists and checking them twice, trying to see who has been naughty or nice.

But who am I kidding? I know you're ready. Surely, after all these centuries, you got this down to an easy system. Right?

Seriously though, it just seems like yesterday we were doing this. I hope you had a great summer and you're well rested, as the game is afoot, so to speak. I've got a lot of work planned for you this year. Yes, I know this is a long list and you probably can't fill it completely, so all I ask is that you do your best, just like you always do.

You'll also see this is not going to be a typical Christmas wish list. I appreciate this is a particularly busy time of year for you, but I'm afraid that, for many people, Christmas has lost its meaning and I am hoping this may help. So here goes.

First off, Santa, this year I'd like you to give all politicians the wisdom, courage and strength to make decisions based on compassion and understanding, not take the politically-expedient route as they often do. In their haste to cut deficits, balance budgets and reduce taxes, governments sometimes lose sight of the people directly affected by their decisions, the people who trusted them with their votes.

I'm talking about the real people; the ones who struggle every day to make ends meet and still come up short. Surely, in a country like ours, everyone is entitled to health care within a reasonable time frame, a good education for all children and a basic quality of life, but sometimes those promises fail to materialize.

Speaking of our great nation, it should not be acceptable for one single person to be homeless. Unfortunately, statistics reveal hundreds—maybe even thousands—of homeless people roam the streets of larger cities such as Halifax, Montreal, Toronto and Vancouver. It's disheartening to think that such a thing can be true, but we know these are the facts.

So, dear Santa, could you please take care of the homeless. Poverty is a heinous plague, but one basic need for all humans is shelter from the elements. Some people need help in meeting that necessity. It's going to take a great deal of ingenuity and political will to find solutions to this escalating problem, but surely, we can do better.

Speaking of shelter, Santa, I'd like you to find some way of making sure all our senior citizens receive some relief from the ever-rising costs of living so that they can remain comfortably in their homes. You and I both know it's a sad commentary on our society when senior citizens must forego their medication and groceries so they can heat their homes.

But it's happening all around us and it appears the people who have the power to make a difference (the politicians) don't seem too concerned. Maybe they'll get the holiday spirit. Let's hope so.

My next wish would be for all the little boys and girls who don't receive gifts on Christmas morning. I understand this happens for many different reasons, which I don't have the space to get into right now, but since Christmas is supposed to be for the children, how can we allow this to happen?

We must applaud local groups and charities for their efforts in helping to make sure the season is a little merrier and brighter for everyone. It's a long list and I don't want to name names for fear of missing someone, but the people behind all these efforts are surely deserving of praise and thanks for their generosity in trying to address this serious need.

While the holidays are supposed to be a time of happiness and family togetherness, we know many people spend Christmas alone. This is a big wish, Santa, but could you make sure everyone has a friend for a few hours this holiday? No one should be alone at Christmas.

And one more wish, Santa. This year, I'm asking that you take care of all the animals suffering unspeakable abuse at the hands of neglectful and mean-spirited owners who don't deserve pets. Let's not forget those animals waiting for their forever homes, where they will find love and warmth.

I get it that Christmas is upon us, but how can we talk about being happy and joyful when there is so much pain and sorrow in the world? How can we find happiness and peace when there are people among us who would bring so much horror and violence into the lives of innocent people?

Speaking of friendship, it wouldn't hurt to sprinkle a little of that holiday feeling over the remaining 364 days of the year. Everyone is so happy and generous during the Christmas season, but after the holidays they seem to lose that feeling. Perhaps you could encourage everyone to try a little harder to keep that spirit alive throughout the year.

As for some of my other wishes, the list is an onerous one. But if you're interested, here goes. Could you please end the wars, stop the famine, curb the crime rate and find cures for all the terrible diseases that inflict so much pain and suffering upon the world? Can you give humans the wisdom and desire to address the impending environment catastrophe that we're facing?

If you can't do that, could you at least bring some peace of mind to those who are suffering? They need to know someone cares and is reaching out to them.

So, there you have it, Santa. This may not be a typical list of wants, but it is my wish list. Somehow, some way, we must put humanity back into the human race and that's the view from here.

I believe there are angels among us

April 13, 2022

We celebrate and observe a long list of special days, weeks and months throughout the year connected to a long list of important causes, all of which deserve our support. However, there is one month in particular that carries a significant amount of importance and that is April, or Organ Donation Awareness Month.

Why is this important? At any given time, approximately 4,400 Canadians await a lifesaving organ transplant. Each year, more than 250 Canadians die waiting. One donor can save eight lives through organ donation and provide tissue for up to 75 patients.

Things are bit different in Nova Scotia than they are in other provinces, as Nova Scotia's opt-out system goes against prevailing practice in Canada. Currently, organ donation in other jurisdictions is based on the "opt-in" system, in which individuals must sign up to be organ donors while they are alive in order for their organs to be harvested for transplantation upon their death. Whether or not someone has registered as a donor, by common practice, the next of kin still may have the final say on whether their organs can be donated.

However, in April 2019, the Government of Nova Scotia passed the Human Organ and Tissue Donation Act. The legislation was proclaimed on June 30, 2020, and was enacted on January 18, 2021.

On that date, Nova Scotia became the first jurisdiction in North America to implement a policy of presumed consent for organ donation. This means all people in the province are considered organ donors unless they opt out. Children under the age of 19 are exempt from the law.

Even though the idea of organ donation can sometimes evoke an emotional response in many people because it often means someone has died, it is an important topic that deserves our full attention and careful, fact-based discussions. In the end, donating an organ or organs ultimately means giving the gift of life to someone else, maybe even someone you know and love, like a family member or a close friend.

This topic has become very personal for my family, with a close family member having undergone transplant surgery to receive a new kidney less than one month ago. Because of the importance of this issue, I want to share this personal story that revolves around my wife's sister, Dale, and Dale's husband, Bruce MacLeod.

While Dale and Bruce have lived in Langdon, Alberta, a bedroom community about a half-hour outside of Calgary, for the past decade, they both grew up right here in Liverpool. Both went to school here and held down a variety of jobs in the area until they moved west in search of better wages, as many Maritimers do. Both have large families here at home, as well as an extensive network of friends, so this is very much a local story.

They were doing well in Alberta until 2016, when Bruce's health took a turn for the worse and his kidneys started to fail, complications from other health issues. He started peritoneal dialysis at home that year. In July, 2018 he started hemodialysis, which meant a complete change in lifestyle, with three trips to the hospital every week.

Unless you or someone you love has gone through this, you may not fully appreciate what this means to dialysis patients. Let's just say your life, as you knew it, will be turned upside down, as you face many challenges that most of us cannot even comprehend. Those who experience it, or have family members on dialysis, know it is a hard way to live, but thank goodness for medical science.

Bruce had to accept that the only way he would ever have a normal life again would be through organ donation, and so his name was added to the transplant list. Despite a series of setbacks, in 2019 an angel entered their lives when one of Dale's co-workers heard of Bruce's plight and volunteered to offer one of her healthy kidneys if she was a match.

Now you have to understand that while they are all very close friends now, in 2019 Niki Kitcher had no personal connection to Dale and Bruce. She wasn't family and had only just met Dale at work. Despite the fact that they were basically strangers, her offer was genuine and one of the most selfless acts of generosity I have heard of in recent years.

Niki started testing to donate in 2019 and, lo and behold, she was a perfect match. With that, the donation process was underway, but because of COVID, the operation was delayed indefinitely.

However, once the pandemic slowed down, the transplant procedure was put back into action and, after more rounds of testing, the operation finally took place in a Calgary hospital on March 23.

Today, Bruce says, the surgery has completely changed his life.

"It's amazing to think how someone could do something so selfless as to donate a life-saving organ to another person," he says. "I went from doing hemodialysis at the hospital three times a week, for four hours each time, to no longer having to do dialysis at all. Receiving this kidney has made me feel revived. I am not as tired as I was, my colour is better, and my kidney function is now at a normal level. I feel so much better already in such a short time."

To say thank you to this wonderful person who gave Bruce his life back seems inadequate. I mean, how do you thank someone who does something so sincere simply for the sake of helping another human being?

I have no doubt that Dale and Bruce have expressed their gratitude to this woman many, many times and will continue to do so for years to come. She is now an important part of their lives. What an amazing gift Niki has given Bruce, and what an inspiration she should be to others.

When I think of this story, I am reminded of the lyrics from a song by the legendary country music group Alabama, *Angels Among Us*:

> *Oh, I believe there are angels among us*
> *Sent down to us from somewhere up above*
> *They come to you and me in our darkest hours*

To show us how to live, to teach us how to give
To guide us with the light of love

Even if you don't know someone suffering from kidney disease or any of a long list of other diseases that may be destroying someone's life, organ donation must be something that everyone should consider, because a patient somewhere, perhaps right next door, could be waiting for you, and that's the view from here.

Let's talk about forerunners this Halloween

October 16, 2023

Growing up in rural Nova Scotia, I was exposed to all kinds of beliefs and superstitions that today seem bizarre and, in some cases, even funny to many people. Most of these traditional beliefs are often dismissed out of hand by nonbelievers.

However, as I've researched and written about these traditions and old wives' tales, I've come to understand that they are a valuable part of our heritage, as they reflect a time before science had discovered a logical explanation for many of the strange phenomena that exist in the world. I've also discovered that we can learn a great deal about our past through this oral history. There is a treasure trove of interesting and valuable information waiting to be gathered, but you must listen and keep an open mind.

The world was a much different place in past centuries than it is today. It was a time when earlier generations had to rely on the cycles of the moon and the sun for clues about what to expect from the approaching seasons. They observed the behaviour of the birds, animals and insects to tell them what type of weather was on the way.

Earlier generations also looked for signs to explain other life occurrences, including sickness and death, love and marriage, the births of their babies and even what might bring them good luck or bad luck.

Perhaps it was because my grandmother, God rest her soul, was from a different era, but I don't think I've ever met anyone quite as superstitious as she was. Naturally, then, that meant as a child I was exposed to all kinds of weird and wonderful beliefs, and I have been fortunate to use those traditions as the basis of a writing career that has spanned many years and that I greatly enjoy.

One of the most fascinating topics that I've researched and written about is forerunners. Now, some of you will know what a forerunner is but others may not, so seeing as Halloween is less than a week away, this is the appropriate time to discuss the topic.

Some of the most common themes in Nova Scotia folklore are superstitions that deal with signs and omens of death. It seems that literally every occurrence, no matter how innocent or innocuous it appears on the surface, can be interpreted as a forewarning that death is coming in the very near future for someone in the family or a close personal friend.

These harbingers of death can take many forms and always present themselves to the receiver without warning, but always leave a sense of foreboding in their wake. The warnings can take the shape of an animal, such as a large black dog, or they can be a subtle incident such as a framed picture falling from the wall and shattering to pieces or a window slamming shut for no visible reason. They can also be a sound like a bell tolling in the distance or three knocks on your door or window.

According to old wives' tales, the signs can also be less subtle. For instance, when a bird slams into a window and dies, it can mean that someone you know will die in less than three days, as, according to tradition, three days is the accepted period for death to strike. To take this belief a step further, it is said that if a bird gets into your house, it's a sign that someone in the house is about to die.

Earlier generations believed that these signs and omens were sent to us as a warning in an effort to prepare us for an imminent tragedy. Those who believe in such things take these warnings very seriously and fret for three days until the allotted time passes or, sadly, until a death occurs.

These superstitions are embedded in our culture and those of us raised in rural Nova Scotia would have been exposed to this oral history, often without even realizing that we were being schooled in such old-world beliefs.

Of all of the omens of death that exist in rural communities, none are taken more seriously or leave such a deep-seeded sense of foreboding and heart-wrenching dread than forerunners. For anyone who may not know, forerunners come in many shapes and sizes or they can also be a sound like three knocks from an unknown source. Forerunners can also be a voice, one of the most common of which comes in the form of someone whispering your name in your ear even though no one else is present.

However, the common forerunners reportedly take the shape of another person, usually a black, shadowy figure and often without any distinguishable facial features, leaving one to wonder who—or what—it was.

Dr. Helen Creighton, the grand-dame of Nova Scotia folklore and the inspiration to a legion of fans and researchers, describes forerunners as "warnings of something about to happen."

Dr. Creighton, who collected many examples of forerunners, explains, "A picture falling off the wall could be a sign. Hearing someone whisper your name could be a signal. Hearing three distinct knocks could be a warning."

Forerunners, then, are an important part of Nova Scotia's folklore and have their foundation in what is a very real phenomenon. Many people have had them and some, who do not believe in ghosts, seemingly have no hesitation believing in forerunners.

The facts that people do not talk about forerunners for fear of appearing foolish, and that people do not know how to recognize them, may have something to do with why, in recent years, we do not hear as much about them.

In fact, Dr. Creighton, in her book *Bluenose Ghosts*, suggests that forerunners may indeed be the most common supernatural event to occur in Nova Scotia.

I always tell people if you have ever experienced a forerunner, you will know it, because it leaves behind a sense of unease unlike anything you may have experienced in the past. It's an indelible feeling of dread and foreboding that can shake your foundation and leave you fearing for impending news of someone's demise.

I have experienced a forerunner firsthand, but the story is much too long to get into in this space. However, I am currently researching a book on forerunners that will be published next year and I would love to hear your stories of encounters with this paranormal phenomenon.

When it comes to topics that we don't understand or that may defy logical explanations, I encourage everyone to keep an open mind and not pass judgment on those who believe such traditions. After all, there are things in this universe that cannot be easily explained and maybe, just maybe, the occurrence of forerunners is one of them, or at least that's the view from here.

The view from here on

A world-wide pandemic

Vernon Oickle

Remain calm, don't panic and grab the toilet tissue

March 18, 2020

They say not to panic, but how can one remain calm when a deadly disease is spreading around the world quicker than you can shake a stick?

It's downright frightening when you hear that people are dying, trips are being cancelled, public events are being closed down, schools and universities are shutting down, businesses are telling employees to work from home and thousands of people are being quarantined.

This is scary stuff, especially since it's unlike anything we've ever seen before. Other virus emergencies, such the SARS outbreak in 2003 and the H1N1 pandemic in 2010, were bad enough, but this new COVID-19 virus, also known as the coronavirus, has spread more rapidly and appears to be more deadly than previous diseases.

But even in the face of all of this, it is important to think rationally, take precautions and to be prepared. I think the only way to calm the fears is to consider the facts as we know them and please, let me be clear here: I am not an expert on any of this. I'm just one middle-aged man trying to keep my family safe, but here's what I do know.

As people stock up on supplies that they think will help them get through this health crisis, it has led to a shortage of items including hand sanitizer, rubbing alcohol, facial masks and, of all things, toilet tissue.

While we're like everyone in hoping that the virus will not reach our community, admittedly, my wife and I have purchased extra supplies in the event that the worst-case scenario should happen. We stocked up on food, medications and other things that we would need to get us through two or three weeks, but seriously, it had never even crossed our minds that we should have an extra supply of toilet tissue on hand in the event of such an emergency.

Now that I think of it, though, it makes perfectly good sense that you must have a good supply of toilet tissue in case you can't get out of your home for an extended period of time, so take heed and make sure you stock up.

Being stocked up on these essential items in the event that you have to take extraordinary precautions is not something any of us want to think about, but as we listen to the news, it has become painfully clear that it is something we should do.

The other thing we should do is make sure we are listening to the right people and getting the facts from those who are experts in the field of contagious disease and those who are public health experts.

While social media may be a good source of communication and entertainment, the platforms are also notorious for spreading false information so it is essential to find a source of information you can trust and then pay attention for regular updates.

There are lots of myths and mistruths circulating about the COVID-19 virus but here are a few things we do know:

- In December 2019, cases of pneumonia were reported in Wuhan, China, caused by a new virus that had not previously been seen in humans. The illness was caused by the novel coronavirus (SARS-CoV-2) and is called COVID-19.
- In the past three months, that virus has spread rapidly around the world. As of March 5, 2020, a total of 34 cases of COVID-19 had been confirmed in Canada and the virus continues to expand globally.
- Nova Scotia launched a website dedicated to the latest information about the coronavirus in January. The Government of Canada has set up a novel coronavirus information line at 1-833-784-4397 so you can get constant updates on the virus.
- Nova Scotia's health-care system is actively monitoring and testing for potential cases of the novel coronavirus (COVID-19).
- On March 4, Nova Scotia's Regional Centres for Education collectively decided to cancel all school-organized student trips to international destinations until April 30. This included all trips to international destinations scheduled for this week's March Break.

This is a rapidly-developing story, so things are likely to change, but at the time of writing this column on March 8, there have been no confirmed cases of COVID-19 in Nova Scotia and officials continue to insist the risk to Nova Scotians remains low.

Since most of us are not health experts we have to trust someone, and in this case that someone has to be Dr. Robert Strang, the chief medical officer of health for Nova Scotia.

"We have well-established plans in place and, as with H1N1, we are actively engaged and working with our partners so we can adapt our response as the situation with the virus evolves," Dr. Strang says. "Although it may seem overly simple, good hygiene remains the best defence against respiratory viruses, such as COVID-19."

According to information from the government, the work currently underway includes:

- Implementing a patient screening process for use by front-line health-care workers.
- Monitoring and investigating potential cases.
- Applying effective public health and infection control measures.
- Establishing working groups focused on disease surveillance, health system impact monitoring, and models of care, supplies and resource management.
- Working with Nova Scotia's Emergency Management Office and other non-health partners on business continuity planning.
- Sharing accurate, up-to-date information with Nova Scotians. You can find accurate, up-to-date information and fact sheets at novascotia.ca/coronavirus

I get it that, as this public health crisis continues to escalate, people are scared. I'm scared; we're all scared, but the best defence against this virus is to know the facts, then exercise caution, listen to the medical advice and take care of your personal hygiene, and that's the view from here.

Vernon Oickle

Pandemic notebook #1: don't touch your face

March 25, 2020

When I was a youngster, I used to chew on my fingernails and my parents would always scold me. "Don't bite your nails," they'd tell me.

That's sound parental advice right there, but anyone who has this nasty habit will know that it's not that easy to kick. In fact, even today when I get stressed, nervous or worried, my natural reflex is to bite my nails.

I usually catch myself but it's a challenge and sometimes, when I slip up, even my wife has to scold me. But I point out to her that I am only human and sometimes I don't even realize I'm doing it. I admit it's a curse.

Just imagine how hard that I—and many others like me with the same habit—have to work to keep our fingers away from our faces as all the medical experts have told us we must do during this time of crises as the COVID-19 virus spreads quickly around the world. It's not easy to do. Go ahead, try it.

I understand all the experts insist that one of the best ways to avoid catching the coronavirus is for people to avoid touching their face, but the fact is, people touch their face all the time. It's a normal thing to do and, although I haven't counted, I bet we touch our faces hundreds of times throughout the day.

You touch your face to scratch it, to wash, to inspect pimples or moles and if you're a man, to shave. Bottom line: people touch their faces. It's natural.

However, based on all we've heard and read over the past weeks, other than avoiding people who have the virus, the best way to protect yourself from getting COVID-19 is not touching your face and constantly washing your hands with soap and hot water. So, pay attention and take heed.

The other way to protect oneself is social distancing. That's another tough challenge, as humans are naturally social beings, and we tend to congregate in large group settings for any variety of reasons. However, this life as we know it must change for the foreseeable future, so, again, in or-der to reduce the spread of this dangerous virus, it is our responsibility to do as the experts and authorities have told us to do.

I get it that there's a lot of information and misinformation floating around. Between social media and the constant barrage of chatter coming from the 24-hour news channels, it's easy to tune out. There is a tendency toward information overload, but I would caution everyone to pay atten-tion during this crisis and to make sure that you are getting your advice from well-informed, knowledgeable people.

And be careful of spreading misinformation yourself. For instance, if you don't know that something on social media is factual and from a reli-able source, then don't share it. People are frightened enough right now that they don't need to read something that's full of inaccurate informa-tion and half-truths.

I was recently challenged by a reader to get the facts on this potentially deadly virus, but unfortunately, I am like most people right now. I, like you, must rely on the doctors and politicians to tell us what they know or what they think we should know. Or maybe it's more like what they think we can handle, but having said that, I do believe our governments are relay-ing the best information they have.

We know this is a new virus that spreads rapidly through social con-tact. We also know that as of a few weeks back (when I was writing this), there was no known cure, so in a crisis such as this, we have no choice but to put our faith and lives in the hands of those who are in a position of knowledge and power.

It's the best system we have and, quite honestly, I would rather listen to these authorities than some so-called "expert" on Facebook about whom we know nothing and whose knowledge is sketchy.

I'm sure it's far from perfect, but we must trust that the people we've elected are prepared for this crisis and we have to believe that doctors and researchers are giving us the best medical advice they have right now.

Indeed, with so much information out there, the real facts are hard to decipher when it comes to COVID-19. Even the World Health Organization, Centers for Disease Control and other experts don't often agree; so, In-ternet pundits have stepped in to fill the void, with mostly garbage, as one reader rightly pointed out.

The reader is also right that some of this information is misleading, some dangerous, and mostly it's wrong. We do know the virus is quite contagious, like the flu, and that there have been deaths from it, like the flu, mostly in patients who are already immune-compromised. The death rate even among these groups is about two to three per cent, but it appears difficult to get an accurate percentage there.

The spread of this virus across the globe has led to the cancellation of just about every major gathering in the world. It has brought global travel to a screeching standstill. It has and will continue to impact the economy. It has resulted in the shutdown of all sporting and entertainment events. It has caused countries to close their borders to travellers and visitors. It has meant mass quarantines.

In some cases, hysteria has set in, as evidenced by the hoarding of toilet paper, hand sanitizer and face masks, but I am not the type of person who believes in downplaying people's fear or dismissing their anxieties. To some, these actions seem irrational, but if it's what some people must do to make themselves feel better in this time of crisis, then don't be so quick to criticize.

Most of us were not alive during the Spanish Flu pandemic of 1918 that swept around the world and left millions dead in its wake, which means this current medical crisis is unlike anything most of us have seen.

The only choice we have, then, is to trust in those who are supposed to be in the know. We must be vigilant with our own personal hygiene, avoid large social gatherings and follow any advisories issued by the authorities, because this virus has changed our lives as we know it for the foreseeable future and that's the view from here.

Pandemic notebook #2: COVID-19, and fear, arrive

April 1, 2020

As I begin this column on March 15, we are on uncharted waters and in a place none of us could have ever imagined we'd be in. But here we are and, with so much going on around the world, I've found the only way I can keep any perspective on this crisis is to write things down, so here's another peek into my pandemic notebook.

March 15: The provincial government announces that the first three pre-sumptive cases of COVID-19 have arrived in Nova Scotia, in the process setting off a shockwave of panic and hysteria unlike anything we've seen in our lifetimes, if ever in our history.

Also on this day, in an unprecedented move, the provincial government announces it is closing all schools and day cares in the province until at least April 6, at which time they will reassess the situation.

At this point, everything remains a mystery as this virus spreads across the globe.

March 16: In what has become the new normal for the foreseeable future, daily government briefings confirm that one of the previous presumptive cases is, indeed, COVID-19 while at the same time announcing two new presumptive cases. This brings the total cases in Nova Scotia to five. We brace for that number to go much higher in the coming weeks[2].

Also on March 16, we started asking Nova Scotians to report on our fellow citizens by urging people to call department of health offices if we knew of someone who had been out of the country but was refusing to self-isolate for fourteen days as mandated by the government.

This really is a sad commentary on people. Surely anyone who has been out of the country must know how dangerous this virus is. We are in this together, folks, and we are counting on everyone to do their part to keep everyone safe.

On the brighter side, amid mounting fear and uncertainty, many people in every corner of the province have stepped up to help others, especially seniors and those who are quarantined. Helping our fellow citizens is what Nova Scotians do best.

March 17: Happy St. Patrick's Day. Certainly not the celebrations everyone was hoping for. As the country moves to close its borders to international visitors, people were doing their best to cope with the new reality amid the ever-mounting crisis. Two more presumptive cases are announced on this day bringing the total to seven, but officials quickly told us that we should expect that number will continue to grow until we flatten the curve, a phrase that has become the rallying cry against this silent invader that has brought humanity to its knees.

Also on this day, the provincial government takes extraordinary meas-ures to prevent the spread of the virus. These include ordering the closure

---

2   And, unfortunately, it did.

of all bars, mandating that business in all restaurants be limited to take out service only and limiting the size of groups to no more than fifty. We expect that number is likely to change.

March 18: A new day with new challenges as reality sets in—we are in for a long haul as the virus continues to spread and the number of cases continue to rise, both globally and here at home. Canadians everywhere scramble to get home for fear of being stranded in a foreign country.

The government announces another five new cases in the province, bringing the total to twelve, and orders major restrictions and wide-sweeping closures including all bars, hair salons, barber shops and gyms. The word came that we should expect more restrictions as everyone battles to slow the spread of this virus that has changed our existence.

We are in new territory, folks. This is unlike anything we've ever seen in our history, not even with the Spanish Flu in 1918.

March 19: In an effort to halt the spread of COVID-19, the Prime Minister announces the border between Canada and the U.S. would be locked down to all but essential traffic starting on Friday night. Whoever thought it would come to this?

Also, as of today, provincial officials confirm that Nova Scotia has five confirmed cases and nine presumptive cases of COVID-19, for a total of fourteen. The message is also very clear—we should prepare to maintain these stringent rules as countries around the world essentially shut down and Canadians outside the country ponder their options, worrying when —or if—they will get home.

If you know someone who still hasn't made it back to Canada, our thoughts are with them as the window of opportunity for travel is all but closed. We pray they will be safe wherever they are.

March 20: Government officials announce Nova Scotia has five confirmed cases and ten presumptive cases of COVID-19, for a total of 15. We also learned that the province is testing daily and has had 1,546 negative test results.

March 21: The number of cases here in Nova Scotia continues to rise. Officials announce there were now nine confirmed cases and 12 presumptive cases of COVID-19, for a total of 21. We are also told that this is just the beginning of the crisis and that we should expect these numbers to rise over the coming weeks.

March 22: Today, we enter a whole new level in this crisis as the provincial government officially declares a state of emergency and brings in a wide-ranging list of orders that citizens are required to follow at the risk of substantial fines.

There is now screening at all entry points to our province for all travellers, including those returning from other parts of Canada, and it is now mandatory that they quarantine for 14 days. Social gatherings of no more than five people are also part of the new rules.

On this day, we also learn that seven new cases were identified on March 21, and all were travel-related or connected to an earlier case. To date, Nova Scotia has 28 positive test results and 2088 negative cases.

And so ends our first week of living in our new world. These are scary times, indeed, but we must remain vigilant and hopeful. While these daily news briefings and updates can be unsettling as they reveal more startling statistics from here at home, across the country and around the globe, they are also helpful, as reality has set in that is that this our life for the foreseeable future.

I will say that through all this emotional stress and turmoil, despite a few people who have tried to take advantage of the situation or the few who have refused to accept the reality and follow directives, most Nova Scotians have responded to the needs of their fellow citizens with kindness and caring.

That's all we can ask. After all, that's the Nova Scotian way and that's the view from here. God speed to you all.

Pandemic notebook #3: Living in a state of emergency

April 8, 2020

So, my friends, we have now entered the second week of the pandemic crisis and, as of March 23, we are in our first day of the state of emergency as the COVID-19 crisis continued to worsen.

Never could we have imagined the situation would get to this, but it is our new reality.

That being said, we must make the best of the situation and remain hunkered down. We each have a role to play in this crisis, as we are in this together. If you don't follow the rules and do as you're told, then you not only put your own health and wellbeing in jeopardy but also the safety of everyone around you. So be careful and be diligent.

As with last week, I am continuing to keep track of the latest updates on this crisis and keeping track of the numbers as they come in. I suspect by the time this column is published, the crisis will have gotten worse, but I think it's important to keep all these numbers in perspective.

March 23: On this day, we learn that 13 new cases were identified as of March 22. The cases were travel-related or related to earlier reported cases. Several of the new cases were connected and involved groups or families who have returned to Nova Scotia following travel outside of Canada.

We also learn that the 41 individuals affected range in age from under ten to their mid-70s. Cases have been identified in all parts of the province. One individual remains in hospital. At this point, there had been no spread within communities.

March 24: We are told that ten new cases were identified as of March 23 and, like before, the cases are travel-related or connected to earlier re-ported cases. None of these cases are from spread within the community.

This latest news brings the total of confirmed cases to 51 individuals and, as of this date, one individual has recovered, and their case is considered resolved.

Author's note: And then this happened. On March 24, I received notice from my editor that the newspaper was shutting down and suspending operations indefinitely because of the virus, so I never finished or published this column. The next issue wouldn't be published until later this year, on October 13.

A brave new world

October 13, 2020

Dear friends, thank you for welcoming me back into your homes every week.

Oh, how I've missed talking to you. It is wonderful to reconnect with all you awesome people again after all this time of feeling cut off and isolated from the rest of the world.

I recognize this opportunity to express my views and my thoughts, and to share my opinions in print every week, as a true privilege and an absolute honour. I also recognize that this opportunity comes with an awesome responsibility.

I appreciate that this responsibility also comes with a tremendous burden, and I know that I must never take it lightly. I certainly do not, nor do I ever take it for granted.

If our experiences throughout the current pandemic have taught us anything about life and our circumstances, it is that such opportunities can disappear very quickly and without warning. So, I relish the faith that the publishers have shown by inviting me to return to their pages of this fine publication every week. I am humbled, and very excited to be here.

It is hard to believe that it has been six months since you last heard from me, and I hope you have all been well. So much has changed in our word during that time that it's difficult to wrap one's head around all of it.

But this is the world in which we find ourselves, so we had all better find a way to embrace it and make the most of our situation. The facts are quite clear—we are a very long way from getting back to the world we once knew.

And as for returning to "normal," whatever that it is, I'm afraid this is the normal. We must accept this truth because, honestly, what other choice do we have?

I really don't want to start our new journey together by stating the obvious, but I feel compelled to repeat what so many people have been saying for so many months: that this *is* the reality.

Let us make peace with that fact and make a commitment to work to-gether to keep everyone safe and healthy, because, that is the number one priority, is it not?

If achieving that reality means wearing a mask in all public buildings and on public transportation, then let's just do it. Don't make the situation worse by causing a scene, as we've seen in so many places. Instead, listen to the medical advice. Don't make a fuss by refusing to wear a mask when you're out and about. Just do it.

If this reality means maintaining a distance of six feet between yourself and everyone else, then let's just all take a few steps back and give every-one their personal space. I understand most of us are affectionate by nature and enjoy being close to others, but if keeping a small circle around yourself will protect you and everyone else, then why not do it?

If this pandemic means having our temperature checked when we enter a public building to engage in a function with other people around, then just step up. It's really a painless process.

If the situation means being extra diligent in our personal hygiene, then please, just wash your hands. Really, folks, at this stage in our lives, no one should have to tell us to do that. We all learn at a very early age to wash our hands, so this isn't anything new.

If the rules call for the use of hand sanitizer wherever you go, then make it so. Seriously, what's the big deal?

Parents, if the situation demands that you set a good example for your children, then please be the parent your children need you to be. If you take precautions, then your children will take precautions. If you complain and refuse to follow the rules, then your children will do likewise.

And finally, if the current health risks means that we should be good citizens and make every possible effort to protect our friends, neighbours and family, why wouldn't you want to do that? Why not be the best person you can be? You really don't want to spread this dreadful disease, do you?

Seeing that on this past Monday we observed Thanksgiving in Canada, we must take a few minutes to express our thanks and gratitude to all of those who have worked so tirelessly throughout this crisis to protect us, including front-line health care workers, first responders and a long list of people who provided the essential services we needed throughout this ordeal.

And we would be remiss if we didn't pause to recognize political lead-ers at all levels of government who provided the leadership and guidance to ensure our safety. Sure, we experienced our ups and downs throughout the state of emergency, but the bottom line is that because of the efforts and sacrifices by everyone in this province, Nova Scotia—in fact, all of Atlantic Canada—is one of the safest, if not the safest place, on earth.

Now, that's something to be thankful for.

Despite our current state of comfort, with only a few active cases of the virus in this province, we must not take this success for granted, nor can we let our guard down. As we've seen in other jurisdictions, this disease can rise up and kick our butts without notice. And when it strikes, it can leave a swath of death and suffering in its wake. So be diligent and be mindful of the rules.

We have no idea how long this pandemic will last, which means until they find an effective vaccine, we must do everything we can to keep everyone safe and healthy. To that end, we must accept the new world order.

It is our duty. It is our responsibility. It is our moral obligation to protect ourselves and to protect everyone around us, and that's the view from here (in the middle of a pandemic).

How things have changed

November 4, 2020

My, oh, my. How the world has changed in these times of COVID-19 and amid all the safety precautions that we must take.

Just thinking about where we were a year ago, compared to where we are today, makes one's head spin. It's a world we could not have ever imagined, but it is our reality and we must adjust to the way we do things today.

And it's often the little things that cause us the greatest consternation. For example, when shopping for fresh produce at the local supermarket, try opening those thin, plastic bags without licking your fingers.

Go ahead. Just try it.

Not so easy, is it?

For me, the effort usually ends in frustration. I usually just pass the bag to my wife and ask her to open it.

For her it's just further proof that I have very little patience.

So, what else is new?

Nancy is used to my little foibles. She usually just grimaces and remarks, "Why do you make things so complicated for yourself?"

I usually just smirk and shrug. And then I sheepishly remark, "I dunno. Guess maybe it's just me."

Clearly, after all these years I trust that she just takes it all in stride.

And if you think that I struggle with opening plastic bags in the supermarket, you ought to see me trying to come to terms with technology. As I quickly point out to anyone who will listen to me, I am technologically challenged.

I don't think it's that I can't handle it; it's just that I panic and when faced with a new way of doing things, I tend to think back to the good ole days and remember a time when we could order our food by simply scanning the menu and telling our server what we wanted.

But oh no, not anymore. Even the simple pleasure of ordering from a menu has gone high-tech thanks to the pandemic.

A few weeks ago, the whole family went out to enjoy lunch at a gluten-free café-style bakery in Halifax. Called Odell's, it's really a great place to eat and we like to go there whenever we're in the city because Nancy has celiac disease, and she can have anything off their menu.

Truthfully, the food's awesome and if anyone struggles with such an infliction or is sensitive to gluten, it's really the place to visit. You won't be disappointed that you did.

However, while the food is awesome, their method of dealing with customers in this age of COVID-19 clearly confirms that I must adapt to the times, or I risk being left in the Dark Ages.

At Odell's, once you take your seat at the table—which are spaced to meet safety protocols—the menus posted on the walls all around the establishment give you clear instructions on how to place your order.

So, while I sat there like the proverbial bump on a log waiting for our server to bring us menus, everyone else at the table had figured it out and had tuned into this new way doing things. While I was stuck in the past, they were getting ready to place their orders.

I had to catch up or risk not being served. That was not going to happen, as I was pretty darned hungry.

But seriously, it's not really that complicated and, all kidding aside, in this current situation, it's a great way to do business.

Basically, you use your phone, and their instructions take you to a website on which you build your order, including what you want on your burger or how many pieces of fish you want with your chips, what you'll have to drink, what you'll have for dessert, and so on.

We designated our son to place the order for all of us, and once everyone decided what they wanted, he simply sent it directly to the kitchen. No fuss, no muss and no physical menus were exchanged.

It was pretty cool, actually, and this one example illustrates how we can and must adapt to the challenges we face in this pandemic era. There are many others, especially for those of us who are fortunate enough to be able to work from home on occasion.

You think I struggled with opening a plastic bag or ordering my lunch from a menu? You should have seen me when I had to deal with setting up for my first Zoom meeting. It was like dropping me in a jungle and telling me to find my way home.

Can you say lost? That's exactly what I was when someone first suggested using Zoom. I knew nothing about the program that allows you to have virtual meetings right in your home, but once I figured it out, I have come to appreciate how fortunate we are that we live in this age of technology.

Seriously, if you have to endure the hardships of struggling through this pandemic it's better to do so with all the modern technology at our fingertips. Just imagine what the world was like a century ago when the Spanish Flu ravaged the world. Except for a handful of people who were alive a hundred years ago, none of us can even begin to image the challenges they faced.

Our current situation may not be perfect, but we are fortunate that technology allows us to keep in touch with our loved ones and it allows us to work and play in a way that was not even imaginable during the pandemic a century ago.

It seems this will be our reality well into the foreseeable future. For me, then, the reality is simple. If we must live with this, then we must also find a way to adjust to the new way of doing things, and that's the view from here.

Vernon Oickle

A holiday season like no other

November 25, 2020

Well, friends, the holiday season is upon us once again, albeit with a sense of foreboding, apprehension and angst unlike anything we've ever experienced.

This year, as people undertake their Christmas preparations, they do so under the spectre of a growing public health crisis and the threat of the unknown caused by a deadly virus that has forever changed our world. Anyone waiting for things to get back to "normal" had better accept reality, because I'm afraid this is the new normal.

As the COVID-19 virus continues to surge into the feared second wave that we had been warned was coming, Nova Scotians, indeed, people around the globe, must be diligent. We must do everything we can to mitigate the spread of this deadly virus. That means curtailing most of our traditional holiday celebrations, and we must do it now.

As Prime Minister Justin Trudeau said in a recent interview, "If you want to gather with your loved ones at Christmas, even in a restrained way, we're going to have to make sure that we change the trend lines on this COVID crisis right now."

The fact is, this crisis will mean a Christmas like none we've ever seen, one in which family gatherings will be limited at best, where mingling with friends will be forbidden, and where holiday parties and celebrations will be scaled back, if not cancelled all together.

Let's be honest. This is going to be a difficult Christmas for most of us. At a time when we like to be with family and friends, we could find ourselves in a lockdown situation in which we are sequestered to our own homes and can only have contact with those we live with.

This time of year can typically be a whirlwind, but this year, because of the pandemic, the pressures will be even more intense. In the next few weeks, as the frenzy gains momentum we can expect that hurried pace to intensify until it reaches the crescendo on December 25. The challenge is to make your preparations while at the same time following all public health protocols. This must be a top priority for every one of us.

With less than a month remaining until the Big Day, however, we can expect that pace to only grow more intense and, by this stage in the game, it is safe to say that if you haven't yet begun your holiday preparations, then it is time to kick it into gear.

Perhaps it's because I'm growing older, but each year now, as we head toward that magical day, my mind turns to those Christmases of my childhood, and I'm reminded of what a special season it was for family and friends.

It will be extra special this year, as we celebrate amid a pandemic, something that none of us could have ever imagined we'd be doing. I also think that celebrating Christmas amid a public health crisis will intensify whatever feelings we're experiencing, both positive and negative.

Christmas will not be the same this year, this is true, but it could always be worse, right? Be thankful that any apprehension and fear we're suffering is mixed with gratitude for being healthy, and be thankful that we live in a part of the world where the crisis has largely been kept under control. Be also grateful that you will be with your close family, if even only by telephone. There are many around the world who will not be as fortunate, not only because of COVID but for a myriad of other reasons.

Through all of this, we must remember that Christmas is still a special time of year, one that can still be filled with brightly-coloured lights, an assortment of delectable treats to please every discerning taste and, of course, gifts. So even if you can't all be together this Christmas as you normally would, you must make the most of it and think that next Christmas will be even more special.

Under the current circumstances, though, it will become increasingly more important to hang onto those other qualities of Christmas that may not be quite as tangible as a present under the tree, but are perhaps even more important.

While many people are lamenting about the holidays quickly approaching because it creates increased financial hardships for them, an elderly friend recently pointed out that as her children have grown up and mostly moved onto other places with their own families, it's often a challenge for them to stay excited about the holidays.

However, she long ago learned that Christmas isn't about material things. It's about being connected with those she loves and those she holds dear. Of course, her first priority is to be with her children and their families, but if that isn't practical or possible, as her children are spread across the country and beyond and cannot come home for the holidays because of the virus, then they will find a way to connect through technology. Even if it's a phone call, they will keep in touch.

As a widow, she added, Christmas becomes an especially trying time for her, but she has found that nurturing good friendships and celebrating the season with those special people are ways she copes with the holidays. Usually, she adds, she has a wonderful time each year and would encourage others to find people with whom they enjoy spending time because, for her, the worst part of the holiday would be spending it alone.

Her message is simple—if you know someone who may be alone this Christmas, find a way to connect and let him or her know you are there for them. Once you connect, keep in touch with them because this is going to be an especially tough year for everyone.

Not to downplay the plight of those who suffer alone during the holidays, because I know this a major issue for a great number of people in all of our communities, but I think the message here is universal: if you know someone who is feeling isolated during the season, it's important to find a way to reach them.

In some communities, there are volunteer groups and service organizations that will help with this problem, but many of these options will be curtailed this year because of the pandemic.

Those of us who are fortunate to have our families and loved ones around during the holidays can reach out to those in our communities who we know are alone and isolated. Drop off care packages or call them on the phone. It's amazing what a conversation can do for someone who is feeling cut off from the rest of the world.

There is no question that the quickly-approaching holiday celebrations will be different this year, but we have no choice except to rise to the challenges and make the most of things, or at least that's the view from here.

'Tis the season to be thankful

December 9, 2020

Well, friends, I don't know about you, but as Christmas fast approaches, I'm feeling a little anxious and sentimental all at the same time.

I'm sure my feelings of anxiety have a lot to do with the growing emergency resulting from the second wave of the COVID-19 pandemic and the fact that we're looking at a holiday season unlike any we've ever experienced before, but I feel the need to reflect upon what this special time of year means to me.

Despite all of the challenges we've faced this year—and there certainly have been many—there is still much to be thankful for, and we must take the time to reflect upon those positive things. So, as we struggle to get into the festive mood during these COVID times, let us pause and think of the things that are important to us, those things that we hold dear.

Instead of dwelling on the dark side of life, as we are apt to do during this crisis, with Christmas quickly approaching I challenge you to make a list of ten things that bring you joy and happiness this holiday season. I'll give you my list:

1. My family. Those of us who are fortunate to be surrounded by family this holiday season are lucky indeed. There is nothing in the world more important to me than my wife and my two sons. Even if we may be experiencing a different type of Christmas this year, I know that I am truly blessed to have them in my life. After them, everything else on this list pales in comparison.
2. I am truly grateful for my health. Who knows what the future holds, but I count my lucky stars every day that I am in relatively good health right now (knock on wood).
3. Close friends. We can all use a good friend, and I am thankful that I have a few wonderful people in my world whom I can truly rely upon, both in the good times and the bad times. Acquaintances are a dime a dozen, but a real good friend is someone to truly

219

treasure. (Thank you to our special friends. You know who you are.)

4. The fact that I'm still able to do the type of work that I love. Is there anything more depressing than getting up every day and going to a job that you really despise? On that note, I know that I am lucky to have been able to carve out a career doing what I love. I've faced some challenges along my career path, but who hasn't? When life throws you a curve ball, you have two choices —let it defeat you or meet the challenge head on and change course. I am grateful that the stars aligned for me to find a way forward.

5. That we live in Nova Scotia. Even before the pandemic struck earlier this year, I always considered myself fortunate to have been born and raised in this province. Seriously, is there any other place you'd rather be right now than in Nova Scotia? I should say not.

6. The fact that scientists have found promising new vaccines to confront the coronavirus. This time last year, who could have predicted that twelve months later the world would be waged in a war with a deadly virus that has basically changed our lives forever? The past nine to ten months have proven to be more challenging than anything we could have ever imagined, but, despite it all, scientists have given us the best Christmas present ever—hope that a vaccine is on its way and that by next year this time, we'll be back to semi-normal ... whatever that looks like.

7. The fact that we have dedicated doctors, nurses, first responders and other front-line workers who often put their own lives on the line to protect and serve others. In these unprecedented times of uncertainty and fear, we must express our deep, deep gratitude to those who put service to others above themselves. Let's say this together—thank you and God bless!

8. The fact that I live in a community filled with caring people who will help others in their time of need. I have always known that people in my home community and, truthfully, throughout Nova Scotia, are generous, thoughtful and helpful people, but honestly, the past several months have proven beyond a doubt that Nova Scotians are among the best when it comes to caring for others. Nova Scotians will rise to any challenge, and, in my books, that is something for which we should all be grateful. Thank you, one and all.

9. We take so much for granted, but if this pandemic has taught us anything, it's that we should be grateful that we live in a place where the essentials of life—food, shelter, clean water, a safe environment, and a relatively crime-free community—are mostly a sure thing. I know there are some who struggle to survive and it falls on society to do better to help these people, but, by and large, the average person is getting by and, honestly, is there much more we can ask for these days?

10. Finally, I am grateful that I still have sufficient faculties to write this column every week. Even after forty years of working in the newspaper industry in some capacity, writing this weekly diatribe still brings me a great deal of pleasure as it provides an outlet to express my thoughts and opinions—my view from here. I hope it brings you some pleasure to read it.

So that's my list of ten things for which I feel blessed this holiday season. I suspect many of the items on my list will be the same as those on your list, but when life seems dark and all hope appears to be lost, I urge you take out a piece of paper, find a pen or pencil, and make your own list. I promise you that the exercise will make you feel better.

And once you have completed your list, put it in a prominent place where you can see it. When the challenges of the world seem too much to bear, review your list and remember to be thankful for what you have and understand that there is some light in the darkness.

No matter what challenges life throws at us, it is important to remember that we still have much to celebrate this holiday season, and that's the view from here.

Vernon Oickle

The life you save by wearing a mask could be your own

January 20, 2021

It has been a year since this nightmare began. On the eve of that grim anniversary, we must all be in agreement that our world is a totally different place today compared to how it was twelve months ago.

Last year, even as we followed news about a mysterious and potentially-deadly virus rising in China, none of us could have ever imagined that our lives were about to change into the foreseeable future and possibly forever.

According to Health Canada, the first Canadian case of the novel coronavirus was reported on January 25, 2020, in a Toronto man who had recently travelled to Wuhan, China.

The day of his January 22 flight from Beijing, Health Canada reported that major Canadian airports in Montreal, Toronto and Vancouver had introduced new screening measures for passengers returning from China with flu-like symptoms. The man didn't have any symptoms when he arrived, but the next day he became so sick that he required a trip to the hospital.

A year later and here we are. Our world has been turned upside down and we live a life that we could never ever imagined.

Millions of people around the world have become very ill and hundreds of thousands have died from this virus, including nearly 17,000 in Canada and 65 in Nova Scotia. Our schools, jobs and social lives have been negatively impacted in ways that it will take years to recover from. Travel, both domestic and abroad, has been curtailed, if not derailed indefinitely.

There's no doubt that this virus poses threats unlike anything we had ever experienced. The only thing that comes close to what we're experiencing is the Spanish Flu pandemic in 1918-1920. For most of us, that means we must put our trust in the hands of the politicians who must make the decisions on how we live under the shadow of a deadly disease that has been ravaging the world for the past year.

Additionally, it means putting our faith in the doctors and scientists who have worked tirelessly for months, if not years, to find treatments and cures for such a virus. It is their job and responsibility to protect us from this deadly threat and, quite frankly, I would prefer to put my trust in these experts with years of experience than in someone on the internet spewing potentially-deadly conspiracies with their messages that masks, social distancing and vaccines don't work.

Many things about this pandemic concern me, but one of the biggest issues that really raises my ire are those people who, after all this time and after all the evidence that has been laid before them (if they choose to believe it), refuse to take precautions such as wearing a mask when they're out in public.

I get it that people have freedom of choice, but I do not understand why it so hard for people to understand that masks save lives and that the life they save may actually be their own. The sad reality with this issue is that it has become so decisive, leading to arguments and confrontations, both public and private.

I've witnessed these arguments and I've been involved with these debates. It's clear that some people either can't or don't want to understand why they should wear a mask. In some cases, it's as if people are looking for a confrontation.

I just don't understand that way of thinking. How in the heck did we ever get here? At this point, wearing a mask in public should be automatic. There is no debate on that.

For the record—and I know some people want to listen to the facts—the World Health Organization (WHO) says people should wear a mask because they are a key measure to suppress transmission of the virus and save lives.

"Masks should be used as part of a comprehensive 'Do it all!' approach including physical distancing, avoiding crowded, closed and close-contact settings, good ventilation, cleaning hands, covering sneezes and coughs, and more," WHO says. "Depending on the type, masks can be used for either protection of healthy persons or to prevent onward transmission."

According to WHO, masks should be worn in areas where the virus is circulating, and when you're in crowded settings where you can't be at least one metre from others, and in rooms with poor or unknown ventilation.

"It's not always easy to determine the quality of ventilation, which depends on the rate of air change, recirculation and outdoor fresh air," WHO says. "So, if you have any doubts, it's safer to simply wear a mask."

WHO also says you should always clean your hands before and after using a mask, and before touching it while wearing it. While wearing a mask, you should still keep physical distance from others as much as possible. Wearing a mask does not mean you can have close contact with people.

For indoor public settings such as busy shopping centres, religious buildings, restaurants, schools and public transport, you should wear a mask if you cannot maintain physical distance from others, as outlined by WHO.

"If a visitor comes to your home who is not a member of the household, wear a mask if you cannot maintain a physical distance or the ventilation is poor," the guidelines also recommend.

They also urge that when outside, you should wear a mask if you cannot maintain physical distance from others. Some examples of this situation include busy markets, crowded streets and bus stops.

It has been proven that masks work and that they save lives. As a member of society, everyone has a responsibility to do their part to ensure the health and wellbeing of their fellow citizens. No matter how many rights you enjoy, you do not have the right to threaten the safety of anyone else.

We live in a democracy and I believe in freedom of choice. I believe we have the right to make decisions about how we live our lives. However, your rights and freedoms end when your decisions can have a negative impact on me or the people that I love, and that's the view from here.

My, how things have changed in just one year

March 10, 2021

This time last year, Canadians, like citizens in most other nations around the world, were trying to come to grips with a new and deadly virus that was sweeping over the globe, leaving in its wake a swath of death and despair unlike anything we had seen in modern times.

The first Canadian case of the novel coronavirus was reported by Health Canada on January 25, 2020, in a Toronto man who had recently travelled to Wuhan, China, the epicentre of the outbreak.

The day of the man's January 22 flight from Beijing, major Canadian airports in Montreal, Toronto and Vancouver had introduced new screening measures for passengers returning from China with flu-like symptoms. The man didn't have any symptoms when he arrived, but the next day, he became so sick that he required a trip to the hospital.

On March 11, 2020, the World Health Organization (WHO) declared COVID-19 a global pandemic, pointed to more than 126,000 cases of the coronavirus illness in over 110 countries and territories around the world, with the sustained risk of further global spread.

On March 15, 2020, Nova Scotia announced the province's first three presumptive cases of COVID-19. That will be a year ago this coming Monday and, boy, have things changed over the past twelve months. It has been a time of immense and unprecedented upheaval that most of us could never have imagined we'd ever experience.

The world as we knew it before March 15, 2020 no longer exists. Instead, during the span of one year as fear and panic about the unknown took hold, we went from washing our hands every five minutes to washing our groceries when they came into the house to hoarding toilet paper and disinfectant wipes to standing in long line ups at the grocery store to buy hamburg.

Things are different now from what they were a year ago, but most people understand that the precautions we presently take are to protect us from a disease that, as of February 28, 2021, has resulted in 1642 cases and 65deaths in Nova Scotia.

Just look at our lives now.

For starters, even though there is great resistance from some people, we are mandated to wear masks whenever we go out in public. There are no exceptions to that rule and, from what I've seen, it appears most people are following that directive.

In fact, while contact with other people is not strictly forbidden, health officials everywhere strongly recommend that we keep a minimal distance of six feet from each other.

It is also strongly recommended that we avoid shaking hands and hugging other people. That's a tough order considering that we are social beings who crave interaction with other humans, but this virus is easily transmitted, so we must avoid such physical contact.

In just one year, the coronavirus has impacted our lives in so many ways that it is now almost impossible to imagine a world without these precautions. Because of COVID-19, people who work in public places sit or stand behind plastic barriers or wear total face shields. In some places, such as a hospital waiting room, you now sit in an individualized plastic cubicle, and in addition to wearing masks many people also wear rubber gloves in public places for protection.

This is now a world where the words quarantine, self-isolation and social distancing have become common in our everyday vocabulary. Many things in our lives function differently today than they did just twelve months ago. We now live in a world where video conferencing and on-line classes and meetings are more common than face-to-face gatherings.

Social gatherings in general have either been eliminated or greatly downsized, with all group functions practically being wiped out. When you do attend any public activity, you must keep your distance from others. In fact, chairs are now placed six feet apart and roped off to prevent contact.

Our schools, especially in their extra-curricular activities, now operate under a strict set of guidelines with sporting and social events being curtailed or eliminated altogether. Forget about large groups in the bleachers cheering on the team and don't even think about holding a school dance or get-together. For now, these are things of the past.

And then there is the impact the pandemic has had on the economy, with businesses being forced to find new ways to operate or, sadly, being forced to shut down altogether. Even those of us who are fortunate to have jobs have had to adjust and, thankfully, working from home has now become an acceptable norm.

Let's not forget how the pandemic has impacted travel. It will take years, maybe decades, for that sector of the economy to recover, and it goes without saying that visits to foreign destinations will remain but a dream until this virus is under control.

The reality is that our lives have changed profoundly in so many ways that it's almost impossible to wrap one's head around the sheer volume of it all. But the truth is, this virus makes people gravely ill, and many people die from it. Despite all of those conspiracy theorists and deniers who insist none of this is real or that it's an elaborate government experiment, the current precautions are being undertaken for the right reasons: to save lives.

We're all tired of talking about the coronavirus. We're exhausted, both physically and mentally, from so many people telling us what to do all the time. It wears us down, but this is our new norm so we must continue to be diligent, and we must be mindful of how our actions can impact the wellbeing of others.

When you get tired of hearing about the virus, or frustrated over being told to follow the rules, just think about how all of this has impacted the people and families of those who have gotten sick or died from the disease. Think of health care workers and those on the front lines who must face these challenges day in and day out. These people are exhausted.

I'll be the first to admit that some of these adjustments are difficult, but considering the grave possibility of contracting a deadly virus, it is only common sense that we all do our part to protect not only ourselves, but also our family, friends and neighbours.

We have seen how quickly this virus can spread and get out of hand, but life changed one year ago. We must accept that fact and that's the view from here.

What do you do when COVID hits close to home

April 21, 2021

For the past year, we've heard of COVID-19 cases being reported all around the world, including hundreds right here in Nova Scotia, but we took comfort in the fact that there were no reported cases in our community.

All of that changed on March 31, when it was confirmed that a travel-related case was reported in Liverpool.

Your immediate reaction?

Panic.

It was the natural reaction.

Our community had worked so hard for the past year to keep the potentially-deadly disease at bay, but now it had come home. With such a highly contagious disease, we knew it would happen someday, but as long as there were no confirmed cases close by, we could take comfort in thinking that the longer we could keep it out of our community, the safer we'd be.

The inevitable was bound to happen, however.

So, for a few minutes on March 31, Facebook lit up with speculation, accusations, finger-pointing and assigning blame. But eventually, as calm, rational and reasonable voices joined the discussion, a sense of relief took over and people began to understand that, as long as everyone continued to practice COVID-19 protocols and follow the established rules, people in our community would remain safe.

That really is the key, isn't it? Remain diligent. Don't jump to conclusions, learn the facts and avoid spreading speculation, as that only serves to fan the flames of fear during these volatile times.

Once the panic subsided and people came to realize that the fear of a major outbreak, while potentially very real, had become overblown in the immediate release of the news that a local case had been confirmed, people began to focus on those who were, in fact, impacted by the virus.

Hopes and prayers were quickly turned to the individual who had tested positive as well as the immediate family involved and anyone who may have had direct contact with them. Within a day or so, as it became clear that there was no major outbreak, a sense of calm replaced the fear and people went about their business.

Like most Nova Scotians, people in my community are resilient, supportive and caring. They will rise to meet any challenge and they will always be there to help their neighbours. If the people at the centre of this story needed help, then they would surely receive it. We don't turn our backs on our neighbours in their time of need, even in the middle of a pandemic.

Fortunately, the people immediately impacted by this case had, by all accounts, taken the proper steps and there were no major health concerns. Because proper procedures had been followed and because people had been alerted, our community appears to have been spared a potential tragedy, despite the initial fear we all experienced when the news first broke.

Dealing with COVID-19 is a new challenge for everyone, so it only stands to reason that, with everything that has transpired over the past year, people would be on edge. We've been inundated with the horror stories of people coping with this dreadful disease and we've had to deal with the constant barrage of disturbing images of people suffering through the pandemic.

The situation is frightening and surreal, sometimes leaving us numb and shocked, to the point that it has often become too much to process. The pain is palpable, so it only stands to reason that when the disease landed on our doorstep, people would have questions and, yes, they would panic.

But if there's one thing we've learned over the past year, it's that people, when they work together and support each other, can overcome many obstacles. We've seen people face challenges by knocking down barriers and by pulling together and leaning on each other.

We knew the day would come when COVID-19 would come to our community. We would have been naïve to think otherwise.

It is true that living through this pandemic is unlike anything most of us have ever experienced, but it is also true that if we embrace our neighbours and help them deal with this burden, we will all be stronger when we emerge on the other end.

Fear of the unknown, like what we've been facing throughout this ordeal, can be a powerful force. It can cause us to do and say things that we may not have previously done or said.

However, through all of this, we must never lose our capacity to understand or to demonstrate compassion when circumstances call for it, and that's the view from here.

Accentuate the positive

May 12, 2021

Nova Scotians have worked extremely hard over the past year to keep COVID-19 numbers under control, and we had been very successful. With a low case count throughout the latter part of 2020 and into early 2021, we were the envy of the rest of Canada.

In recent weeks, however, the bubble burst and we now find ourselves in the midst of a crisis that seems daunting and, in truth, scary as hell.

The past couple of weeks, with a total lockdown of everything except essential services, have been tough, let's be clear about that. While we once could take comfort in believing that we had been successful in keeping the virus at bay, we've now seen a record number of cases, some very serious. It became very clear that we have a long way to go in our fight against COVID-19.

Adding to the sadness and disappointment is the fact that, after a tough year of feeling trapped and depressed, we were all looking forward to a summer of freedom with less stringent rules and regulations, basically hoping to break out of the crisis in which we had been trapped since last March. Clearly, we misjudged this potentially-deadly virus that has all but shut down our society.

And the fear, almost a constant companion with us since the spring of 2020, is now even more palpable as, once again, we anticipate a summer filled with anxiety and angst because, honestly, we don't know what to expect next. Even if case numbers fall, we must remain mindful of the potential threat that could rise up on any given day and knock us to our collective knees.

Most government and health officials agree this third wave of COVID-19 is more severe than the first two. It is more contagious and virulent, and potentially more lethal. Where once it seemed the virus mostly attacked the more vulnerable in our society, such as the aged and infirm and those with existing underlying health issues, this current strain has targeted the younger, healthier population. It is worrisome, indeed.

There are a number of issues we could tackle here, such as the economic implications and long-term fallout of a total lockdown. There are many things to consider as people's livelihoods and futures hang by a tenuous thread. The recovery will be long and it will be arduous.

There is also debate over the need to wear masks whenever we're out and about, and also the urgency in getting vaccines into as many arms as possible and as quickly as possible. There are certainly many things to discuss, not only both of these very serious topics, but also other health issues including our mental wellbeing throughout all of this.

In fact, I could devote an entire column to any of those issues mentioned above, but the truth is, we are all tired of talking about the pandemic and what it means to us. We know we must pay attention and follow the rules as this crisis unfolds and escalates, but for our own mental health and wellbeing we also must think about the brighter side of things and, yes, even in this midst of all this darkness, there is a brighter side. You just have to look for it.

I have a good friend who continues to stress that throughout this ordeal it is important to accentuate the positives, and I think he's onto something. Continuing to reside in that negative space created by the COVID-19 crisis is not good for one's mental health, as our capacity to process the constant barrage of dark and oppressive news will reach a breaking point. To offset that mental fatigue, I think it's time we talk about some of the positive things that we have in our lives.

Let's be grateful that even though the pandemic took a turn for the worse, we have been fortunate here in Nova Scotia that political and health care leaders have taken charge with decisions that, while tough, were necessary to get us through this dark crisis. For the most part, their efforts were successful as we have fared fairly well when compared to other places in the country.

But political issues aside, on a more positive note let's just all be grateful that we reside in such a beautiful place and that, even under lockdown, we all have access to outdoor spaces that offer a reprieve from the darkness.

If you are in good health and you opened your eyes this morning and put your feet on the floor, then those are many positives for which you must be grateful, as many people in this world are not as fortunate. And if you are not well, then be grateful that you have access to a good health care that, while it sometimes comes up short, by and large provides top quality care when needed. Many places in the world would envy what we have.

Think about those around you—your family and your friends. If you have people in your life who care for you, then there is nothing more important in this world. There are many people in our communities who are alone and isolated. That's tough enough when times are good and these people may be able to get out and about, but during this dark period when they are confined to their homes, their loneliness must be extreme.

If you know someone in that situation, reach out to help him or her, even if it's just a phone call to let them know you care. Sometimes a friendly voice can go a long way to helping another person out of the doldrums.

It is often said that there isn't much in life that is free, but the important things come without a price tag and those are the things for which we must be grateful.

The sunshine on your face. The laughter of children. The uplifting melody of music. The birds cheerfully chirping. The array of spring colours bursting forth following a cold winter. The cleanliness of spring showers that wash our cares away. The smell of flowers as their perfume fills the air. The smell of the freshly-mowed grass as it wafts through the spring air. The aroma of homemade bread right out of the oven. The thunder of the waves crashing on the shore. The spectacular hues as the sun kisses the day goodnight. The stars that wink at us from way up there on a clear night.

These are the things that money can't buy, and these are some of the many positives that we must accentuate, especially now.

Our lives changed dramatically when the COVID-19 virus arrived here in the spring of 2020 and we're still struggling with the many challenges that came with it. And while the future remains a mystery, the present is very clear. We all must find a way to cope with this crisis and dwelling on the negative is not only not helpful, but it is also not healthy.

Sometimes it's the littlest things that can get you through the day and sometimes that's all you need. We must, to use old phrase that seems apropos at this time, stop and smell the flowers and that's the view from here.

Enjoy your own backyard

June 23, 2021

It really is true that most of us don't appreciate the things that are right in front of us, but if the pandemic has taught us one thing, it's that we should consider all the things we do have instead of the things we are missing.

COVID-19 has created many obstacles and challenges since last spring, but now that summer is here and the restrictions have somewhat loosened, I suggest that you take advantage of the season and enjoy the things that we have right here in our backyard.

For starters, I suggest a day of sightseeing and exploring in this great region of Nova Scotia. I am willing to admit that, even after all these years of researching and writing about the South Shore, I never grow tired of the amazing things you can discover in the region.

You don't have to travel far to enjoy a day of beautiful scenery, local history, great food and outdoor recreational opportunities. I often enjoy taking an hour or so just to tour my hometown, the Port of the Privateers. I like to view the historical district at Fort Point, and always marvel at the important structures I find there, such as Perkins House and the Fort Point

Lighthouse. We have many gems right here in our own town, if you look for them.

With the region's rich heritage that spans several centuries, it doesn't matter where you live in the South Shore because every town, village and community is steeped in such history. Just go exploring around your own backyard and I am sure you will be amazed at what you discover. When was the last time you did that?

When my wife, Nancy, and I want to go on a longer excursion, we like to visit Cape Forchu near Yarmouth. It is nearly a three-hour drive from Liverpool, but if you have never been to Cape Forchu, I highly recommend you go this summer as it is well worth the drive.

Cape Forchu, with its lighthouse perched high atop the weather-beaten rocks, is indisputably one of the most beautiful places in the province. The naturally-stunning vistas highlighted by the powerful waves of the Atlantic crashing on the rocks and the pristine scenery you'll discover there will leave you awestruck, as we always are whenever we visit.

We have already planned a trip there someday soon to enjoy the unspoiled beauty of this spectacular place on the southern tip of Nova Scotia. With the crispness and cleanliness of the cool, clean, salty air and the rugged natural beauty, Cape Forchu is surely one of the province's best natural treasures.

After leaving this piece of paradise, we like to travel back along the South Shore by way of the Lighthouse Route. You might be able to work in a stop in Tusket to tour the Argyle Township Court House and Gaol, depending upon COVID restrictions, of course. For those who don't know, a gaol (pronounced 'jail') is a place of confinement and the historic structure in Tusket is Canada's oldest standing courthouse. It was built in 1805 and operated as a working courthouse and jail until 1944.

If you are inspired by local heritage, then I would highly recommend a visit to this museum that was such an integral part in the history of this region. Not only is the unique structure a gem to behold, but it also has an interesting story to tell. Even if you are not a history buff, you will still enjoy a tour of the building complete with a visit to the jail cells. Add it to your list of must-see places.

Leaving Tusket, you can travel further along the Lighthouse Route, a spectacular journey for both locals and visitors to enjoy. I never grow tired of the panoramic views along the way. Often times, the fog will hang over the coastline, providing jaw-dropping scenery that always creates a visual feast for anyone who enjoys nature in all its glory.

We also make it a point to stop at the famous Shag Harbour UFO crash site. Along with its unique place in the region's paranormal culture, the location also affords you a spectacular view of the Atlantic Ocean and all its glorious beauty.

Again, you should check on their COVID protocols before you plan to visit, but if you like seafood, I can recommend just the place to stop for lunch: Capt. Kat's Lobster Shack in Barrington Passage. If you are looking for a place to enjoy lobster or any type of seafood dish, then this is the place to go. Their lobster rolls are among the best I have ever eaten. If I had to choose one word to describe them, it would be scrumptious.

Once you've enjoyed lunch, head to Barrington for a stop at the Barrington Woollen Mill, where the scenery alone is worth taking in, but it is the history that's really impressive. Powered by a water-driven turbine, the mill washed, picked, carded, spun, dyed and wove the wool. The mill was a thriving producer of woollens in the late 19th and early 20th centuries and is now a delightful museum.

From that picturesque location, head to the Black Loyalist Heritage Centre in historic Birchtown. The Centre, with its mandate "to ensure the chronicles and contributions of Black Loyalists share a place with other communities that shape Canada's cultural mosaic", is not just a museum. It is an experience to be embraced as it gives us the opportunity to discover a part of this region's heritage that went largely forgotten until just a few decades ago.

If you have never been, then you should check on the status of their COVID restrictions and make plans to check it out this summer. The only caution I would offer here, is to make sure you allow sufficient time to take it all in. To fully appreciate the history and legacy of the Black Loyalist settlers, you should give yourself several hours to spend at the Centre, as it is absolutely worth the investment of time.

Moving on from Birchtown, we always enjoy a visit to the Loyalist town of Shelburne. There, you can explore historic Dock Street, which features the highest concentration of pre-1800 wooden buildings in Canada. Again, speaking of things we take for granted, the waterfront and streetscape of this picturesque South Shore town are gems just waiting to be discovered and you owe it to yourself to make a visit.

From Shelburne, our route takes us on a side-trip to the historic town of Lockeport, with its beautiful beach. You can easily spend an afternoon there.

The trip then brings us back to Liverpool. We always leave Highway103 at Port Mouton to follow the Lighthouse Route, where you can soak up the spectacular beauty of the Summerville Beach and Hunts Point areas. This truly is a piece of paradise.

Back in Liverpool, if you're not too tired, there's always something special to discover. In recent years, Cosby's Garden Centre, with the concrete sculptures created by the talented Ivan Higgins, must be seen to be believed. To say I am always impressed with Ivan's marvellous creations would be an understatement, indeed. I would recommend a visit to this special place, as it is simply amazing.

In a future column, we'll take a trip in the other direction because, no matter how often we make these trips and regardless of how often we visit these destinations, I am always thoroughly impressed with what we find on the South Shore. When I recall the pleasure these journeys bring us, I'm prompted to remind those of us who call this place home that we should never take for granted the view from here.

So, now what?

July 21, 2021

I think we can all agree that living the past fourteen months under the dark cloud of uncertainty and fear has more than tested our patience and personal strength.

This pandemic has actually tested our resolve as human beings.

It's tested our abilities to cope, to cooperate, to be understanding, to be compassionate, and to be supportive of one another.

Simply put, it has tested our ability to be good people.

It has not been an easy journey, but I think, for the most part, we would all agree that people have risen to the challenges that we've faced because of COVID-19. This fight for survival gives me faith in humanity, but now we all need a break.

I hope I am not tempting fate, but it appears as though we are coming out of the long, dark tunnel that is the pandemic. It sure feels that way. What with falling case numbers, the loosening of travel restrictions, the return to larger events and the opening of most facilities, you can sense a shift in the world.

I also understand that there are many more steps to be taken on this long and arduous road to full recovery, but on the off chance of jinxing our progress, I would like to talk about what we do now that the world appears to have reopened for business.

As the reduced restrictions suggest that we can return to a normal, albeit adjusted, existence, what are the things that you're most looking forward to?

Contact with other people is an essential part of the human condition so first and foremost, for me, returning to a semblance of normalcy means getting together with family and friends without worrying about acquiring a potentially deadly disease from them or me making them sick. It's clear that, for the foreseeable future, we will have to remain vigilant to protect ourselves and each other, but at least we can gather with those we love.

With our world opening up, even ever so slightly, it means we can visit some of our favourite places and attractions in Nova Scotia without the fear of becoming infected. That's not to say we can let our guard down, but at least we are moving in the right direction.

The loosening of restrictions means that we'll be able to go to theatres and enjoy the movies, a favourite pastime for my sons and me. I've missed going to the movies. There's nothing like seeing an action sequence on the big screen and eating popcorn in a dark room. Surely, we'll have to accept safety protocols, but I'll see you at the movie, folks.

Just as I enjoy going to the movies, I also get excited at the prospect of visiting historical museums and learning about our heritage. It's encouraging to know that we can once again visit museums, galleries and other cultural facilities. It has been a long lockdown, folks, so embrace your culture. It's what makes us who we are.

In the same cultural vein, I am also looking forward to attending festivals and events that celebrate our diversified heritage and shared experiences. These annual activities are such an important part of our lives that their absence over the past 14 months has left a large void in our world, a void that is difficult to fill. It will be fun and exhilarating to enjoy the wide variety of festivities that the South Shore and, indeed, all of Nova Scotia has to offer.

Another thing I enjoy is dining in restaurants, especially while we're touring around the province taking in the spectacular sights. It's wonderful to think that we'll be able to visit some of our favourite dining places this summer and enjoy our favourite foods. That's exciting for anyone who enjoys a good meal prepared by someone else, especially when we have so much to celebrate.

While I don't attend many large sporting events or concerts these days, I know a lot of people who enjoy those activities and it's exciting to know that if I see an event I want to attend, I can now do that, providing I follow the safety rules that include social distancing and wearing a mask.

That's the same thing with travelling. Even before the pandemic, I hadn't gotten out of the province much, but it is comforting to know that the country (and the world, for that matter) is slowly opening up again, so that if I want to take a trip to, let's say, visit family in Alberta, I can do so.

Over and above all these wonderful experiences, however, the one thing I am looking forward to the most is the return to not living in constant fear every day, twenty-four hours a day. It is time to get out from under this dark, oppressive cloud that we've endured for the past year and a half.

This has been a long journey for everyone, and I am not saying that it's over. In fact, I believe we still have a way to go before we can say we've returned to normal (whatever that normal is), but it does seem as though we are now in a different place than we were a year ago or six months ago or even a month ago, for that matter.

We should be thankful for where we are right now. We should also be thankful for the scientists, medical professionals and leaders who guided the world through this darkness and out the other side.

We should embrace the opportunity to get on with life, even if things are a bit different than they were before the arrival of COVID-19 rocked our world, and that's the view from here.

United we stand, divided we fall

September 22, 2021

In recent weeks I've been hearing this great advertisement on the radio from an insurance company, talking about community, and it got me to thinking, just what is a community?

On the map, a community is defined by geography. People who live in a certain neighbourhood, village or town, and a county or region such as the South Shore are all part of a community.

Those of us who call the province of Nova Scotia our home are part of a larger community; we're all Nova Scotians or Bluenosers.

You can consider the Maritimes or the Atlantic Region a community just as you can consider the country of Canada a community. Looking even further you can say every one of us on the planet is part of a much larger community—the community of humans.

But that's taking the literal definition of the word. A community can be defined in many other ways.

Those of us with a common history, heritage or culture are part of a community, just as those who share a common goal, objective, cause or theme are a community.

And those who strive to overcome the same challenges, battle the same threats or climb the same obstacles are part of a community, just as those who celebrate the same successes are part of a community.

Members of a group, organization or fraternity are a community. People who work for the same company are part of a community and those who attend the same school or institution are part of a community.

The same can be said for people who practice the same religion or share the same faith. Those people are part of a community.

Those common threads that connect us in some way help us form a community, and if we all work together then our community is strong and prosperous. However, if we fight from within and tear each other down, then our community becomes weak and may crumble.

My philosophy is a simple one: our community is only as strong as we make it, and we do that by working together and being supportive of each other.

Conversely, then, it stands to reason that our community is only as strong as our weakest link in the chain and these days, our collective community faces a major threat.

Yes, the COVID-19 pandemic poses many serious physical threats to our health and wellbeing. We've been under attack for the past year and a half by this relentless disease that comes after all of us. The threat is real and challenges our collective resolve to survive, but we've been fighting, mostly, as a united community.

However, beyond the physical threat, the virus threatens our community in another serious way—it threatens to fracture our support and love for one another. There are many issues to this pandemic, issues that are now pitting neighbour against neighbour, family against family and friend against friend.

When such rifts form it becomes difficult to repair the resulting divide, so be very careful here. We have started down a slippery slope, a slide that could be difficult to stop as it gains momentum.

There are two sides to every debate, and that is true with this virus that has forever changed our lives. There are those who argue that the virus is real and those who believe it is a conspiracy designed by government or a mysterious world-wide cabal to control us and to thin the herd.

There are those who continue to wear a mask for protection and those who, even after all this time and despite government mandates, refuse to wear them as they argue masks are unhealthier than the disease itself.

And there are those who have received the vaccine as they see it as the best defence against COVID-19, but there are also those who refuse to take it saying they believe it is more harmful than the virus itself. They argue it is their right to refuse the vaccine as it's their body and no one, not even government, can force them to put something in their body that they don't want.

That issue is a separate argument, but the point is this rift is real. And sadly, it's growing larger every day.

I cannot think of anything in recent history that has fractured our community more than this virus. Without debate, it has united us on many fronts as people have largely pulled together to protect themselves and their neighbours. However, right now the wedge over masks and vaccines is growing wider and threatens the very foundation of our community.

I truly believe that while people have the God-given right to form their own opinions and to make decisions that impact themselves, there comes a point where you also have to do what's best for the community as a whole, and that means doing your part to protect and secure those in your community.

For the most part, I think people want to do what's right and they want to help others, but the hatred and animosity that have developed over the past year and a half are so real they are palpable. I blame a lot of that simmering angst on social media, with its venom and vitriol fuelling the argument and driving that wedge even deeper.

What we've seen happening in recent months is not good for us as individuals and it's certainly not good for our collective community. As we move forward, we must always be respectful of each other in our community, and we must find a way to co-exist in harmony. We must continue to understand and support one another, not spew hatred at each other, for that helps no one.

Throughout history, people have faced many threats. They persevered and they've overcome the challenges. This pandemic will end. We don't know when and we're not sure how, but at some point in the future, the threat from this particular virus will be over.

The end may come through the natural evolution of the human species or as the result of the vaccine or maybe even some other form of treatment that hasn't been developed yet. Regardless, when it does end, we want our community to be strong and healthy because, make no mistake, when this pandemic ends, there will be new threats.

The message is clear—the more united we remain the stronger our community remains, or at least that's the view from here.

Let's focus on the things we can control

March 23, 2022

We live in perilous times.

Between the pandemic that had basically shut down our lives for the past two years and now the devastating war in the Ukraine, we wonder what is happening right now. We long for better times when, despite on-going issues, the world still seemed like a much friendlier place, and we wish we could go back there.

We should worry about our futures and those of our children and grandchildren, but the harsh truth is that we cannot change world events. While we can watch them unfold, express our dismay, pass judgment and make our opinions known to those decision makers who tell us they are in control, there is little else we can do.

Some things are just beyond our reach.

But while we all have an obligation to remain informed and engaged in these events that impact the entire world, we must also accept that, in the larger scheme of things, our hands are mostly tied as we rely on our leaders to do the right thing, even when it seems the "right thing" is not always what we would recommend.

Yes, we can commiserate and express our unhappiness. We should talk about it as it's unhealthy to keep our emotions bottled up inside. We should be angry, but we simply must accept that as the universe unfolds, it's important to let go of the darkness and embrace those positive things in our lives. Working to improve our world closer to home is a good counterbalance for those things beyond our control.

We live in a free and democratic country, so while we have every right to complain about and criticize those things we disagree with, we should not spend all our time and energy dwelling on the negative issues. Instead, it would be healthier and more productive to focus on the many positive things that we have in our lives—and there are many. We should embrace them.

While the world is seemingly spinning out of control right now, we would be wise to take stock of the wonderful things that contribute to our quality of life here in Canada because, by comparison to other parts of the world, we have it pretty darned good.

Every time I hear someone complain about our current situation or how bad they have it or how inconvenienced they feel, I think, yes, all of that may be true from one perspective, but what about …

The love, comfort and support you receive from your family and friends?

When you are feeling down and out, or the burden is becoming just too much, I would encourage you to think about those important people in your life and be grateful that you have someone who cares for you and who will stand by you no matter what. That's a quality that no amount of money can buy and nothing else can replace.

We would all do well to remember that, because there are so many people out there in the world who do not have such support.

The reality that you woke up this morning in a warm, safe house and you could go about your daily tasks of getting ready for work and seeing the kids off to school is reason to be grateful.

You went through your normal routine of dressing, eating breakfast, probably checking all your social media accounts for updates on world events and then you went off to live your day. Pretty normal, right? Just remember how lucky you are to be able to enjoy that routine while hundreds of thousands, maybe millions, don't have a home or food or a job to go to.

The fact that we live in a relatively safe environment where bombs are not dropping from the sky and nobody is shooting at us; where buildings aren't collapsing around us and our neighbours are not being killed in front of our eyes, is a lot for which we should be grateful.

Here on the South Shore, we all live in relatively safe communities where people can freely go about their business and daily routines without having the constant fear of being attacked or, worse, killed. Sure, we do have crime, but in comparison to some areas of the world—and even other parts of our own country—our region is pretty secure.

The reality that, even though the price of groceries has reached higher levels than most of us have ever seen before, we are fortunate enough to be able to put food on our tables. We are also fortunate that we can drive to the supermarket, where we can safely find pretty much everything we're looking for. We should not take that convenience for granted.

And while we know there are many serious issues in the health care system, most of us still have unencumbered access to medical care. There may be a shortage of doctors, nurses and other health care professionals and there may be longer-than-we'd-like delays and wait times, but, at the end of the day, most Canadians do find some relief for what ails them. Not every place in the world can deliver the same level of care.

Maybe some people won't see this as an important quality or they won't believe it to be true, but here in Canada, we have access to a free and uncensored media that is not controlled by the government. This may be contrary to what some people think, but the uncensored flow of information is vital to a free democracy and that information keeps us informed and contributes greatly to our quality of life.

For those of you with children, think about the schools, teachers and other professionals who provide them with a good education to prepare them to meet the future world. There are challenges, especially in this age of COVID, but surely a quality education is something to embrace, especially because there are so many other places in the world where children learn on the streets and have never seen the inside of a classroom.

As for quality of life, while our environment may be under attack on various fronts, we are still fortunate to live in a beautiful place with fresh air, clean water and largely-unpolluted land. While there is an urgency to slow the degradation of the natural places around the world and to stop global warming, it's also true that, for the most part, we live in a pristine environment. This is an added bonus on the list of positive attributes that make our lives better.

There are also many places where rampant and crippling poverty prevent people from getting the simple basics of life, let alone the many luxuries we enjoy every day. Think of that the next time you complain about your problems.

For those who go to work every day to a job that you love and enjoy, you should add that to your list of positives as well because there are places around the world where you are told what you're going to do every day.

The same holds true for people who like to travel. Sure, during the pandemic there were strict guidelines, and the movement of people was pretty much shut down for two years, but the situation is getting better with the travel industry swinging into high gear. That means you'll be pretty much able to travel to most of the places you enjoy and see family and friends you may not have seen for a few years.

Indeed, the world may be a little off kilter these days. There are things that we can't change, but I urge you to pause and reflect upon those qualities that give you a better life. I'm sure after some introspection and letting go of the things you cannot change, you'll see things in a different light, or at least that's the view from here.

What do you do when COVID comes home?

August 10, 2022

Well, it happened.

After two and a half years of living in fear and loathing of getting COVID-19, and after taking precautions to avoid catching the virus, the dreaded disease finally showed up on our doorstep a few weeks ago as both my wife, Nancy, and I tested positive.

Honestly, we were surprised at the results because, despite the more relaxed public COVID mandates in Nova Scotia, my family continues to take precautions such as wearing masks whenever we go inside a public building.

We have also taken advantage of the vaccines and boosters as they become available, and we will continue to do so. We were very diligent in our efforts to avoid infection but, somehow, it still found us. It almost seems like it was inevitable.

I know that despite the abundance of scientific evidence that's available there are many people who choose to believe that COVID-19 is a huge, world-wide conspiracy, and they also refuse to believe that masks and vaccines are safe. You are free to believe whatever you wish, just as my family and I are free to do likewise. The bottom line is that we should all respect each other's opinions and decisions.

However, at age 60, both Nancy and I choose to believe that it is safer to protect ourselves as best we can, so we will continue to take whatever precautions we can. We choose to trust science and medicine.

Now, there are those who argue that if these precautions are so safe and effective, how did we get COVID?

That's a very good question that we can't explain nor easily answer except to point out that public health officials are now warning that this new variant is much more transmissible and aggressive than previous forms of the virus so again, it almost seems inevitable that we are all likely going to get COVID.

The fast-spreading BA.5 subvariant of Omicron and its close relative BA.4 now make up approximately 95% of COVID cases in Canada and the U.S. While provinces have lifted mask mandates and ended measures meant to contain the spread of the virus, Canada's public health officials have warned of an increase in hospitalizations as the highly transmissible Omicron subvariant circulates around the globe.

Instead of arguing that the precautions don't work, I would counter that had we not received the vaccines, my wife and I may have been dealing with a more serious case of the disease. We can argue this until the proverbial cows come home, but as it was, Nancy and I consider ourselves very lucky to have had a somewhat mild case of the disease, which seemed much like a very bad head and chest cold with extreme fatigue.

In fact, if I had to identify one symptom of the illness that affected me the hardest, I would say it was the extreme lethargic feeling I suffered for more than a week, with a serious lack of energy and ability to focus. The best way to describe the feeling is to say that it felt like I was dealing with serious sleep deprivation and all I wanted to do was rest.

For Nancy, while she was also very tired, she suffered more with the cough and chest congestion than I did, but she agrees it was as if she had a really bad cold. We also agree, though, that it is something we do not want to experience again.

We know that every case is different and none of this is meant to diminish the seriousness of this potentially deadly disease. In truth, we consider ourselves lucky to have suffered what we considered minor symptoms in comparison to what some people say they have experienced.

Despite the gains that have been made in medical research and treatment, the coronavirus still poses a very serious threat to humans. While great strides have been made in dealing with the disease that crippled the world for more than two years, it's clear that COVID-19 is here to stay and that we will have to learn to live with it.

What that means for us moving forward is still not clear and, while some continue to debate and dismiss the seriousness of the virus, it is abundantly clear that it can find you no matter what precautions you take.

This virus is all around us and is still infecting a significant number of people. For instance, from July 19 to July 25, hospitals in Nova Scotia reported a significant jump in the number of patients who tested positive for COVID-19.

According to Nova Scotia Health, during that period there were a total of 260 patients in hospitals across the province who were positive for COVID-19. That number included 45 patients admitted for treatment of COVID-19 symptoms (nine in ICU), 143 patients admitted for treatment of another health issue but tested positive for COVID-19 and 72 patients who contracted COVID-19 after admission to hospital.

These numbers represented an increase of 64 patients from the previous week, one of the largest week-over-week increases reported in Nova Scotia hospitals since the start of the pandemic.

Nova Scotia also reported five new COVID-19 deaths and a daily average of 272 lab-confirmed cases. Since March 2020, there have been 468 COVID-19 deaths in Nova Scotia. About three-quarters of those deaths happened during the Omicron wave, which began December 8, 2021.

Nova Scotia is considered one of the hottest spots in Canada for COVID right now and a number of deaths are reported every week from the disease, so we would never make light of the situation nor dismiss anyone's suffering.

COVID is a very serious disease and people should still be on their toes when it comes to the virus. They should be aware that the chance of catching COVID is very real, and that's the view from here.

Vernon Oickle

It's time to find your inner light this holiday season

November 30, 2022

As I am writing this column for the November 30 issue of the paper, I can't help but wonder where the past year has gone, but here we are on the cusp of another holiday season and, this time next month, we'll be knee-deep in all things Christmas.

This year, we will be celebrating Christmas without the tight COVID restrictions that we endured the previous two years. We may be dealing with another mask mandate, but you know what? That isn't so bad. Let's be honest, we have gone through worse and most of us survived, so we can do this.

Everything considered, then, let's celebrate the coming season and embrace what Christmas means to us.

The Christmas season is the ideal time to pull together with friends, family and neighbours and to turn away from the darkness that we endured the previous two years. It's time to find the light.

You can interpret that observation as you wish. If you are a spiritual person with deeply-held religious beliefs, I'm sure the light will mean something completely different than it does to those who may not have a similar deep-seeded faith. But that's okay, because if you don't hold any particularly strong religious beliefs, then that light can be something else such as your loved ones and your family traditions.

Regardless of where you find that respite from the darkness, Christmas is the time of year to celebrate and observe all that is good in your life. With Christmas less than one month out, let's think about those things that are near and dear to us, those things that make us smile, give us peace, those things that give us joy and make our hearts sing.

We all have trials and tribulations in our lives. We all face challenges, and we all have obstacles that we must overcome, some worse than others. And it goes without saying that humanity has had more than its fair

246

share of darkness over the past couple of years since COVID arrived on our shores, but let's put that behind us once and for all. Let's find that inner strength to smile and rejoice in the season.

So, what do the holidays mean to you?

For me, the holidays are about sharing in the warmth and love of family and friends. Nothing is more important than our loved ones, and they must be our priority, with a focus on spending quality time with those who mean the most to us. Christmas is the perfect occasion to rally around one another and embrace the warmth of those close to us.

The season is also about helping others in need, extending a hand to our neighbours and reaching out to those who may be alone, shut in or struggling to make ends meet. Here in our piece of the world, Nova Scotians largely do that throughout the year, but during the holidays we go the extra mile to make sure everyone enjoys a bit of happiness at this special time.

Christmas is also about embracing family values and our traditions that have been passed down to us from earlier generations. We may celebrate other special occasions throughout the year, but no other season brings out the traditions quite like Christmas, and that's important because it allows us to remember our collective past while at the same time celebrating all that is good. Connecting with our roots allows us to remain grounded and gives us a solid base from which to face a new year.

The list of traditions we observe during the holidays is long and runs the gamut from decorations, to giving gifts, to attending religious services, to welcoming Santa into our homes, to trimming the tree, to preparing feasts and hosting seasonal gatherings. No matter which traditions you celebrate or which you choose not to observe, these activities are all part of the collective season that is Christmas, and the key is to do things that bring you closer to your loved ones.

A major component of all holiday celebrations are the seasonal foods. Perhaps it's just me, but there are some foods that seem to taste better during Christmas than at any other time of the year. While those dishes are important parts of our annual traditions, preparing our favourite family recipes also allows us to honour and remember those loved ones who are no longer with us.

For me, it's my mother's three-bean salad. While the recipe is simple enough to follow, she loved it and prepared it every Christmas for as long as I can remember. So, as a way of keeping her memory with us during the holiday season, I prepare Mom's bean salad every Christmas. It's usually the only time of the year I make it, keeping it as a special tradition just for the holidays.

Even to those who do not consider themselves to be spiritual people, the holy season fills us with faith and hope and a sense of peace. The season gives us a rallying point around which we can count our blessings, put our lives into perspective, pull our loved ones close and honour whomever or whatever you worship. It's about believing in something beyond the normally restrictive confines of our day-to-day lives.

In the material world in which we live, Christmas is also about having faith in our humanity. Even when events and circumstances such as what we've gone through over the past few years conspire to tear us down and test our resolve, this special season allows us to pause, take a deep breath, step away from the stress, gather our thoughts, and regroup so that we can face a new year filled with hope and the belief that there will be a better tomorrow.

And I do believe there will be a better tomorrow.

No matter how busy life has become or how dark the times may seem, Christmas is that one time of year when all of that negativity can melt away. It may only be for a few days, but it's a welcome respite from our hustle-bustle world, and that's the view from here.

The coronavirus virus: three years later

March 1, 2023

Three years ago, Canadians, like citizens in most other nations around the world, were trying to come to grips with a new and potentially-deadly virus that was sweeping over the globe, leaving in its wake a swath of death and despair unlike anything we had seen in a century.

Things are different now than they were three years ago, when mounting tensions and high emotions ruled the day, but most people understand that the precautions we took were to protect us from a disease that—as of the time of writing this column on February 18, 2023—has resulted in more than 140,000 documented cases and 746 confirmed deaths in Nova Scotia.

Just look at what we went through.

For starters, even though there was great resistance from some people, we were mandated to wear masks whenever we went out in public. There were no exceptions to that rule and for the most part, from what I saw, the vast majority of people followed that directive.

In fact, while contact with other people was not strictly forbidden, health officials everywhere strongly recommend that we keep a minimal distance of six feet from each other.

It was also strongly recommended that we avoid shaking hands and hugging other people. This virus is easily transmitted so such physical contact was to be avoided.

In just two years, the coronavirus impacted our lives in so many ways that it is now almost impossible to imagine a world before its arrival. The words quarantine, self-isolation and social distancing became common in our everyday vocabulary. Many things in our lives function differently today than they did three years ago. During the pandemic, we lived in a world where video conferencing and on-line classes or meetings were more common than face-to-face gatherings. If fact, some people are still doing business in that way.

Social gatherings in general were either eliminated or greatly downs-ized, with all group functions practically being wiped out. When we attended any public activity, we were to keep our distance from others. In fact, chairs were placed six feet apart and roped off to prevent contact.

When they could open, schools, especially extra-curricular activities, operated under a strict set of guidelines, with sporting and social events being curtailed or eliminated altogether.

And then there is the impact the pandemic had on the economy. Even those of us who were fortunate to have jobs had to adjust and, thankfully, because of technology, working from home became an acceptable norm.

Let's not forget about how the pandemic impacted travel, which is still suffering from the impact. It will take years, maybe decades, for that sector of the economy to recover, and visits to some foreign destinations remain under scrutiny, three years later.

Our lives have changed profoundly in so many ways that it's almost impossible to wrap one's head around the sheer volume of it all. But the truth is, this virus made people gravely ill, and many people died from it. Some people are still getting very sick and some are still dying.

Despite all of those conspiracy theorists and deniers who insisted none of this was real or that it was an elaborate government experiment or just the regular flu, the precautions were undertaken for the right reason: to save lives.

Even though we are now seeing the end of this plague, we must still be vigilant as it is clear this virus is going to be with us for a long time so we must adapt and learn to live with it. We must remain strong and—as we have learned during this difficult time—we must support each other.

I'll be the first to admit that some of these adjustments were difficult, but considering the grave possibility of contracting a deadly virus, it was only common sense that we all did our part not only to protect ourselves, but also our family, friends and neighbours.

We all saw how quickly this virus could spread and get out of hand, but life changed three years ago. We must accept that fact, and that's the view from here.

The view from here on

Democracy and Canada

Vernon Oickle

Being Canadian

July 1, 2015

So friends, today, July 1, is Canada's 148th birthday. I hope you all enjoy your time off, and if you have to work, I hope you still manage to find a way to celebrate the birth of our great nation.

Each year, Canadians take advantage of the holiday to kick back and relax by the pool, take a trip to the cottage or maybe visit the beach, hold a barbecue or perhaps join one of the celebrations that are traditionally held in communities across the nation.

Food, fireworks and fun are the top priorities on Canada Day, but July 1 isn't just about a day off. Nor is it just a time to relax or to frolic. It is also a day to celebrate the birth of one of the best countries in the world.

As Canadians, we take a great deal for granted, but each year as we're enjoying the festivities we should also pause and take stock of the things that make this country so great.

We may complain about the governments we elect—and most of us certainly do our fair share of that—but it's because we live in a country where freedom of speech is guaranteed through our democracy that we enjoy the right to criticize the people we elect to represent us.

Furthermore, it's because we live in a democratic society that we even get to elect our governments in the first place, but please don't take that right for granted. What has taken generations to build up could be torn down before our very eyes if we're not careful and if we're not mindful of whom we elect.

This is an important year for democracy in our country, as we lead up to a federal election in October. It's essential that as a Canadian you pay attention to the issues and become engaged in the process. Listen to the candidates, consider the leaders' strengths and weaknesses, and understand the party platforms, but, most importantly, become engaged in the process.

While voting for our government is paramount to our democracy and freedom of choice is an essential pillar of our society, there's more to being a Canadian than exercising that right. In the lead-up to Canada Day, I have been thinking about what it means to be a Canadian, and here's what I've come up with.

Being Canadian means we have the freedom to speak up for the things we believe in or against the things we don't like, regardless if it's counter to the ruling government's position, and we can do that without fear of reprisal.

Being Canadian means that, even if we disagree with what someone else is saying, we will defend their right to say it. (Unless it's spreading words of hatred or instigating violence. We won't tolerate that.)

Being Canadian means we can choose whatever profession or career we wish without someone else telling us what we're going to do.

Being Canadian means our children are not required to join the military when they reach a certain age.

Being Canadian means we have reasonable access to a free and adequate education up to Grade 12.

Being Canadian means we can access health care when we are ill, even if the system is not without flaws and we sometimes have to wait.

Being Canadian means we can freely travel throughout this great country with ease.

Being Canadian means we can live anywhere in this great nation that we choose to live.

Being Canadian means we can mostly travel to any part of the world we wish to travel without the government telling us we can't leave the country.

Being Canadian means we have the right to assembly and the right to protest. We even have the right to protest our government's actions.

Being Canadian means we have the freedom to practice whatever religion we believe in.

Being Canadian means we support equal rights for all nationalities.

Being Canadian means that we prefer peace over force to settle disputes.

Being Canadian means that we will freely lend a hand to our neighbours in their time of need, both in this country and beyond our borders.

Being Canadian means we get to bask in the varied and vast natural beauty that is this great country.

Being Canadian means we coexist in a melting pot of varied cultures.

Being Canadian means we get to elect our government every four or five years.

Being Canadian means we get to support the party and candidate of our choice and we have the right to keep that vote a secret.

Being Canadian means we get to run for elected office if we choose.

Being Canadian means that if you are female, you don't have to fear for your life just because of your gender.

Being Canadian means we expect fair and swift justice for all.

Being Canadian means we believe that everyone is innocent until proven guilty.

Being Canadian means that we embrace our heritage and work to preserve it for the benefit of future generations.

Being Canadian means we revere hockey almost as if it's a religion.

Being Canadian means our many national symbols, including the maple leaf, the RCMP, the beaver, our anthem and our flag instill pride in us.

Being Canadian means that in striving to be a tolerant society, we reject discrimination based on race, colour, culture, religion, age, ability, gender or sexual orientation.

Being Canadian means that we can send our children outside to play in the yard without fear of them being shot or send them off to school knowing that a bomb won't drop from the sky and level the building.

Being Canadian means that I get to express these thoughts and feelings in writing every week in this space without fear of reprisal or repercussion, or at least that's the view from here.

A thought or two on democracy

August 19, 2015

I believe that we live in the greatest nation in the world. We are fortunate to live in a country where we have so many rights and freedoms that we take most of them for granted.

A case in point is our right to vote.

Every four or five years we get the opportunity to decide who is going to govern our province or country, yet following the federal election call on August 2, I was absolutely disheartened, disturbed, discouraged, disgusted and dismayed to hear so many people openly declare that they don't follow politics and so won't be voting in this or any election.

Instead, they believe "all politicians are crooks" and that "they are only out to line their own pockets" or "take care of their friends."

Now, I will concede that over the years we have seen some dirty politicians who, indeed, were only in the game to further their own causes. I'll also acknowledge that we've experienced a litany of scandals in recent decades that have led to the current level of cynicism and distrust in politicians.

It's likely that these scandals have turned some of us off to politics as we've continued to struggle while the rich and powerful seem to become richer and more powerful, but it isn't accurate to paint every politician, either new or seasoned, with the same brush. Furthermore, anyone who snubs their nose at their right to vote is doing a grave disservice to democracy in this country.

I will also say, however, that having an eleven-week election is more than a little excessive by most modern standards (at least in this country) and there's no doubt that by election day on October 19, most of us will be feeling a little fatigued, but there really is no good excuse not to vote.

We should never take our right to vote for granted. Our forefathers and foremothers fought and died for our right to vote and to now turn your back on your right to vote is an affront to everything they sacrificed. Seriously, as a Canadian, you should be proud and honoured to cast your vote in every election at every level, be it municipal, provincial or federal.

As Canadians, we should be asking ourselves, where did we go wrong? What is so bad that it causes so many people not to vote in an election? Somewhere in the course of this country's history, our democracy went off the tracks, but we must find a way to put it back on the rails, for if we fail to do so, our democracy will be in jeopardy.

There are nations around the world where the people never have a say on who governs them. There are places in the world where citizens are shot, hanged, tortured or disappeared for even suggesting that they should have a say in who runs the country. And there are nations in the world where elections are outlawed and where proponents of democracy are thrown into prison, where they spend years and are often never heard from again.

People in these countries can only dream of what we have here and what we take for granted, so never snub your nose at democracy.

No matter which party you support or candidate you get behind, you should think of your ballot as your way of passing judgment on the previous government and consider it your opportunity to help decide who will run things for the next four to five years.

So, you don't like the current system. I get that. But nothing will ever change if you don't vote. On the other hand, if you like the current system, you could jeopardize the status quo by refusing to vote. There is a lot at stake here, as democracy is fragile.

Voting is serious business and, yes, in a democracy such as ours here in Canada, no one is going to force you to vote. Even though mandatory voting has been suggested in the past, it hasn't happened yet because—get this—we live in a democracy. It's your choice to vote or not, but voting is a right that you should always honour, because when you don't vote you allow hypocrisy to reign supreme.

I understand that people are cynical and I appreciate why they think that they've been shafted by governments in the past, but the simple truth remains that if you don't cast your vote then you allow someone else to make that important choice for you and in the end you're stuck with whatever government other people choose.

It's true that you may not get the government you want. It's also true that your candidate of choice may not win, but by voting you've at least expressed your opinion. Voting is your way of standing up and saying you want change, or you support the current government's plans, but by not voting you let someone else make that decision for you.

Furthermore, by not voting, you're basically saying, "Okay, I don't like what you're doing to me, but give me more of the same."

At least by voting you're standing up for your right to demand change or to keep the status quo, whichever option you support. The power is ultimately in your hands.

Would you let someone else pick out what car you'll buy? Would you let someone else decide where you're going to live? Would you let someone else decide how you are going to invest your money or where you're going to spend your vacation? Would you let someone decide where you'll spend your retirement years without at least having your input on the decision?

My guess is that you'll answer "no" to all these questions and if so, then why would you let someone else decide for you who will run the country for the next four to five years? Why would you do that without at least having your say? Because that's exactly what you're doing when you don't vote.

There's a lot riding on every election, and this is especially true at the federal level, where decisions are made that affect the country's overall financial status and its position on the world stage.

The federal government makes decisions regarding our nation's security and determines whether we go to war, and where we will stand on many international issues. The federal government makes policies that affect our laws, our economy and the environment. The federal government manages our national parks and institutions. And, most importantly, the federal government protects our constitutional and charter of rights while safeguarding our freedoms.

These are issues that are not to be taken lightly and you, as a Canadian, should want your voice to be heard on these and many other important issues. This is how democracy works, but it doesn't work if you don't vote.

When Canadians go to the polls on October 19, we will elect a government and a leader to represent the values and vision of our country. Voting is the truest form of democracy that we have. By putting pencil to paper you will join people across Canada to vote for the candidate and the political party you think will best lead our country.

You owe it to yourself and to future generations to vote. You also owe it to the memory of those who fought on your behalf to ensure you have the right to vote. Your right to vote should never be taken for granted, or at least that's the view from here.

It's time to become engaged

October 7, 2015

I was recently sitting in a local coffee shop somewhere on the South Shore, enjoying my coffee and muffin. I was just minding my own business when I overheard a conversation between two gentlemen about the upcoming federal election.

And no. I do not consider that to be eavesdropping as the verbal exchange was taking place at a table directly behind mine and well within earshot. We were in a public place, after all, and they were becoming rather loud, so I didn't consider it to be a private meeting.

It was a lively and colourful conversation that covered many political topics, including the local candidates running for office in the riding of South Shore-St. Margaret's. After dismissing the "other" parties in the race because these two men decided they were non-factors in the local campaign, they proceeded to dissect the three mainstream parties and discussed how they were going to vote, if they voted at all because, as they reassured each other, not voting was a real option for them.

Especially in this election, they made a point of stressing.

The men, whom I did not recognize, also discussed the strengths and weaknesses of the national leaders, as well as who they felt was to blame for the current sputtering state of the economy in this country (their views were diametrically opposite on this point, I might add) and the prospects of economic recovery for the country and, more specifically, for the province of Nova Scotia.

The two parties involved also commiserated with each other and talked about how they feel disenfranchised by the political process. Both agreed that they were not being heard on the issues, although almost in the same breath, they also agreed that they pay very little attention to politics, and told each yet again that they were even contemplating not voting on October 19.

It makes one shake one's head. Therein lies the problem.

Yes, I totally agree with these gentlemen that governments at all levels must communicate their business in an expedient, concise and clear manner that's accessible to every constituent. It comes with the job for which they were elected. And while I'm sure it's a challenge to reach everyone, it's the duty and responsibility of every elected member to keep us all informed.

However, at some point, it's also the responsibility of us, the electorate, to search out the information and, if we don't understand it, to ask questions. It's our responsibility to become engaged in the political process, especially now while we're in the midst of an election.

It seems to me that at some point our society became too dependent upon government to do everything for us. Now, instead of the government working for the electorate, it appears the electorate is working for the government.

How did that happen?

It happened because we—and I'm speaking in general terms here—have collectively become complacent and have effectively removed ourselves from the political process. We have abdicated our duty as voters and come to rely too heavily on those we elect to always provide us with the answers instead of taking on some of the responsibility to find them for ourselves.

It's time to reverse that trend because, in truth, we're as much to blame for the current disconnect as the politicians we elect and the bureaucrats who work for government. I'm not naïve. I know the system does not always work as it's supposed to, but we must do our part.

Past experience has proven that not all governments do what's in the best interest of the electorate, nor does every politician do the right thing. Only through engagement with those whom we elect can we be sure they follow the best process and, ultimately, take best course of action.

It's also true that no government can be everything to everyone and, as we know, sometimes a government must make unpopular decisions. In such cases, it's important that we engage the decision-makers and learn as much as we can about the process.

Sometimes, even when we don't like or don't agree with such a decision, we may learn that the course of action government has taken really is in the best interest of the municipal unit, province or country.

The two gentlemen in the coffee shop were right in observing that governments, no matter the level of responsibility, are there to do what's best for the people they were elected to represent. But they're wrong in their assertions that every politician becomes tainted once they assume power and, in truth, during these times of political discord, it is critical to remain engaged and connected.

Now is not the time for voters to withdraw themselves from the political process. When it appears that the process has gone off track, then it's up to the electorate to act, not step away from the problem.

In an ideal democracy, we would have swift and unfettered accountability when our governments lose their way, but we know that's often not the case. Instead, we must wait every four or five years to exercise our right to vote and to abdicate that right only furthers the disconnect you may feel.

It is true that no one can force you to vote, at least not yet, as we do not have mandatory voting in this country. However, instead of sitting around a coffee shop complaining about not being informed, get out there and talk to the candidates, attend debates and forums, read the material, check out their websites, study the platforms and become engaged.

It's a two-way street. True, if the candidates want your vote, it's in their best interest to connect with you. However, it's also true that it's impossible for any candidate (no matter the party) to find every voter in a riding as geographically large as is South Shore-St. Margaret's.

We can't put all the responsibility on the candidates. As a voter you owe it to yourself to become involved and informed, or at least the view from here.

What is an average Canadian?

February 3, 2016

I have a lot of pet peeves, but one of my biggest is politicians and bureaucrats who use the phrase "average Canadians" to describe everyday working Joes like you and me.

I'm sure they don't mean to sound condescending, but the term smacks of elitism and suggests that those people in a position of authority and power are somehow better than the rest of us. In fact, though, it's the "average Canadian" who really makes this country tick.

Furthermore, it's those "average Canadians" who gave said politicians and bureaucrats their power and authority in the first place, so they would do well not to lose sight of that reality.

I understand that some Canadians are better financially positioned than others and that some, because of the country's societal, economic and political structures, have more authority than others, but the little hairs on the back of my neck stand at attention every time I hear one of those influential individuals refer to the rest of us as average.

For the record, I consider myself to be an average Canadian. As the old saying goes, I put my pants on one leg at a time, I work hard to provide for my family, and I have hopes and dreams just like most people I know. However, for the sake of argument and because our leaders continue to use the colloquialism, let's look at what makes an average Canadian.

From my perspective, an average Canadian is someone who has respect for his fellow citizens regardless of cultural, ethnic, social, economic, religious or geographical differences.

An average Canadian also recognizes and embraces the reality that we live in a multicultural country where the fabric of our society is woven together by people from around the globe.

Average Canadians also understand that our unique and diverse culture is what creates the "Canadian" society.

An average Canadian obeys the laws of the land and follows the rules under which we are governed without scheming to cut corners for personal gain or advancement, or to the detriment of others. We also understand that when someone breaks those laws, they will be punished accordingly.

At the same time, the person who works hard and strives for success, no matter their field of work or area of interest, is an average Canadian.

An average Canadian is the person who embraces who they are and, while working to make a positive contribution, puts the wellbeing of their family and friends ahead of everything else.

An average Canadian tries to help improve the world by helping to make their own community a great place to live, work and raise a family.

An average Canadian will respond to the needs of others by making a positive contribution through volunteering and offering their time and abilities to make positive changes in their community.

An average Canadian will become engaged in the issues that impact their lives and the communities where they live. They will step up to the plate when circumstances call for action and they will celebrate success when it happens.

Those who reach out to assist their neighbours and open their homes and hearts to others in their hour of need are truly average Canadians.

Average Canadians are those who can debate and discuss the issues but still respect those who have opposing viewpoints.

Average Canadians are resilient and resourceful, responding to a challenge with optimism and faith that they can build a better future for themselves, for those they love and for the country as a whole.

Average Canadians also know that not every battle has an easy outcome, but when problems arise, these citizens demonstrate a great deal of ingenuity and creativity in looking for solutions.

Above all else, the average Canadian will not go down without a fight, especially if it's for a cause in which they believe, such as human rights and equality for every citizen of this great nation.

Average Canadians embrace their heritage and respect their roots, while at the same time understanding that to go forward one cannot stay mired in the past. However, we believe you must know where you came from to know where you're going.

Average Canadians show compassion, and they are typically forgiving of those who have made mistakes, for we understand that no one is perfect.

While being appreciative of the rights and freedoms we enjoy in this great nation, the average Canadian understands that we are part of a global community, which means that what happens in other parts of the world will often impact us. We also understand that when circumstances warrant, we, as a nation, must react accordingly.

Average Canadians support the idea that our nation can be a sanctuary for those who have no country.

I know it's just a figure of speech, but as I said, whenever I hear this term, I wonder what makes an above average Canadian. No matter your lot in life, what you do for a living, your cultural or ethnic background or your level of income, we're all "average" Canadians in that we all want the same thing—a country that lets us be us, or at least that's the view from here.

Oh Canada! You look great at 150

June 28, 2017

On July 1, Canada celebrates its 150ᵗʰ birthday, and for those of us fortunate to call this great nation our home, there is much to celebrate.

It may be an over-generalization, but for the most part I believe Canadians take a great deal for granted. On the eve of this milestone birthday, I was challenged recently by a friend to come up with a list of 150 things that immediately make me think of Canada. The catch was that I had to do it without referring to the Internet or asking anyone else for suggestions.

Easy, right?

Sure, I thought. I could do that, so I immediately accepted the challenge and quickly began jotting down my ideas.

In the initial stages, the task was a breeze, as I could string off a relatively long inventory of things that immediately scream "Canada." But as the list grew, I confess to having a few struggles, and along the way I was tempted to ask for help.

In the end, though, I was able to compile a list of 150 people, places, things and quality of life ideals that immediately make me think of Canada. I'll admit though, the challenge wasn't as easy as I thought it would be.

In no particular order then, here is my list of 150 things that instantly make me think of Canada when I hear them:

(1) Freedom (2) Democracy (3) Diversity (4) Multiculturalism (5) Maple Leaf (6) Hockey (7) Home (8) Equality (9) Peace (10) Acceptance.

(11) Tolerance (12) Beauty (13) Nature (14) United (15) Nationalism (16) Canadian Bacon—the name says it all (17) Poutine —not really one of my favourites, but those who like it, like it a lot (18) Tim Hortons—that will be a medium double, double (19) Friendly (20) Neighbourly.

(21) Beaver (22) Moose (23) Bluenose (24) Charter of Rights (25) Trudeau—father and son (26) Resources (27) Northern Lights (28) Donairs—so tasty (29) Terry Fox (30) Health care.

(31) Clean water (32) Great Lakes (33) Rocky Mountains (34) Red and white (35) Toonies (36) Loonies (37) "Eh!" (38) Clean air (39) Insulin (40) Royal Canadian Mounted Police.

(41) Baby pablum—I actually knew it was invented by a Canadian. Guess I had heard that little tidbit somewhere along the way (42) Nanaimo Bars—love them! (43) Standard Time—invented by a Canadian in Halifax (44) BlackBerry (45) Canadarm (46) Great White North (47) Acadians (48) Snowmobile (49) Snow blower (50) Garbage bags—yes, these were actually invented by a Canadian.

(51) Caesar—the drink, not the salad, was also invented in Calgary (52) Calgary Stampede (53) Kerosene—invented by a Nova Scotian (54) Paint roller—another Canadian invention (55) The Robertson screw (56) Alkaline battery—I confess to cheating on this one. I recently heard this on the television (57) Egg carton —first used in BC. Another piece of not-so-useless information I acquired along the way (58) Peanut butter—is there anything better on toast? (59) McIntosh apple (60) IMAX theatre.

(61) Instant replay—yes, it was used first in Canada (62) Superman—an American hero created by Canadian artist Joe Shuster (63) Canola (64) Crispy Crunch (65) Coffee Crisp—my absolute favourite chocolate bar (66) Prosthetic hand (67) Foghorn (68) Lighthouses (69) The goalie mask—first used by Jacques Plante in 1959. I saw this in a book, so technically I didn't cheat as the rules stipulated no Internet and no help from a friend (70) Lacrosse—I remember that from school.

(71) Trivial Pursuit (72) Plexiglas—don't ask me how I knew that. I just knew it was a Canadian invention. Must have read it somewhere. (73) Telephone (74) The zipper (75) Robert Stanfield

(76) Joey Smallwood—makes me think Newfoundland and that makes me think Canada (77) Banff (78) Rideau Canal (79) Freedom of choice (80) Freedom of speech.

(81) Penicillin (82) Zambonis—yes, they are a Canadian invention. (83) Rink rats (84) Velcro (85) Toques (86) Mr. Dress Up (87) The Friendly Giant (88) Romper Room (89) CN Tower (90) Confederation Bridge.

(91) Peggy's Cove (92) PEI potatoes (93) Lobster (94) Port aux Basques (95) Chris Hadfield (96) Roberta Bondar (97) Stephen Lewis (98) Ken Taylor (99) #99 (100) William Shatner.

(101) Toronto Blue Jays (102) Toronto Raptors (103) Toronto Maple Leafs (104) Montreal Canadiens (105) Ottawa—the nation's capital (106) Wheat (107) Prairies (108) Polar bears (109) Canoe (110) Northwest Passage.

(111) Hudson Bay (112) Beaver tails—the kind you eat (113) Rogers Centre (114) Joseph Howe (115) Sir John A. Macdonald (116) Louis Riel (117) Tommy Douglas (119) Canada Goose (120) CBC.

(121) Hockey Night In Canada (122) Don Cherry (123) Stompin' Tom Connors (124) Anne Murray (125) Hank Snow (126) Snow Birds (129) Voyageurs (130) Métis.

(131) Bannock (132) Buffalo (133) Trans Canada Highway (134) Peace Tower (135) Lester Pearson (136) Stanley Cup (137) Grey Cup (138) Maple syrup (139) Rush—I'm talking about the iconic Canadian band, not the speed at which we travel in traffic (140) Bachman Turner Overdrive—better known by some as BTO.

(141) Port Royal (142) Perogies (143) Rick Hansen (144) Sidney Crosby (145) Molson Canadian (146) Gordon Lightfoot (147) Neil Young (148) The Guess Who (149) Air Canada (150) Canadian Tire.

So, there you have it. This is my list of 150 things that make me think of Canada as soon as I hear them.

These were in no particular order. In fact, I just jotted them down over a few days as they popped into my head, but I think you must agree that all these things are proof that Canada is, indeed, the greatest country in the world, or at least that's the view from here.

Go ahead and embrace your Canadian pride

January 18, 2023

When Team Canada beat Team Czechia 3-2 in dramatic overtime fashion to take the gold medal at the IHF Junior Championships in Halifax on January 5, a groundswell of patriotism swept the nation in fine fashion, as citizens far and wide professed their pride at being Canadian.

And rightfully so, as there was a lot of glory in which to bask. The national pride was palpable. What a wonderful story.

The fine, young hockey players who comprised Team Canada set an awesome example for every Canadian to emulate. Sportsmanship. Dedication. Determination. Hard work. Commitment. Positive attitude. Pride in country.

All these qualities were on full display every time the members of Team of Canada put on their jerseys and took to the ice. I will be the first to admit that I don't know much about hockey, but it is clear even to this occasional band-wagon-jumper that, with this core team of young talent taking to the ice, the future of this country's beloved sport is in good hands.

After three years of darkness, upheaval and uncertainty in our futures due to the pandemic, Canada most assuredly needed that golden victory. While the young players, their coaches, their managers, sponsors and all those who supported the team's efforts deserve every bit of adulation they received, we would do well to remember that there are many reasons for which we should all be proud to be Canadian.

Throughout this country's relatively short history, and in the more recent past, there have been times that Canadian patriotism has been front and centre. We most assuredly swell with pride every time a national team takes to the world stage and the country's anthem is played. It's a force that pulls us together like no other.

We burst with limitless enthusiasm when our athletes compete at the Olympics, and we pump our chests with unbridled pride when those athletes step up on a podium at the Olympics, as we should, for, medal or not, these fine young women and men have worked hard to achieve their goals.

They have earned and rightfully deserve our respect.

Over the centuries, athletics and sports have been the great unifier, but there are many other reasons to be a proud Canadian. For instance, you should be proud of every selfless act of bravery and kindness that sets Canadians above other nationalities.

There are many.

We should all also be proud every time Canadians lay down the welcome mat to provide a safe haven to displaced immigrants who have been forced from their homes for reasons we cannot even begin to understand, chief among them oppressive regimes, natural disaster, famine and war.

We are lucky to live in such a great country that we rarely have to worry about these life-threatening obstacles, and we should be proud to share with others what we take for granted.

And be proud of Canada's international reputation as a peacemaker not a fighter. In these uncertain times, when it seems as though our very existence is being threatened by war, disease and environmental disaster, let us embrace the fact that Canada is a leader in the fight for our future. If that's not reason to be proud, then I don't know what is.

Over the decades, Canadians have given us many reasons to beam with pride in movies, music, literature, visual arts, medicine, science, politics, the military, business and, as we've already said, sports. The list of outstanding contributions Canadians have made is very long, and there is little doubt that there are many, many reasons for which to be proud.

It should not take winning a gold medal at an international tournament to inspire our pride in country, but I get it. Not many people want to openly display that patriotism on their chests for fear of reprisal from a small group of vocal rabble-rousers, but these days there are far too many people openly disparaging our great nation. Such an attitude serves little purpose, and that simmering negativism often festers below the surface, usually leading to discontentment and confrontation.

In a democratic nation such as Canada, every citizen has the right to express their displeasure in our leaders and elected officials for decisions they've made, but just because you don't like or don't agree with something that's been done doesn't mean you should profess your hatred for country. Differing opinions is one thing; aggression for the sake of aggression is another thing altogether.

For sure, not everything is perfect in this country. We'd all like a better life with lower inflation, a more affordable cost of living, cheaper food and fuel, better access to quality health care, and less government interference and taxes; but seriously, when you compare Canada to most other countries around the world, you should readily agree that we've got it pretty darned good here at home.

So go ahead and embrace your pride and, instead of dissing the country, as many so often do these days. We should all take the opportunity every now and then to openly express our patriotism.

I am not afraid to admit that I am a proud Canadian. Are you?

Every citizen of this country should loudly and proudly proclaim their patriotism, or at least that's the view from here.

Acknowledgements

This book was more than 40 years in the making. It started with my formal journalism education at Lethbridge Community College, beginning in September 1980 and culminated with my last weekly column in *The South Shore Breaker* in October 2024. It was quite a ride, and I can honestly say I would not change a thing about the experience. My time in the community newspaper industry was challenging and exhilarating, but, most of all, it was rewarding.

There are a lot of people I could single out who played an important role in my journalism experience, but I want to reserve these thank-yous for those who helped make this book a reality, starting with Andrew Wetmore, my extraordinary editor at Moose House Publications. It was Andrew who pitched the idea for this collection of columns, so I have much appreciation for him, as I do for Moose House publisher, Brenda J. Thompson. Thank you both from the bottom of my heart for your ongoing support.

Thank you to the very talented Rebekah Wetmore for the beautiful cover design. You surprise me with every book we do.

Thank you to the very talented photographers whose images appear in this book—Linda Mason for the front cover photo; Betty Meredith for the image on the back cover; and Chris LaRocque for the author photo. I appreciate your talents very much.

Thank you to the very thoughtful and insightful Kim Kierans, who has long been a strong advocate for local newspapers and the important role they play in our communities. The kind words you wrote in your foreword touched me in many ways.

Finally, a special thank you to my family, and especially my wife, Nancy, who has been with me throughout this whole journey. I love you all very much.

Vernon Oickle

About the author

Vernon Oickle was born and raised in Liverpool, Nova Scotia, where he continues to reside with his wife, Nancy, and their family. Growing up in a small town in rural Nova Scotia, Vernon had always wanted to pursue a career as a newspaper reporter.

After completing high school in 1979, he attended Lethbridge Community College in Alberta. He graduated in 1982 with an honours diploma in Journalism and returned to Liverpool, where he worked at the local weekly newspaper, *The Advance*, for 13 years before becoming the editor of the *Bridgewater Bulletin*. His community newspaper career spanned 33 years.

Vernon is an award-winning journalist and editor, and is the author of 46 books, many of which collect and preserve the heritage and culture of Atlantic Canada. His best-selling books include *Ghost Stories of the Maritimes, Ghost Stories of Nova Scotia, More Ghost Stories of Nova Scotia,* the *Nova Scotia Outstanding Outhouse Reader, South Shore Facts and Folklore, Strange Nova Scotia, The Bluenosers' Book of Slang, Red Sky at Night, Forerunners: Harbingers of Death in Nova Scotia* and *Grandma's Home Remedies.*

He also writes fiction in the popular "Crow" series, based on the old Maritime poem *One Crow Sorrow.* In 2024, the seventh book in the series, *Seven Crows for a Secret Yet to be Told*, won an International Impact Book Award, taking first place in the Historical Mystery/Thriller category.

In addition to his long list of newspaper awards, in 2012 Vernon re-ceived the Queen Elizabeth II Diamond Jubilee Medal, recognizing his contributions to his community, province and country; and in 2015 he received a Distinguished Alumni Award (Community Leader) from Leth-bridge College. He was inducted into the Atlantic Journalism Awards Hall of Fame in the spring of 2020.

As a testimony to his outstanding career, in 2014 the South Queens Middle School in his hometown, Liverpool, announced the creation of the Vernon Oickle Writer's Award, to be given annually to a student who ex-cels in the art of writing, either fiction or non-fiction.